Better Homes and Gardens®
SALAD BOOK

BETTER HOMES AND GARDENS BOOKS
NEW YORK   DES MOINES

© Meredith Corporation, 1969. All Rights Reserved.
Printed in the United States of America. Second Edition. Fifth Printing, 1972.
Library of Congress Catalog Card Number: 71-4016
SBN: 696-00110-1

CONTENTS

On the cover: Chunks of blue cheese top the succulent vegetables in Summer Salad Bowl.

Left: Plan for generous helpings when the main dish is Deviled Beef Toss.

This Low-calorie Symbol appearing throughout the Salad Book identifies accompaniment salads, main dish salads, and salad dressings that will fit well into a calorie-controlled menu. For a complete listing, see the Index.

Better Homes and Gardens
TEST KITCHEN

Our seal assures you that every recipe in the *Salad Book* is endorsed by the Better Homes and Gardens Test Kitchen. Each recipe is tested till it rates high in family appeal, practicality, and deliciousness.

RAINBOW OF FRUIT SALADS

Fruits as colorful as the rainbow brighten any dinner table. Combinations can be chosen to add a splash of color to the meal and a sunny flavor to the menu. In this chapter, sketches and pictures showing arrangements of fresh and canned fruits help the food artist.

Fruit-studded salads can be planned for any colorful course in the menu. Side dish salads compliment a hot dish. Try them arranged, molded, frozen, or refrigerated. When a baked dish doesn't seem appealing, feature fruit as the main dish.

Fruit salads such as the multilayer gelatin salads add a dazzling note and flavor contrast to that buffet menu. Use the purchasing guide and quantity recipes to aid planning and preparation for the party.

Fruit and Orange Fluff is one of the easiest salads to prepare. Just whip up the dressing from an instant pudding mix, then serve with a luscious mixture of cut fresh fruit.

SIDE DISH SALADS

FRUIT AND ORANGE FLUFF

Try the salad shown on previous page—

1 35/8- or 33/4-ounce package
   instant vanilla pudding mix
2 cups cold milk
1 cup dairy sour cream
1/2 teaspoon grated orange peel
1/4 cup orange juice
   Sliced unpared pears*
   Quartered nectarines *or* peaches*
   Whole fresh strawberries
   Seedless green grape clusters
   Fresh dark sweet cherries
   Fresh blueberries

To prepare dressing, slowly beat pudding mix and milk in mixing bowl with rotary beater till well blended, about 1 to 2 minutes. Gently beat in sour cream. Fold in orange peel and juice. Chill.

To serve, center small bowl of dressing in large shallow bowl. Arrange fruits around. To keep cold, place fruit bowl atop bowl of crushed ice. Makes 3 cups dressing.

*To keep fruit bright, use ascorbic acid color keeper or dip in lemon juice mixed with a little water.

MELON SALAD

1 3-ounce package cream cheese,
   softened
2 tablespoons mayonnaise or
   salad dressing
2 tablespoons milk
1/4 cup diced celery
2 tablespoons chopped pecans
1/2 cup frozen whipped dessert
   topping, thawed
3 cups chilled melon balls

With rotary beater, beat together first 3 ingredients till smooth and fluffy. Add celery and nuts; fold in thawed topping. Chill. Divide melon balls into 6 lettuce cups; top each serving with cheese mixture. Serves 6.

CHEESE-TOPPED PEARS

1/2 cup plain yogurt
1/4 cup cream-style cottage cheese
2 tablespoons mayonnaise or
   salad dressing
1 tablespoon blue cheese
1 29-ounce can pear halves,
   drained and chilled

Blend together first 4 ingredients. To serve, spoon a little cheese mixture over center of each pear half. Makes 3/4 cup dressing.

MELON SUPREME

1 131/2-ounce can pineapple tidbits
1 cup small cantaloupe balls
1 cup small watermelon balls
1 cup sliced, peeled fresh
   peaches*
   . . .
1/4 cup mayonnaise or salad
   dressing
1 tablespoon confectioners' sugar
1/4 teaspoon grated lemon peel
1/2 cup whipping cream, whipped

Drain pineapple, reserving 2 tablespoons syrup. Mix fruit together; chill. Blend together reserved syrup, mayonnaise, and sugar; beat with rotary beater till smooth. Stir in lemon peel. Fold chilled fruit into mayonnaise mixture. Fold in whipped cream. Chill. Makes 6 to 8 servings.

SWISS APPLE SALAD

Combine 4 medium unpared apples, diced*; 1 cup diced Swiss cheese; 1/2 cup diced celery; 1 cup dairy sour cream; and dash salt. Chill thoroughly. Serves 6 to 8.

CORING FRESH PEARS

For neat looking fresh pear halves, core them with a melon ball cutter or teaspoon.

FRUIT-TOPPED PINEAPPLE

This Hawaii-inspired recipe is certain to win family acclaim—

  1 8½-ounce can pineapple slices
  1 3-ounce package cream cheese, softened
  2 tablespoons mayonnaise or salad dressing
  1 medium banana, peeled and diced* (1 cup)
  4 maraschino cherries, quartered
  ¼ cup snipped pitted dates

Drain pineapple, reserving 1 tablespoon syrup. Beat cream cheese, mayonnaise, and reserved pineapple syrup together till smooth. Fold in banana, cherries, and dates. Arrange one pineapple slice on each of 4 lettuce-lined plates. Top each slice with the cheese-fruit mixture. Makes 4 servings.

GINGERY FRUIT SALAD

  2 cups sliced, peeled fresh peaches
    or nectarines
  ¼ cup sugar
  1 teaspoon lemon juice
  1 3-ounce package cream cheese, softened
  ½ teaspoon ground ginger
  1 to 2 tablespoons milk
  3 cups torn mixed salad greens
  1 cup chilled fresh raspberries
  ½ cup chilled fresh blueberries

Place peach slices in bowl; toss with sugar and lemon juice. Cover and refrigerate about 1 hour. Drain peaches, reserving syrup. Cover peach slices and refrigerate. To prepare dressing, add cream cheese and ginger to reserved syrup; beat till smooth. Stir in milk till dressing is desired consistency. Chill.

Place salad greens in salad bowl. Arrange peach slices, raspberries, and blueberries atop greens. Serve with dressing. Serves 6.

A mound of vibrant raspberries highlights the fresh fruit arrangement of Gingery Fruit Salad. Set the fruits atop an interesting variety of salad greens and pass the spicy fruit dressing.

BASIC WALDORF SALAD

    2 cups diced apple
    1 cup 1-inch julienne celery
        sticks
    ½ cup broken walnuts
    ¼ cup mayonnaise
    1 tablespoon sugar
    ½ teaspoon lemon juice
    ½ cup whipping cream, whipped

Combine apple, celery, and nuts. Blend
together mayonnaise, sugar, lemon juice, and
dash salt. Fold in whipped cream; fold into
apple mixture. Chill. Makes 6 servings.

Date-marshmallow Waldorf: Prepare Basic
Waldorf Salad, reducing celery to ½ cup;
add ½ cup snipped pitted dates and 4 marshmallows, quartered.

Red Grape Waldorf: Prepare Basic Waldorf
Salad, adding 1 cup halved and seeded red
grapes to the apple mixture.

Orange Waldorf: Prepare Basic Waldorf
Salad, reducing celery to ½ cup; add ½
cup orange slices or mandarin oranges.

FRUIT REFRESHER

    ½ cup brown sugar
    ¼ cup honey
    ¼ cup dry sherry
    2 tablespoons lemon juice
    1 teaspoon grated lemon peel
    2 medium unpared apples, sliced
    2 medium nectarines, peeled
        and sliced (1½ cups)
    2 medium pears, pared and
        quartered (1½ cups)
    2 medium bananas, peeled and
        sliced
    1 cup dark sweet cherries, halved
        and pitted

In saucepan, combine first 5 ingredients;
cook over low heat 5 minutes, stirring occasionally. Remove from heat and cool.
    Combine fruits. Pour dressing over; toss
lightly. Cover; chill thoroughly, stirring occasionally. Drain, reserving dressing. Serve
fruit on lettuce-lined plates. Pass dressing.
Makes 6 to 8 servings.

APPLE-MELON TOSS

Combine 2½ cups cubed unpared apples,
1½ cups small cantaloupe *or* honeydew
balls, and ½ cup sliced celery.
    Blend together ½ cup dairy sour cream
and ⅓ cup mayonnaise or salad dressing;
stir in 2 ounces blue cheese, crumbled (½
cup). Add dressing to fruit mixture; toss
lightly. Chill. To serve, spoon into lettuce
cups. Makes 4 or 5 servings.

FRUIT-FILLED ORANGE

    6 large oranges
    1 medium banana, peeled and
        sliced
    6 plums, pitted and sliced
    1 cup sliced seedless green
        grapes
    Fresh mint sprigs
    Honeyberry Dressing

Slice tops from oranges; cut slices from bottoms to make oranges sit flat. With grapefruit knife or paring knife, remove orange
sections and combine with banana, plums,
and grapes. Refill orange shells with fruit
mixture. Trim salads with sprigs of mint.
Pass Honeyberry Dressing. Serves 6.
    Honeyberry Dressing: Beat ½ cup jellied
cranberry sauce till smooth. Stir in ¼ cup
honey and 1 tablespoon orange juice.

Mint sprigs garnish Fruit-filled Orange. Drench
the fruit mixture with Honeyberry Dressing.

PEAKED PINEAPPLE SALAD

2 cups melon balls
1 cup sliced pitted dates
2 medium bananas, peeled and
    sliced (2 cups)
¼ cup chopped macadamia nuts *or*
    chopped toasted almonds
       . . .
1 cup whipping cream
2 tablespoons sugar
1 tablespoon lemon juice
    Dash salt
1 20½-ounce can pineapple slices,
    chilled (10 slices)

Combine melon balls, dates, bananas, and nuts. Whip cream with sugar, lemon juice, and salt till soft peaks form. Fold into fruit mixture. Top each lettuce-lined plate with one pineapple slice; pile fruit mixture over. Makes 10 servings.

FRESH FRUIT AND CREAM

Have all ingredients and salad bowls well chilled. Line individual salad bowls with a bed of coarsely shredded lettuce. For each serving, arrange rings of fresh pink grapefruit sections; fresh white grapefruit sections; fresh strawberries; watermelon cubes; figs with centers filled with seeded purple grape halves; and papaya slices.

Garnish with sprigs of watercress frosted with confectioners' sugar. Serve with Whipped Cream Dressing.

Whipped Cream Dressing: Combine 1 cup mayonnaise or salad dressing; ½ cup whipping cream, whipped; and 1 teaspoon honey. Tint with red food coloring to a delicate pink. Makes 1½ cups dressing.

SHERRY SPICED PEARS

Drain one 29-ounce can pear halves, reserving ½ cup syrup. In saucepan, combine reserved syrup, 1 cup brown sugar, ½ cup dry sherry, 2 tablespoons vinegar, 1 tablespoon chopped candied ginger, and ¼ teaspoon ground cinnamon. Stir mixture over medium heat till sugar is dissolved. Add drained pear halves and simmer 5 minutes. Serve pears hot or cold.

CINNAMON-APPLE SALAD

Prepare these crimson red salads in the fall when apples are at their best—

½ cup (4 ounces) red cinnamon
    candies
2 cups water
6 small tart apples, pared and
    cored
       . . .
1 3-ounce package cream cheese,
    softened
2 tablespoons milk
1 teaspoon lemon juice
⅓ cup pitted dates, snipped
1 8¾-ounce can crushed pine-
    apple, drained (¾ cup)
2 tablespoons chopped walnuts

In a 3-quart saucepan, cook cinnamon candies in water till dissolved. Add apples and cook slowly, uncovered, just till tender, about 15 to 20 minutes, turning once during cooking. Refrigerate apples in syrup several hours, turning once.

Blend together cream cheese, milk, and lemon juice till smooth and creamy. Add dates, drained pineapple, and walnuts. Drain apples; stuff centers with cream cheese mixture. Serve on lettuce-lined plates. Serves 6.

ORANGE-PEAR SALAD

Toasted sesame seed decorates the top—

1 cup dairy sour cream
2 tablespoons honey
¼ teaspoon grated orange peel
       . . .
2 large oranges, peeled
6 pears, pared, halved, and cored
1 head Bibb lettuce
1 tablespoon toasted sesame seed

To make dressing, blend sour cream with honey and orange peel. Cut each orange into six slices. For each salad, spread one orange slice with sour cream-honey dressing; top with second orange slice.

Insert orange "sandwich" between two pear halves; place on lettuce-lined plates. Top with remaining dressing. Sprinkle with sesame seed. Makes 6 servings.

FRESH FRUIT BOWL

In large lettuce-lined salad bowl, arrange 6 small pared watermelon wedges as dividers. Between dividers, place separate mounds of peach slices*, bias-cut banana slices*, halved avocado rings*, cantaloupe and watermelon balls, orange sections, and halved pineapple rings.

Center salad with flaked coconut. Tuck in sprigs of mint for garnish. Serve with Blue Cheese Fluff Dressing.

*To keep banana, avocado, and fresh peach slices pretty and bright, use ascorbic-acid color keeper or dip pieces in lemon juice mixed with a little water.

Blue Cheese Fluff Dressing: Mash 2 ounces (½ cup) blue cheese with rotary beater; gradually beat in ⅓ cup salad oil till smooth. Beat in ½ cup dairy sour cream, 1 tablespoon lemon juice, and ½ teaspoon grated lemon peel. Add milk, if desired, to make fluffy consistency. Chill. Makes 1¼ cups dressing.

GREEN AND GOLD SALAD

    1 medium papaya
    1 cup salad oil
    ⅓ cup tarragon vinegar
    ¼ cup sugar
    1 tablespoon lime juice
    ½ teaspoon *each* salt, dry mustard,
        and instant minced onion
    ¼ teaspoon paprika
    4 cups mixed salad greens

To peel ripe papaya, dip in boiling water one minute, then place in ice water. With tip of paring knife, pull away peel. Cube papaya, reserving seeds.

To make dressing, place remaining ingredients *except* papaya and salad greens in blender container. Cover; blend thoroughly. Add 1½ tablespoons papaya seeds; blend till seeds are size of coarsely ground pepper. Chill. Combine papaya and greens. Toss with desired amount of dressing. Serves 6.

An arrangement of brilliant red anthuriums sets the mood for a festive Hawaiian Isle dinner. Exotically-dressed Green and Gold Salad creatively complements pork roast and baked bananas.

SLIM-TRIM FRUIT TOSS

2 medium oranges, pared and
   sliced
1 cup halved strawberries
1 cup cubed watermelon
½ cup plain yogurt
¼ cup low-calorie strawberry
   jelly
1 to 2 drops red food coloring

Combine first 3 ingredients; chill. Beat together yogurt and jelly; blend in food coloring. Serve fruit on lettuce-lined plates. Pass
dressing. Makes 4 to 6 servings.

CREAMY AMBROSIA SALAD

2 medium oranges, pared and diced
2 medium bananas, peeled and
   sliced
1 cup halved seedless green
   grapes
½ cup pitted dates, snipped
¼ cup frozen whipped dessert
   topping, thawed
¼ cup mayonnaise or salad
   dressing
¼ cup flaked Toasted Coconut
   (see Index)

Drain diced oranges. Combine oranges with
next 3 ingredients; chill. Fold dessert topping into mayonnaise; fold into fruits. Spoon
into crisp lettuce cups; sprinkle with coconut.
Makes 4 to 6 servings.

PINEAPPLE-CHEESE SALAD

1 20½-ounce can pineapple chunks
1 16-ounce carton (2 cups) cream-
   style cottage cheese
2 cups miniature marshmallows
½ cup pitted dates, snipped
1 tablespoon lemon juice
6 to 8 whole pitted dates

Drain pineapple, reserving ¼ cup syrup.
Combine reserved syrup and next 4 ingredients. Mound cheese mixture on lettuce-
lined plates; arrange pineapple chunks
around. Top each serving with one whole
pitted date. Makes 6 to 8 servings.

FIG FRUIT SALAD

½ cup dried figs
1 8¾-ounce can crushed pineapple
1 3-ounce package cream cheese,
   softened
1 tablespoon mayonnaise or salad
   dressing
1 tablespoon honey
     . . .
2 medium unpared apples, diced
2 medium bananas

Steam figs in a sieve over hot water about
20 minutes; cool. Clip stems; cut figs in thin
strips. Drain pineapple, reserving 2 tablespoons syrup. Beat syrup, cheese, mayonnaise, and honey together till smooth. Toss
figs, apples, and drained pineapple with
dressing. Chill. Before serving, peel and slice
bananas; toss with fruit mixture. Serves 6.

PEAR WALDORF SALAD

2½ cups diced unpared pears
1 tablespoon lemon juice
   Dash salt
1 cup diced celery
½ cup raisins
¼ cup coarsely chopped walnuts
¾ cup mayonnaise or salad
   dressing

Sprinkle pears with lemon juice and dash
salt. Add celery, raisins, and nuts. Toss with
mayonnaise; chill. Makes 6 to 8 servings.

PINEAPPLE STYLES TO KNOW

Crushed: Fruit is cut in very small pieces
just right for molded salads and dressings.
Tidbits: Slices are cut into small wedges
that are more dainty than chunks. Add to
tossed salads and fruit cups.
Chunks: Even, spoon-size pieces cut from
thick slices are available canned or frozen.
Frozen chunks should *not* be used when preparing gelatin salads.
Spears: Lengthwise strips make good additions to salad plates and trays.
Slices: Rings are cut from the pineapple
cylinders. They can be used in, under, or
atop salad combinations.

LOW-CAL FRUIT BOWL

1 grapefruit, chilled
2 oranges, chilled
1 ripe medium banana
1 cup chilled sliced fresh
    strawberries
½ cup chilled honeydew balls
    Mint sprigs
    Low-cal Snow Dressing

LOW CALORIE • LOW CALORIE

Peel and section grapefruit and oranges, reserving juices. Peel and slice banana; brush with reserved fruit juices. Combine grapefruit and orange sections, banana, strawberries, and honeydew balls in lettuce-lined bowl. Trim with mint. Serve with Low-cal Snow Dressing. Makes 4 servings.

Low-cal Snow Dressing: Combine 1 cup plain yogurt, 1 teaspoon lemon juice, and dash salt. Stir in non-caloric liquid sweetener equal to 4 teaspoons sugar. Chill.

TROPICAL APPLE SALAD

1 cup diced unpared red apple
1 cup diced unpared yellow apple
1 large banana, peeled and sliced
1 cup sliced celery
½ cup broken walnuts
½ cup flaked coconut
¼ cup mayonnaise or salad
    dressing
1 tablespoon sugar
½ teaspoon lemon juice
    Dash salt
½ cup whipping cream, whipped
    Romaine leaves

Combine apple, banana, celery, walnuts, and coconut. To prepare dressing, blend together mayonnaise, sugar, lemon juice, and salt. Fold whipped cream into mayonnaise mixture; gently fold into apple mixture. Chill.

Arrange romaine in bowl; spoon in salad. Garnish with additional unpared apple slices, if desired. Makes 6 servings.

← **A profusion of red and yellow apples,** bananas, celery, nuts, and coconut in a creamy dressing tempts every hungry palate. Tropical Apple Salad measures up to all flavor expectations.

SPICED WALDORF SALAD

3 cups diced apple
2 teaspoons lemon juice
    • • •
1 cup diced, drained canned spiced
    apple rings (6 to 8 rings)
1 cup halved seedless green
    grapes
½ cup chopped celery
½ cup chopped walnuts
⅓ cup mayonnaise or salad
    dressing

Sprinkle fresh apple with lemon juice; add spiced apple, grapes, celery, and walnuts. Fold in mayonnaise. Chill. Serve on lettuce-lined plates. Makes 6 to 8 servings.

MIDDLE EAST PEARS

Sweet and sharp go together in a jiffy—

1 29-ounce can pear halves,
    chilled and drained
1 cup plain yogurt
¼ cup sugar
    Ground nutmeg *or* cinnamon

Place pear halves on lettuce-lined plates. Combine yogurt and sugar; spoon into pear cavities. Sprinkle with nutmeg.

PINEAPPLE CHEESE-WICHES

1 20½-ounce can pineapple slices,
    chilled
1 3-ounce package cream cheese,
    softened
2 tablespoons mixed chopped
    candied fruits and peels
    Curly endive

Drain pineapple slices, reserving 2 teaspoons syrup. Beat cream cheese with 1 to 2 teaspoons syrup till of spreading consistency. Stir in candied fruits and peels.

Blot pineapple slices with paper toweling. Spread cream cheese mixture on 5 pineapple slices; top each with another pineapple slice. Cut each "sandwich" in half. For each salad stand 2 halves on edge on curly endive-lined plate. Makes 5 servings.

Bright red strawberries add flavor and color to an unusual side-dish salad. The combination includes sliced peaches, crosswise slices of kiwi, and whole strawberries on crisp leaf lettuce.

Plump, juicy blueberries and fresh pineapple chunks fill the hollow and cascade down the side of a honeydew melon wedge. Serve this salad in a shallow bowl and pass a fluffy cooked dressing.

Bananas, cut in chunks on the bias, are arranged on lettuce leaves with pitted red plum halves and succulent red raspberries. To keep bananas bright, brush with a little lemon juice mixed with water.

FRUIT COMBINATION GUIDE

Team the fruit with suggested counterparts at the right for a real taste treat. Then, arrange items on different varieties of greens each time. Top with a dressing.

To Go Along With	Choose These
Unpared red apple slices	• Grapefruit sections, sliced avocado, and pomegranate seeds
Unpared red apple wedges	• Cream cheese balls rolled in finely chopped nuts
Apple, diced	• Mandarin orange sections and diced celery
Avocado, peeled and sliced	• Grapefruit sections and persimmon wedges • Sliced tomato
Apricots, halved and seeded	• Red grapes and sliced jellied cranberry sauce • Pineapple chunks and maraschino cherries
Banana, halved lengthwise	• Orange and grapefruit sections and pitted dates • Cottage cheese and salted peanuts
Banana, bias-cut	• Halved red plums, sliced pineapple, red raspberries, and coconut
Figs, halved and seeded	• Raspberries and cream cheese balls rolled in shredded coconut
Grapefruit sections	• Sweetened raw cranberries • Orange sections, pineapple spears, and ripe olives
Honeydew melon, pared and crescent-cut	• Thinly sliced Prosciutto ham
Honeydew melon, pared and sliced	• Raspberry, lemon, or lime sherbet
Melon, pared and sliced	• Fresh sweet cherries, halved green grapes, and chopped pecans • Fruit cocktail and whipped cream
Melon, cubed	• Cottage cheese and fresh strawberries • Raspberries and bias-cut banana slices
Peach, halved	• Blueberries and raspberries • Cottage cheese and candied ginger
Peach, spiced	• Pineapple chunks and apple-mint jelly
Pear, halved	• Shredded American cheese • Sliced plums and blueberries • Halved green grapes and cream cheese
Pineapple, chunks	• Orange sections and fresh strawberries
Pineapple, sliced	• Watermelon chunks and sliced banana

FRUIT ARRANGEMENTS

Combine fresh and canned fruits to create an enticing salad. Line plates with leaf lettuce. Place banana quarters, orange sections, and a peach half on each. Trim with berries.

For a frilly effect, line the plate with curly endive. Make a circle of grapefruit sections around outside edge. Fill center with unpared apple slices and melon balls. Garnish with nuts.

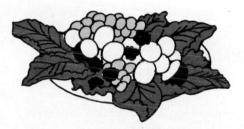

Romaine leaves also make an attractive salad liner. Place leaves in star fashion on each plate. Mound plum halves and cantaloupe balls inside each ring. Insert clusters of grapes and raspberries in any open area.

On each Bibb lettuce-lined plate, arrange banana quarters, crosswise slices of orange, dates, and a few blackberries. To transform the salad into an ideal side dish to serve in winter, substitute grapes for the blackberries.

Center cottage cheese on each lettuce-lined plate. Around it place a pear and peach half, each filled with berries; halved pineapple slices; strawberries; grapes; and mint.

This patriotic salad is red, white, and blue. Atop each leaf lettuce-lined plate place a large pear half. Fill the cavity with blueberries. Set spiced crab apple wedges around each pear half.

←**Chicken salad** hides beneath fresh fruits—orange sections; strawberries; avocado balls; halved limes; and unpared pineapple, sliced lengthwise—for a party-perfect summer main dish. Establish a tropical mood by lining each plate with a bamboo place mat and by garnishing the salad with pineapple leaves and fragrant gardenias. For added refreshment, serve with tall glasses of well-chilled tea.

FRUIT-FILLED MOLDS

BERRY-PEACH MARBLE

 1 3-ounce package strawberry-
      flavored gelatin
 2 cups sliced fresh strawberries
 1 16-ounce can peach slices
 1 envelope (1 tablespoon)
      unflavored gelatin
 2 tablespoons lemon juice
 1 2-ounce package dessert topping
      mix
 2 3-ounce packages cream cheese,
      softened

Dissolve strawberry-flavored gelatin in 1 cup boiling water; stir in 1 cup cold water. Chill till partially set. Fold in berries.

Meanwhile, drain peaches, reserving syrup. Dice peaches. Add enough water to peach syrup to make 1 cup. In saucepan, soften unflavored gelatin in syrup mixture; heat and stir till gelatin is dissolved. Stir in lemon juice. Cool. Prepare dessert topping mix following package directions; beat in cream cheese. Fold in peach-gelatin mixture and diced peaches. Chill till partially set.

Layer strawberry and cheese gelatin mixtures in 7½-cup mold. Swirl knife through gently to marble. Chill till firm. Serves 10.

MELON POLKA-DOT MOLD

 2 3-ounce packages cherry-
      flavored gelatin
 1 tablespoon lemon juice
 1 8-ounce package cream cheese
 ½ cup finely chopped pecans
 2 cups small melon balls

Dissolve gelatin in 2 cups boiling water. Stir in 1¾ cups cold water and lemon juice. Pour 1 cup gelatin into 6½-cup ring mold. Chill till partially set. Shape cheese into 40 balls; roll in nuts. Arrange 9 *each* cheese and melon balls alternately in mold. Chill till *almost* firm. Meanwhile, chill remaining gelatin till partially set; fold in remaining cheese and melon balls. Pour over gelatin in mold. Chill till firm. Makes 8 to 10 servings.

PAPAYA RING MOLD

Dissolve two 3-ounce packages lemon-flavored gelatin in 2 cups boiling water. Stir in 1 cup cold water, one 8¾-ounce can undrained crushed pineapple, and 3 tablespoons lemon juice. Chill till partially set.

Fold into gelatin 1 large papaya, peeled, seeded, and diced (1½ cups), *or* one 15-ounce can papaya, drained and diced; 2 medium oranges, peeled, sectioned, and cut up; and two 3-ounce packages cream cheese, chilled and diced. Pour into 6½-cup ring mold; chill till firm. Makes 8 to 10 servings.

CHICKEN PECAN SALAD

 3 medium peaches, peeled and
      sliced (1½ cups)
 3 cups cubed cooked chicken
 1 cup diced celery
 ½ cup mayonnaise
 2 tablespoons salad oil
 1 tablespoon vinegar
 ¼ cup toasted broken pecans
      Cranberry Ring

Reserve a few peach slices for garnish. Cut up remaining peaches. In large bowl, combine cut up peaches, chicken, and celery. Blend together next 3 ingredients and ½ teaspoon salt; toss with chicken mixture. Chill. Before serving, fold in nuts. Serve in center of Cranberry Ring. Garnish with peaches and parsley, if desired. Makes 6 servings.

Cranberry Ring: Dissolve two 3-ounce packages lemon-flavored gelatin and ¼ teaspoon salt in 1 cup *each* orange juice and water, heated to boiling. Stir in 1 cup cold orange juice. Chill till partially set. Stir in one 16-ounce can whole cranberry sauce. Pour into 6½-cup ring mold. Chill till firm.

Toasted pecans, fresh peaches, and hearty ➔ chunks of chicken fill the center of ruby Cranberry Ring. Adorn the Chicken Pecan Salad with choice peach slices and fluffs of fresh parsley.

FRUITY GINGER ALE MOLD

A red and gold bubbling beauty—

1 3-ounce package lemon-flavored
   gelatin
1 cup boiling water
1 7-ounce bottle (about 1 cup)
   ginger ale, chilled

. . .

1 unpared apple, cut in wedges
½ cup chopped pared apple
½ cup halved seedless green
   grapes
1 8¾-ounce can pineapple tidbits,
   drained (⅔ cup)

Dissolve gelatin and dash salt in boiling water. Cool to room temperature. Slowly add ginger ale. Chill till partially set.

Arrange apple wedges in 5½-cup mold. Pour in a little gelatin mixture. Chill till *almost* firm. Add pared apple, grapes, and pineapple tidbits to remaining mixture. Pour over first layer. Chill till firm. Serves 5 or 6.

Cran-cheese Squares are artfully placed on a marble plate and trimmed with orange sections.

HONEY BANANA MOLD

1 6-ounce can evaporated milk
1 3-ounce package orange-flavored
   gelatin
2 ripe medium bananas
¼ cup honey
3 tablespoons lemon juice

Pour milk into freezer tray. Freeze till soft ice crystals form around edges. Dissolve gelatin in 1 cup boiling water; cool. Peel bananas; mash in large mixer bowl with electric mixer. Beat in honey and lemon juice, then cooled gelatin. Chill till mixture is partially set.

Whip mixture at low speed while gradually adding icy cold milk. Increase to high speed; continue whipping till double in volume and thick. Pour into 4½-cup mold. Chill till firm. Makes 4 to 6 servings.

CRAN-CHEESE SQUARES

1 3-ounce package orange-
   pineapple-flavored gelatin
1 cup orange juice
½ cup whipping cream, whipped
1 3-ounce package cream cheese,
   softened
¼ cup chopped pecans

. . .

1 envelope (1 tablespoon)
   unflavored gelatin
1 16-ounce can whole cranberry
   sauce
2 tablespoons lemon juice
¼ teaspoon ground allspice
⅛ teaspoon ground nutmeg
1 cup orange sections
1 7-ounce bottle (about 1 cup)
   ginger ale, chilled

Dissolve orange-pineapple-flavored gelatin in 1 cup boiling water; stir in orange juice. Chill till partially set. Blend a little whipped cream into cheese; fold in remaining cream. Add nuts; fold into partially set gelatin. Pour into 9x9x2-inch pan; chill till *almost* firm.

Soften unflavored gelatin in ¼ cup cold water; stir over low heat till gelatin is dissolved. Combine next 5 ingredients; stir in gelatin. Gradually stir in ginger ale. Pour slowly over cheese layer. Chill till firm. To serve, cut into squares. Makes 9 servings.

FRUIT-NUT CHEESE MOLD

- 1 20½-ounce can (2½ cups)
  crushed pineapple
- 1 3-ounce package lime-flavored
  gelatin
- 2 3-ounce packages cream cheese,
  cubed and softened
- 1 cup diced celery
- ½ cup chopped walnuts
- ¼ cup chopped canned pimiento
- 1 cup whipping cream, whipped

Heat undrained pineapple to boiling. Add gelatin; stir till dissolved. Slowly add hot mixture to cheese, beating smooth with rotary beater. Chill till partially set. Stir in celery, nuts, and pimiento. Fold in whipped cream. Pour into 6½-cup mold. Chill till firm. Makes 6 to 8 servings.

SPARKLING MELON LOAF

- 2 envelopes (2 tablespoons)
  unflavored gelatin
- 1 6-ounce can frozen lemonade
  concentrate, thawed
- 2 7-ounce bottles (about 2 cups)
  ginger ale, chilled
- 2 tablespoons maraschino cherry
  juice
- 2 cups frozen honeydew balls,
  thawed and drained, *or* 2 cups
  fresh honeydew balls
- 2 tablespoons sliced maraschino
  cherries
- ¼ cup dairy sour cream
- ¼ cup mayonnaise or salad
  dressing

Soften gelatin in ½ cup cold water; stir over low heat till gelatin is dissolved. Add ¾ cup cold water and lemonade concentrate. Slowly add ginger ale. Divide gelatin mixture in half. Stir cherry juice into first half; chill till partially set. Fold melon balls and cherries into partially set gelatin. Pour into 8½x4½x 2½-inch loaf dish. Chill till *almost* firm.

Meanwhile, add sour cream and mayonnaise to second half of gelatin mixture. Beat with rotary beater till smooth. Leave at room temperature till fruit layer in mold is *almost* firm. Then slowly pour sour cream mixture over. Chill till firm. Makes 8 to 10 servings.

ORANGE-PINEAPPLE RING

Molded sunshine to tempt the palate—

- 2 envelopes (2 tablespoons)
  unflavored gelatin
- ½ cup sugar
- ¼ teaspoon salt
- 2 cups orange juice
  . . .
- 2 3-ounce packages cream cheese,
  cubed and softened
- 1 cup cold orange juice
- 1 13½-ounce can (1⅔ cups)
  crushed pineapple

In saucepan, combine gelatin, sugar, and salt; stir in 2 cups orange juice. Stir over medium heat till gelatin is dissolved. Gradually beat hot gelatin mixture into cream cheese; add 1 cup cold orange juice and undrained crushed pineapple.

Chill till partially set, stirring occasionally. Pour into 6½-cup ring mold; chill till firm. Makes 8 to 10 servings.

Made with frozen or fresh honeydew, this Sparkling Melon Loaf is an appetite tempter.

APPLE-CHEESE RIBBONS

1 16-ounce can (2 cups)
   applesauce
1 3-ounce package lime-flavored
   gelatin
2 tablespoons lemon juice

. . .

1 envelope (1 tablespoon)
   unflavored gelatin
1 12-ounce carton cream-style
   cottage cheese, sieved
1 3-ounce package cream cheese,
   softened
¼ cup mayonnaise or salad
   dressing
½ cup diced celery

Heat applesauce and ⅔ cup water to boiling. Add lime-flavored gelatin and lemon juice; stir till gelatin is dissolved. Cool. Reserving *half* of mixture, pour remainder into 8½x 4½x2½-inch loaf dish. Chill till *almost* firm.

In saucepan, soften unflavored gelatin in ½ cup cold water. Stir over low heat till gelatin is dissolved. Blend cheeses and mayonnaise; stir in gelatin and celery. Mix well. Pour into dish over first layer. Chill till *almost* firm. Pour reserved applesauce mixture over cheese layer. Chill till firm. Serves 8.

GOLDEN APRICOT MOLDS

Spiced with cinnamon and cloves—

1 30-ounce can apricot halves
2 tablespoons vinegar
7 whole cloves
4 inches stick cinnamon
1 3-ounce package orange-
   flavored gelatin
1 8-ounce can jellied cranberry
   sauce, cut in 8 slices

Drain apricots, reserving syrup. Add next 3 ingredients to reserved syrup; bring to boiling. Simmer, uncovered, 10 minutes. Strain syrup and measure; add enough boiling water to make 2 cups. Pour over gelatin; stir till gelatin is dissolved. Chill till partially set.

Arrange drained apricot halves in eight ½-cup molds and pour gelatin mixture over. Chill till firm. To serve, unmold on cranberry slices. Makes 8 servings.

ORANGE-GRAPEFRUIT RING

2 3-ounce packages orange-
   flavored gelatin
1 6-ounce can frozen orange
   juice concentrate, thawed
1 11-ounce can mandarin oranges
1 16-ounce can grapefruit
   sections, drained and cut up

Dissolve gelatin in 1½ cups boiling water; add juice concentrate and 1 cup cold water. Drain oranges, reserving syrup. Add syrup to gelatin mixture. Chill till partially set. Fold in oranges and grapefruit. Pour into 6½-cup ring mold. Chill gelatin mixture till firm. Makes 8 to 10 servings.

CRANBERRY MOLD

Relish mold for Thanksgiving dinner—

Dissolve one 3-ounce package *each* cherry-flavored and lemon-flavored gelatin and ½ cup sugar in 3 cups boiling water. Add 1 tablespoon lemon juice and one 8¾-ounce can undrained crushed pineapple; chill till gelatin mixture is partially set.

Fold in 2 cups whole fresh cranberries, ground; 1 small unpared orange, quartered, seeded, and ground (about ⅔ cup); 1 cup diced celery; and ½ cup chopped walnuts. Pour gelatin mixture into 8½-cup mold. Chill till firm. Drain one 20½-ounce can pineapple slices. Serve salad with pineapple slices. Makes 10 to 12 servings.

FRUIT COCKTAIL MOLD

1 17-ounce can fruit cocktail
1 3-ounce package lime-flavored
   gelatin
1 7-ounce bottle (about 1 cup)
   ginger ale, chilled
2 tablespoons lemon juice

Drain fruit cocktail, reserving syrup. Add enough water to syrup to make 1 cup; heat to boiling. Add gelatin and stir till dissolved; cool. Gently stir in ginger ale and lemon juice. Chill till partially set. Fold in drained fruit. Pour into 3½-cup mold. Chill till firm. Makes 4 or 5 servings.

FRUIT-NECTAR SALAD

Dissolve one 3-ounce package lemon-flavored gelatin in one 12-ounce can (1½ cups) apricot nectar, heated to boiling. Add ½ cup cold water and 1 tablespoon lemon juice. Chill till partially set.

Fold in one 11-ounce can mandarin oranges, drained; ½ cup diced unpared apple; and ½ cup halved seedless green grapes. Pour gelatin mixture into 4½-cup mold. Chill till firm. Makes 4 or 5 servings.

FRUITED EMERALD WREATH

A pineapple-studded gem—

   2 3-ounce packages lime-flavored gelatin
   1 20½-ounce can pineapple slices
   2 tablespoons lemon juice
   1½ cups seedless green grapes

Dissolve gelatin in 2 cups boiling water. Drain pineapple, reserving syrup. Add lemon juice to reserved syrup and enough cold water to make 2 cups. Add syrup mixture to gelatin; chill till partially set. Fold in grapes.

Pour gelatin mixture into 6½-cup ring mold. Place pineapple slices on edge, 2 together, at 5 intervals around mold. Chill till firm. If pineapple extends above gelatin, trim off ends before unmolding so mold will sit flat. Makes 10 to 12 servings.

JELLIED AMBROSIA

A gelatin variation of a Southern favorite. Serve with mayonnaise or whipped cream—

In saucepan, mix 1 envelope (1 tablespoon) unflavored gelatin and ¼ cup sugar together; add ½ cup cold water. Stir over low heat till gelatin and sugar are dissolved. Add 1¼ cups orange juice and 1 tablespoon lemon juice. Chill till partially set.

Segment 2 medium oranges, peeled; cut segments in pieces, reserving a few whole segments for garnish. Fold orange pieces; 1 medium banana, peeled and sliced; and ¼ cup flaked coconut into gelatin. Pour into 4½-cup mold. Chill till firm. Unmold; trim with reserved orange segments. Serves 6.

SHRIMP IN AVOCADO RING

Lemon wedges, to serve with the shrimp, make an appropriate garnish—

   1 3-ounce package lemon-flavored gelatin
   1 cup mayonnaise or salad dressing
   1 to 2 tablespoons lemon juice
   ½ teaspoon salt
   2 medium avocados, peeled and sieved (1 cup)
   1 cup whipping cream, whipped
   Lettuce
   Cleaned and cooked shrimp

Dissolve gelatin in 1 cup boiling water. Chill till partially set; whip till fluffy. Stir in mayonnaise, lemon juice, and salt. Fold in avocado and whipped cream. Pour into 5½-cup ring mold or six to eight ½-cup ring molds. Chill till firm.

Unmold on lettuce; fill center with shrimp. Makes 6 to 8 servings.

BLUE CHEESE FRUIT CUPS

   1 16-ounce can fruit cocktail
   2 envelopes (2 tablespoons) unflavored gelatin
   2 cups orange juice
   1 3-ounce package cream cheese, cubed and softened
   ½ cup mayonnaise or salad dressing
   ¼ cup lemon juice
   2 tablespoons sugar
   1 ounce blue cheese, crumbled (¼ cup)
   ½ cup broken pecans

Drain fruit cocktail, reserving 1 cup syrup. Soften gelatin in *half* the reserved syrup. Heat orange juice just to boiling and add to softened gelatin, stirring till gelatin dissolves. Slowly add hot mixture to cream cheese, beating with rotary beater till smooth.

Add remaining reserved fruit syrup, mayonnaise, lemon juice, sugar, and dash salt. Beat gelatin mixture again till smooth. Chill till partially set. Stir in drained fruit cocktail, blue cheese, and nuts. Spoon into ten ½-cup molds. Chill till firm. Serves 10.

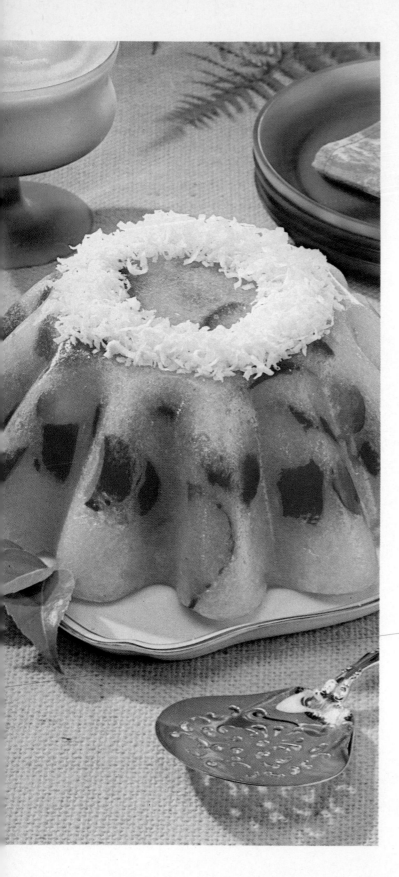

PLUM DESSERT SALAD

2 envelopes (2 tablespoons)
    unflavored gelatin
1 cup sugar
2 cups orange juice
¼ cup lemon juice
2 cups fresh red plums, pitted
    and cut in wedges, *or* 1
    16-ounce can plums, well-
    drained and pitted
Lemon Sauce

Combine gelatin and sugar; add 1½ cups cold water. Stir over low heat till gelatin and sugar are dissolved. Add orange and lemon juices. Chill till partially set. Set pan of gelatin in ice water; beat with rotary beater till light and foamy. Fold in plums. Pour into 6½-cup mold; chill till firm. Unmold; top with wreath of flaked coconut, if desired. Pass Lemon Sauce. Makes 8 servings.

Lemon Sauce: Beat 2 eggs and 1 tablespoon lemon juice together till thick and lemon-colored. Gradually add 1 cup sifted confectioners' sugar, beating constantly. Stir in ½ teaspoon vanilla, ¼ teaspoon grated lemon peel, and dash salt. Makes 1¾ cups.

ORANGE DELIGHT SALAD

Drain one 11-ounce can mandarin oranges, reserving syrup; add enough water to reserved syrup to make ¾ cup. Dissolve two 3-ounce packages orange-flavored gelatin in 2 cups boiling water. To *half* the gelatin add reserved syrup-water mixture; chill till partially set. Fold in oranges and ¼ cup broken pecans. Pour into one 6½-cup mold or ten to twelve ½-cup molds. Chill till gelatin mixture is *almost* firm.

Meanwhile, spoon 1 pint vanilla ice cream into remaining hot gelatin; stir till ice cream is melted. Chill till mixture mounds when spooned. Fold in 1 medium banana, peeled and sliced. Spoon over orange layer; chill till firm. Makes 10 to 12 servings.

Plum Dessert Salad will star at a luncheon or late evening get-together. Crown the mold with a delicate ring of moist coconut and be certain that fluffy Lemon Sauce accompanies each serving.

APPLE RING WALDORF

1 3-ounce package lemon-flavored
   gelatin
1 medium unpared apple
2 teaspoons lemon juice
2 tablespoons chopped walnuts
½ cup miniature marshmallows
⅓ cup chopped celery
½ cup mayonnaise or salad
   dressing

Prepare gelatin following package directions;
chill till partially set. Pour a little gelatin into 6½-cup ring mold. Cut enough thin apple
wedges to fit bottom of mold; lay wedges
with unpared side out, around outside edge
of mold. Chill till *almost* firm.

Dice remaining apple; sprinkle with lemon
juice and fold into remaining gelatin. Fold in
nuts, marshmallows, celery, and mayonnaise.
Spoon on top of first layer. Chill till firm.
Makes 6 servings.

FROSTED FRUIT MOLD

1 3-ounce package lime-flavored
   gelatin
1 7-ounce bottle lemon-lime
   carbonated beverage, chilled
1 8¾-ounce can crushed pineapple
1 medium banana, peeled and
   sliced
¼ cup sugar
1 tablespoon all-purpose flour
1 slightly beaten egg
½ cup whipping cream, whipped
¼ cup shredded sharp process
   American cheese
2 tablespoons grated Parmesan
   cheese

Dissolve gelatin in 1 cup boiling water; cool.
Slowly add carbonated beverage. Chill till
partially set. Drain pineapple, reserving
syrup. Fold drained pineapple and banana
into gelatin mixture. Pour into 8x8x2-inch
pan. Chill till firm.

Combine sugar and flour in saucepan and
stir in reserved syrup and egg. Cook and
stir over low heat till thickened; chill. Fold
whipped cream into egg mixture. Spread
over gelatin. Sprinkle with cheeses. To serve,
cut into squares. Makes 6 to 8 servings.

MOLDED CHERRY RING

1 20-ounce can pitted tart red
   cherries (water pack)
2 envelopes (2 tablespoons)
   unflavored gelatin
Non-caloric liquid sweetener to
   equal ¾ cup sugar
5 drops red food coloring
    • • •
½ cup lemon juice
¼ cup chopped celery

LOW CALORIE · LOW CALORIE ·

Drain cherries, reserving juice; add enough
water to juice to make 3 cups. Soften gelatin
in juice mixture; stir over medium heat till
gelatin is dissolved. Add sweetener, food coloring, and cherries; bring just to boiling.

Remove from heat; add lemon juice. Chill
till partially set, stirring occasionally. Fold
in celery. Pour into 5½-cup ring mold. Chill
till firm. Makes 8 or 9 servings.

CITRUS-CHEESE SQUARES

2 16-ounce cans grapefruit
   sections
2 3-ounce packages lemon-flavored
   gelatin
    • • •
1 8-ounce package cream cheese,
   softened
2 tablespoons milk
⅓ cup chopped walnuts
    • • •
¼ cup halved maraschino cherries

Drain grapefruit, reserving syrup; add
enough water to syrup to make 3½ cups.
Heat *half* the syrup mixture to boiling, then
add to gelatin and stir till dissolved. Add remaining syrup mixture; cool.

Arrange *half* the grapefruit sections in
bottom of 9x9x2-inch pan. Carefully pour
half the gelatin mixture over arranged fruit;
chill till firm. Blend cream cheese with milk
and chopped walnuts. Spread cheese mixture
over firm gelatin layer; chill.

Meanwhile, chill remaining gelatin mixture till partially set. Arrange remaining
grapefruit and cherries on top of cheese layer. Carefully pour partially set gelatin mixture over fruit. Chill till firm. To serve, cut
into squares. Makes 9 to 12 servings.

SEA LIME SALAD

Dissolve one 3-ounce package lime-flavored gelatin in 1 cup boiling water. Gradually stir hot gelatin into one 8-ounce package cream cheese, cubed and softened; beat till smooth. Chill till partially set.

Fold in one 8¾-ounce can undrained crushed pineapple; 1 cup chopped pared cucumber; ¼ cup chopped walnuts; and ½ cup whipping cream, whipped. Pour into 5½-cup mold; chill till firm. Serves 5 or 6.

PEACH-A-BERRY SQUARES

    2 3-ounce packages orange-flavored
        gelatin
    3 medium peaches, peeled and
        sliced
    1 cup fresh or frozen blueberries
    ¼ cup dairy sour cream
    ¼ cup mayonnaise or salad
        dressing

Dissolve gelatin in 2 cups boiling water; stir in 1½ cups cold water. Chill till partially set. Fold in peaches and blueberries. Pour into 8x8x2-inch pan; chill till firm. Blend together sour cream and mayonnaise; spread mixture over firm gelatin. To serve, cut into squares. Makes 9 servings.

GOOSEBERRY CUPS

The piquant flavor enhances a turkey dinner—

    1 16-ounce can gooseberries
    2 3-ounce packages lemon-flavored
        gelatin
    ½ cup sugar
    2 cups orange juice
    1 cup sliced celery
    ¼ cup broken walnuts

Drain gooseberries, reserving syrup. Add enough water to syrup to make 1½ cups; add gelatin and sugar. Heat to boiling, stirring till gelatin and sugar are dissolved. Remove from heat. Stir in orange juice. Chill till partially set. Fold in drained gooseberries, celery, and nuts. Pour into ten ½-cup molds. Chill till firm. To serve, unmold on lettuce-lined plates. Makes 10 servings.

QUICK SET SALAD

A welcome time-saver—

Dissolve one 3-ounce package fruit-flavored gelatin in 1 cup boiling water. Add 8 to 12 ice cubes; stir constantly till gelatin starts to thicken, about 2 to 3 minutes. Remove unmelted ice. Let stand 3 to 5 minutes. Fold in fruits or vegetables; chill till firm.

SWEET APPLE RING

    1 cup apple juice
    1 3-ounce package lemon-flavored
        gelatin
    1 cup cold water
    ¼ teaspoon salt
    ½ cup diced unpared apple
    ¼ cup seedless green grapes
    1 8¾-ounce can pineapple
        tidbits, drained
    ½ cup miniature marshmallows

Heat apple juice to boiling; add to gelatin and stir till gelatin is dissolved. Stir in cold water and salt. Chill till partially set. Fold in remaining ingredients; pour into 4½-cup ring mold. Chill till firm. Serves 4 or 5.

PEAR SALAD RING

Cheese balls make a surprise pear center—

Drain one 29-ounce can pear halves, reserving syrup; add enough water to make 1¾ cups liquid. Dissolve two 3-ounce packages lemon-flavored gelatin in 2 cups boiling water. Stir in reserved pear syrup, 2 tablespoons lemon juice, ½ teaspoon ground ginger, and ¼ teaspoon salt. Chill gelatin mixture till partially set.

Meanwhile, form one 3-ounce package cream cheese, softened, into small balls to equal number of pear halves. Roll balls in ¼ cup chopped walnuts; place 1 ball in center of each pear half.

Pour about a *fourth* of the partially set gelatin into 6½-cup ring mold. Arrange pear halves, ball side down, and 8 thinly sliced green pepper strips (optional) on top of gelatin. Carefully pour remaining gelatin mixture over. Chill till firm. Serves 8.

HOLIDAY WREATH

    1 8¾-ounce can seedless green
        grapes
    1 3-ounce package lime-flavored
        gelatin
    ½ cup chopped celery
    1 envelope (1 tablespoon)
        unflavored gelatin
    ½ cup frozen lemonade
        concentrate, thawed
    ½ cup mayonnaise or salad
        dressing
    1 16-ounce can fruit cocktail
    1 3-ounce package cherry-flavored
        gelatin
        Lemon Mayonnaise

Drain grapes, reserving syrup. Add enough water to syrup to make 1 cup. Dissolve lime-flavored gelatin in 1 cup boiling water; stir in syrup mixture. Chill till partially set. Fold in grapes and celery. Pour into 8½-cup ring mold; chill till *almost* firm. Soften unflavored gelatin in ½ cup cold water; stir over low heat till gelatin is dissolved. Add lemonade concentrate and 1 cup cold water; beat in mayonnaise. Chill till partially set. Pour over lime layer. Chill again till second layer is *almost* firm.

Drain fruit cocktail, reserving syrup. Add water to syrup to make 1 cup liquid. Dissolve cherry-flavored gelatin in 1 cup boiling water; stir in syrup mixture. Chill till partially set. Fold in fruit cocktail; pour over lemon layer. Chill till firm. Serve with Lemon Mayonnaise. Makes 12 to 14 servings.

Lemon Mayonnaise: Combine ½ cup mayonnaise or salad dressing and ¼ cup frozen lemonade concentrate, thawed. Fold in ½ cup whipping cream, whipped.

CRANBERRY WINE SALAD

A luscious mold for luncheons—

Dissolve two 3-ounce packages raspberry-flavored gelatin in 2 cups boiling water. Stir in one 16-ounce can whole cranberry sauce, one 8¾-ounce can undrained crushed pineapple, and ¾ cup port. Chill till partially set. Fold in ¼ cup chopped walnuts. Pour gelatin mixture into 6½-cup mold. Chill till firm. Makes 10 to 12 servings.

CREAMY PEAR-LIME MOLD

    1 4-serving envelope low-calorie
        lime-flavored gelatin
    1 3-ounce package Neufchatel
        cheese, softened
    2 tablespoons skim milk
        • • •
    1 16-ounce can dietetic-pack pear
        halves, drained and diced
    1 medium banana, peeled and
        sliced

Prepare gelatin following package directions. Beat cheese with milk; slowly add gelatin, beating till light and fluffy. Chill till partially set. Fold in pears and banana. Pour into 4½-cup mold. Chill till firm. Serves 6.

APPLE-GRAPEFRUIT MOLDS

    1 8-ounce can grapefruit sections
    1 3-ounce package lime-flavored
        gelatin
    1 cup diced unpared apple

Drain grapefruit, reserving syrup; cut up grapefruit sections. Dissolve gelatin in 1 cup boiling water. Add enough water to reserved syrup to make 1 cup; stir into dissolved gelatin. Chill till partially set.

Fold in grapefruit and apple. Pour into six ½-cup molds. Chill till firm. Serves 6.

CHEESE-NUT RING

    1 3-ounce package lime-flavored
        gelatin
    1 7-ounce bottle (about 1 cup)
        ginger ale, chilled
        • • •
    1 12-ounce carton (1½ cups) small
        curd cream-style cottage
        cheese, *well* drained
    1 tablespoon mayonnaise or salad
        dressing
    ¼ cup chopped pistachio nuts

Dissolve gelatin in 1 cup boiling water. Cool; gently stir in ginger ale. Chill till partially set. Combine remaining ingredients; fold into gelatin. Pour into 3½-cup mold. Chill till firm. Makes 4 to 6 servings.

CANTALOUPE CROWN

  1 small cantaloupe
  1 3-ounce package lemon-lime-
     flavored gelatin
  1 3-ounce package lime-flavored
     gelatin
2½ cups boiling water
 ¼ cup lemon juice
     Dash salt
  1 7-ounce bottle (about 1 cup)
     lemon-lime carbonated
     beverage, chilled

Halve cantaloupe; remove seeds and rind. Cut in wedges about ¾ inch thick at the widest part. Dissolve lemon-lime- and lime-flavored gelatins in boiling water; stir in lemon juice and salt. Cool.

Pour carbonated beverage slowly down side of bowl into gelatin; stir gently to mix. Chill till partially set. Arrange cantaloupe in 6½-cup fluted tube mold. Carefully pour a *fourth* of the gelatin mixture into mold covering bottom of cantaloupe. Chill gelatin in mold till *almost* firm. Leave remaining gelatin at room temperature.

Slowly pour *half* of remaining gelatin mixture into mold; chill till *almost* firm. Pour remaining gelatin into mold; chill till firm. Before unmolding, trim off tips of cantaloupe wedges if extending above gelatin. Makes 8 servings.

APPLE-AVOCADO RING

Spiced apples zip up this two-layered mold—

Dissolve one 3-ounce package strawberry-flavored gelatin in 1 cup boiling water. Drain one 16-ounce jar spiced apple rings, reserving ¼ cup syrup. Add syrup and ¾ cup water to dissolved gelatin; chill till partially set. Dice apple rings, reserving 3 whole rings. Fold diced apple into gelatin. Pour into 6½-cup mold; chill till *almost* firm.

Dissolve one 3-ounce package lemon-flavored gelatin in 1 cup boiling water; add ½ cup cold water and 1 tablespoon lemon juice. Chill till partially set. Fold ½ cup whipping cream, whipped, and 2 avocados, peeled and mashed (1 cup), into lemon-flavored gelatin. Pour over apple layer. Chill till firm. Garnish with reserved apple rings. Makes 8 servings.

STRAWBERRY CUPS

Use fresh or frozen berries—

Drain one 8¾-ounce can pineapple tidbits, reserving ½ cup syrup. Combine 1 cup fresh strawberries, hulled and halved*, and 2 tablespoons sugar; chill till juice forms. Drain, reserving juice; heat to boiling with enough water to make 1¼ cups. Dissolve one 3-ounce package strawberry-flavored gelatin in boiling juice. Stir in reserved pineapple syrup, 2 tablespoons lemon juice, and dash salt. Chill till partially set. Fold in fruits. Pour into six ½-cup molds; chill till firm. Makes 6 servings.

*Or use two 10-ounce packages frozen sliced strawberries, thawed; drain, reserving 1 cup juice. Bring juice to boiling. Dissolve gelatin in boiling juice.

WINTER FRUIT SOUFFLE

  1 3-ounce package lime-flavored
     gelatin
 ½ cup mayonnaise or salad
     dressing
1½ tablespoons lemon juice
  2 tablespoons finely chopped
     celery
  1 16-ounce can grapefruit sections,
     drained and diced
  1 avocado, peeled and mashed

Dissolve gelatin in 1 cup boiling water. Add ½ cup cold water, mayonnaise, lemon juice, and ¼ teaspoon salt. Beat with rotary beater till smooth. Chill till partially set, then whip till fluffy. Fold in celery and fruit. Pour into 4½-cup mold; chill till firm. Serves 6.

HARVEST CREAM

Dissolve one 3-ounce package lemon-flavored gelatin in 1 cup apple juice heated to boiling. Stir in 1 cup cold apple juice. Chill till partially set. Add 1 cup chopped unpared apple and ¼ cup chopped pecans to *1 cup* gelatin. Pour into 5½-cup mold; chill till *almost* firm. Prepare one 2-ounce package dessert topping mix according to package directions; fold into remaining gelatin. Pour over first layer. Chill till firm. Serves 5 or 6.

ORANGE-APRICOT RING

2 16-ounce cans apricot halves
2 3-ounce packages orange-
   flavored gelatin
1 6-ounce can frozen orange juice
   concentrate
2 tablespoons lemon juice
1 7-ounce bottle (about 1 cup)
   lemon-lime carbonated
   beverage, chilled

Drain apricots, reserving 1½ cups syrup. Puree apricots in sieve or blender. Heat reserved syrup to boiling; dissolve gelatin and dash salt in syrup. Add puree, juice concentrate, and lemon juice; stir till concentrate is melted. Slowly pour carbonated beverage down side of pan; mix gently. Pour gelatin mixture into 6½-cup ring mold. Chill till firm. Makes 10 to 12 servings.

HEAVENLY ORANGE FLUFF

2 3-ounce packages orange-
   flavored gelatin
1 13½-ounce can crushed pineapple
1 6-ounce can frozen orange juice
   concentrate, thawed
2 11-ounce cans mandarin oranges,
   drained
1 3¾-ounce package *instant*
   lemon pudding mix
1 cup cold milk
1 cup whipping cream, whipped

Dissolve gelatin in 2½ cups boiling water; add undrained pineapple and concentrate. Chill till partially set. Fold in oranges; pour into 13x9x2-inch pan. Chill till firm. Beat pudding and milk with rotary beater till smooth. Fold in whipped cream. Spread over gelatin; chill. Makes 12 to 15 servings.

Green spinach leaves, crisp and fresh, nestle in the center of flaming Orange-apricot Ring while selected fruits—green grapes, plums, avocado, and

pineapple—encircle it on a large serving platter. Have fun using artistic imagination to make every recipe a treat to eye and appetite.

SALADS THAT MELLOW IN TIME

CINNAMON FRUIT SALAD

Tiny cloud-like puffs of marshmallow enhance this creamy, cinnamon-flavored fruit salad—

- ¼ cup red cinnamon candies
- 2 tablespoons vinegar
- 2 tablespoons water
  Dash salt
- 3 beaten egg yolks
- 2 tablespoons honey
- 1 tablespoon butter or margarine
- 1 tablespoon lemon juice
- 2 cups sliced banana
- 3 cups diced unpared apple
- 1 cup miniature marshmallows
- 1 cup halved seedless green grapes
- ½ cup whipping cream, whipped

In small saucepan, combine first 4 ingredients. Cook and stir till candies are dissolved. In small bowl, combine egg yolks and honey. Gradually stir hot cinnamon mixture into egg yolk mixture; return to saucepan. Add butter. Cook and stir 3 to 4 minutes, or till thickened; cool. In large bowl, sprinkle lemon juice over banana; let stand a few minutes. Add apple, marshmallows, and grapes. Fold in cinnamon mixture and whipped cream. Chill several hours or overnight. Makes 10 to 12 servings.

5-CUP SALAD

A salad that's as easy as its name—

- 1 8¾-ounce can pineapple tidbits, drained (⅔ cup)
- 1 cup drained orange segments
- 1 cup shredded coconut
- 1 cup miniature marshmallows
- 1 cup dairy sour cream

Combine ingredients. Chill several hours or overnight. Makes 5 or 6 servings.

FRUIT GALAXY SALAD

- 1 8-ounce can dietetic-pack pineapple tidbits
- 1 tablespoon cornstarch
- 2 tablespoons lemon juice
  Non-caloric liquid sweetener equal to ¼ cup sugar

. . .

- ½ cup plain yogurt
- 1 cup sliced fresh peaches
- 1 cup diced unpared apple
- ½ cup diced fresh pear
- ½ cup sliced banana
- ½ cup halved seedless green grapes

Drain pineapple tidbits, reserving ½ cup juice. In 1½-quart saucepan, gradually stir pineapple juice into cornstarch. Stir in lemon juice and sweetener. Cook and stir over medium heat till thickened and bubbly; cool. Fold in yogurt, then pineapple, peaches, apple, pear, banana, and grapes. Chill several hours. Makes 8 servings.

CRANBERRY-GRAPE SALAD

Either dessert or salad. Try both ways—

- 2 cups fresh cranberries
- ¾ cup sugar

. . .

- 1 cup seeded halved red grapes
- ¼ cup broken walnuts
- 2 cups miniature marshmallows
- ½ cup whipping cream, whipped

Grind cranberries through food chopper, using coarse blade. Stir in sugar. Cover and chill overnight. Drain, pressing lightly to remove excess juice. Add grapes, nuts, and marshmallows to *well-drained* cranberry mixture. Just before serving, fold in whipped cream. Mound in lettuce cups. Garnish with grape clusters, if desired. Serves 6 to 8.

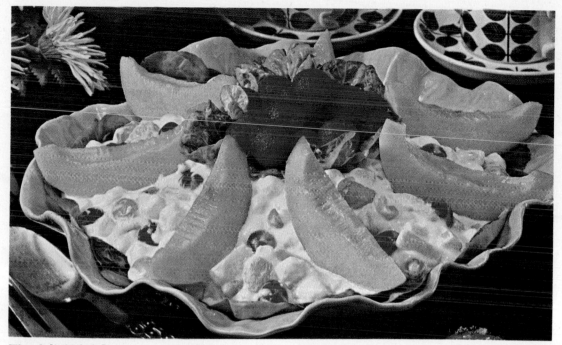

The delightful flavors in 24-hour Salad mingle as the fruits chill leisurely in a fluffy whipped cream dressing. It's a do-ahead salad and perfect for the buffet table. Pile on platter lined with greens and garnish with golden cantaloupe wedges and rosy watermelon balls.

24-HOUR SALAD

  1 20½-ounce can pineapple tidbits
  3 egg yolks
  2 tablespoons sugar
  2 tablespoons vinegar
  1 tablespoon butter or margarine
  1 16-ounce can pitted light
      sweet cherries, drained
  2 pared oranges, cut up and
      drained
¼ cup drained maraschino cherries
  2 cups miniature marshmallows
  1 cup whipping cream, whipped

Drain pineapple, reserving 2 tablespoons syrup. In top of double boiler, beat egg yolks slightly; add reserved syrup, sugar, vinegar, butter, and dash salt. Place over *hot not boiling* water; cook, stirring constantly till mixture thickens *slightly* and *barely* coats a spoon (about 12 minutes). Cool to room temperature. Combine *well-drained* fruits and marshmallows. Pour custard over and mix gently. Fold in whipped cream. Turn into serving bowl. Cover and chill 24 hours. Serves 6 to 8.

CREAMY FRUIT COMBO

  1 cup seedless green grapes
  1 8¾-ounce can pineapple
      tidbits, drained (⅔ cup)
  1 cup pitted dark sweet cherries
  1 cup diced orange
  1 cup cantaloupe balls
  2 medium plums, sliced
⅔ cup flaked coconut
   •   •   •
   Creamy Dressing
  1 cup sliced banana

Combine first 7 ingredients. Fold in Creamy Dressing. Chill 24 hours to allow flavors to blend fully. Fold in sliced banana just before serving. Makes 8 to 10 servings.

Creamy Dressing: In small saucepan, combine 2 beaten eggs, 2 tablespoons orange juice, and 2 tablespoons vinegar; stir in ¼ cup sugar and dash salt. Cook over low heat, stirring constantly, till mixture thickens. Remove from heat and stir in 1 tablespoon butter or margarine. Cool. Fold in 1 cup dairy sour cream. Chill thoroughly.

SALADS FROM
THE FREEZER

APPLE SNOW SALAD

In saucepan, combine one 8¾-ounce can undrained crushed pineapple, 2 beaten eggs, ½ cup sugar, ¼ cup water, 3 tablespoons lemon juice, and dash salt. Cook over low heat, stirring constantly, till thickened. Chill.

Stir in 2 cups diced unpared apple and ½ cup chopped walnuts; fold in 1 cup whipping cream, whipped. Pour into 8x8x2-inch pan. Freeze till firm. Let stand at room temperature 10 to 15 minutes before serving. Cut into squares. Makes 9 servings.

PINEAPPLE MINT FREEZE

- 1 20½-ounce can crushed pineapple
- 1 envelope (1 tablespoon) unflavored gelatin
- 1 10-ounce jar mint jelly
- 1 cup whipping cream
- 1 teaspoon confectioners' sugar

Drain pineapple, reserving syrup. In saucepan, soften gelatin in syrup. Add jelly and dash salt; heat and stir till gelatin is dissolved and jelly melted. If needed, beat to blend jelly. Stir in pineapple. Chill till mixture is thickened and syrupy.

Whip cream with sugar; fold into thickened gelatin mixture. Tint with few drops green food coloring, if desired. Spoon into 8½x4½x2½-inch loaf dish. Freeze till firm. Let stand at room temperature 10 to 15 minutes before serving. Unmold; slice and place on lettuce-lined salad plates. Garnish with fresh mint sprigs, if desired. Serves 8.

← Give the hot summer meal a cool lift by serving Pineapple Mint Freeze for the salad course. Fresh mint sprigs and ruffles of leaf lettuce spruce up this eye-catching, creamy refresher.

DATE-PECAN MOLDS

- 1 8-ounce package cream cheese, softened
- ¼ cup orange juice
- 1 8¾-ounce can crushed pineapple, drained (¾ cup)
- ½ cup snipped pitted dates
- ½ cup chopped pecans
- ¼ cup chopped maraschino cherries
- ½ teaspoon grated orange peel
- 1 cup whipping cream, whipped
- 8 orange slices (cut crosswise)

Beat together cream cheese and orange juice till fluffy. Stir in drained pineapple, dates, nuts, cherries, and orange peel. Fold in whipped cream. Spoon into eight ½-cup molds or one 8½x4½x2½-inch loaf dish. Freeze till firm. Let stand at room temperature 10 to 15 minutes before serving. Unmold each on orange slice. Serves 8.

BERRY-FRUIT FREEZE

- 2 3-ounce packages cream cheese, softened
- 2 tablespoons sugar
- 2 tablespoons mayonnaise or salad dressing
- 1 16-ounce can whole cranberry sauce
- 1 8¾-ounce can crushed pineapple, drained (¾ cup)
- ½ cup chopped walnuts
- 1 cup whipping cream, whipped
- 4 drops red food coloring

Beat cream cheese with sugar and mayonnaise. Stir in cranberry sauce, pineapple, and nuts. Fold in whipped cream and food coloring. Pour into 8½x4½x2½-inch loaf dish. Freeze till firm. Let stand at room temperature 10 to 15 minutes before serving. Unmold; slice to serve. Serves 8 to 10.

Quickest way to freeze salad mixture is in a freezer tray. To serve, cut in wedges or squares.

For round slices, pour mixture into No. 2 or 2½ can (20 to 29 ounce capacity). Freeze till firm.

To remove, let stand out a few minutes. Loosen end of can with opener; push out and slice.

SHORTCUT FROZEN SALAD

Prepare one 3⅝- or 3¾-ounce package *instant* lemon pudding mix according to package directions. Stir in 2 cups frozen dessert topping, thawed; ½ cup mayonnaise or salad dressing; and 2 tablespoons lemon juice. Fold in one 16-ounce can fruit cocktail, drained; 1 cup miniature marshmallows; and ¼ cup chopped pecans. Turn into 9x5x3-inch loaf pan. Freeze till firm. Serves 8 to 10.

CRAN-CHEESE FROSTIES

1 16-ounce can jellied cranberry sauce
2 tablespoons lemon juice
1 3-ounce package cream cheese, softened
¼ cup mayonnaise or salad dressing
¼ cup sifted confectioners' sugar
¼ cup chopped walnuts
1 cup whipping cream, whipped

Beat cranberry sauce and lemon juice till smooth. Pour into 6 to 8 paper baking cups, filling about ⅓ full *or* one 4-cup freezer tray. Beat together next 3 ingredients. Stir in walnuts. Fold in whipped cream and spread over cranberry layer. Freeze till firm. Serve on lettuce. Makes 6 to 8 servings.

RHUBARB FREEZE

A perfect summer special—

In small saucepan, combine 1 cup diced fresh rhubarb, 2 tablespoons water, and ¼ cup sugar. Cover and cook over medium heat about 3 minutes, or till rhubarb is tender, stirring occasionally; cool. Combine rhubarb and one 8¾-ounce can undrained crushed pineapple. Drain mixture, reserving ½ cup of the fruit juice.

Beat together one 8-ounce package cream cheese, softened; ¼ cup sugar; 1 tablespoon lemon juice; 7 drops red food coloring; and reserved juice. Stir in drained fruit and 1 cup miniature marshmallows. Fold 1 cup whipping cream, whipped, into fruit mixture. Pour into eight to ten ½-cup molds. Freeze till firm. Makes 8 to 10 servings.

Keep Cranberry-orange Salad in mind for an extra-easy salad. The flavor combination makes it especially suitable for holiday meals consisting of turkey and all the trimmings. Line the salad plates with crisp leaf lettuce, then garnish each square with a frosty cluster of red grapes.

CRANBERRY-ORANGE SALAD

    1 3¾-ounce package vanilla
        whipped dessert mix
    ½ cup ginger ale
        • • •
    1 cup cranberry-orange relish
        Leaf lettuce
        Frosted red grape clusters

Prepare vanilla whipped dessert mix according to package directions, substituting the ½ cup ginger ale for the recommended amount of water in package directions.

Fold cranberry-orange relish into dessert mixture. Pour into 8x8x2-inch pan. Freeze till firm. To serve salad, cut in squares. Place on leaf lettuce-lined plates. Garnish with clusters of frosted red grapes (see Index). Makes 6 servings.

CRANBERRY BANANA LOAF

An unusual blend of fruit flavors—

    1 16-ounce can jellied cranberry
        sauce
    1 medium apple, pared and grated
    2 medium bananas, mashed
    ⅓ cup sifted confectioners' sugar
    1 teaspoon vanilla
    ¼ cup chopped walnuts
    1 cup whipping cream, whipped

Beat cranberry sauce till smooth; stir in grated apple. Pour into 11x7x1½-inch pan. Fold bananas, sugar, vanilla, and *half* the nuts into whipped cream. Spread over cranberry layer. Sprinkle with remaining nuts. Freeze till firm. Let stand at room temperature 15 minutes; cut in squares. Serves 8.

FRUIT MEAL-MAKERS

GLAZED AVOCADO BOATS

An enticing aroma abounds from this salad—

    1 8¾-ounce can pineapple
        tidbits
    1 *teaspoon* unflavored gelatin
    1 tablespoon sugar
    ¼ teaspoon grated lime peel
    1 tablespoon lime juice
    1 medium unpared apple, diced
    1 orange, pared and diced
    ½ cup diced celery
    3 medium avocados

Drain pineapple, reserving syrup. Combine gelatin, sugar, and dash salt. Heat syrup and ½ cup water to boiling; add to gelatin mixture and stir till gelatin and sugar are dissolved. Stir in lime peel and juice. Chill till partially set. Combine pineapple tidbits, apple, orange, and celery. Halve avocados lengthwise; remove seeds and skin. Place one half on each of 6 lettuce-lined luncheon plates. Spoon fruit into cavities. Drizzle gelatin over. Makes 6 servings.

FRUIT AND CHEESE PLATE

    1 30-ounce can pineapple slices
    1 3-ounce package orange-
        flavored gelatin
    1 3-ounce package cream cheese,
        cubed and softened
    ¼ cup orange juice
    1 tablespoon lemon juice
    1 16-ounce carton (2 cups) cream-
        style cottage cheese

Drain pineapple, reserving syrup. Halve pineapple slices; set aside. Add water to syrup to make 1½ cups. Bring to boiling; add to gelatin and stir till dissolved. With rotary beater, gradually beat hot gelatin into cheese. Stir in juices. Chill till partially set, stirring occasionally. Pour into four ½-cup molds. Chill till firm. Unmold; arrange on 4 lettuce-lined plates with pineapple and cottage cheese. Makes 4 servings.

PAPAYA FRUIT SALAD

Cut 1 large papaya into eighths; remove seeds and membrane. Pare and section 2 medium grapefruit. Peel and slice 2 medium bananas*. Center a generous scoop of lime sherbet on each of 4 lettuce-lined luncheon plates. Arrange papaya, grapefruit, bananas, and 1 cup halved and seeded red grapes around edge. Makes 4 servings.

*To keep bananas bright, use ascorbic acid color keeper or dip in lemon juice mixed with a little water.

FRUITED PARFAIT SALAD

    1 16-ounce package frozen sliced
        strawberries
    1 10-ounce package frozen melon
        balls *or* 1 cup fresh melon
        balls
    1 10-ounce package frozen
        blueberries *or* 1 cup fresh
        blueberries
    1 cup dairy sour cream
    ½ teaspoon grated lemon peel
    1 16-ounce carton (2 cups) large
        curd cream-style cottage
        cheese

Partially thaw and drain frozen fruits separately, reserving ¼ cup strawberry syrup. Prepare dressing by blending together sour cream, reserved syrup, and lemon peel.

Allowing ⅓ cup cottage cheese for each salad, begin layering with *half* the cottage cheese in bottoms of 6 large parfait glasses. Continue layering with dressing, strawberries, a few melon balls, blueberries, remaining cottage cheese, dressing, and strawberries. Top with remaining melon balls. Serve immediately. Makes 6 servings.

Choose Fruited Parfait Salad to be the dazzling attraction at a forthcoming luncheon. There's versatility in this recipe since fresh or frozen fruits can be used depending on their availability.

POLYNESIAN SALAD

LOW CALORIE • LOW CALORIE

1 large cantaloupe
6 heads Bibb lettuce
1 14-ounce can dietetic-pack
    pineapple slices, drained and
    halved
1 medium papaya, peeled and
    thinly sliced
2 medium peaches, peeled and
    thinly sliced*
2 medium plums, thinly sliced
1 medium unpared apple, thinly
    sliced*
2 cups fresh whole strawberries

Chill all fruits and lettuce thoroughly. Cut midsection of cantaloupe into 6 rings. Remove seeds and rind. Remove rind from end pieces of cantaloupe and cut into thin spears. Cut roots from heads of Bibb lettuce leaving heads in one piece.

To assemble salads, spread Bibb leaves apart. Place 1 cantaloupe ring on each of 6 luncheon plates. Top each with a head of lettuce. Tuck slices or spears of the different fruits on end among the Bibb leaves. Fill in with hulled strawberries. Serve with a low-calorie dressing (see Index). Serves 6.

LUNCHEON SALAD

1 20½-ounce can pineapple chunks
2 12-ounce cartons (3 cups)
    cream-style cottage cheese
1 cup halved pitted dark sweet
    cherries
3 oranges, peeled and sectioned
1 banana, peeled and cut in
    sixths*
1 cup halved seedless green
    grapes

• • •

½ cup mayonnaise or salad
    dressing
½ cup whipping cream, whipped

Drain pineapple, reserving ½ cup syrup. Arrange pineapple, cottage cheese, cherries, oranges, banana, and grapes on lettuce-lined plates. Prepare dressing by folding reserved syrup and mayonnaise into whipped cream. Chill salads and dressing separately. At serving time, pass dressing. Makes 6 servings.

APRICOT-CHEESE SALAD

1 30-ounce can apricot halves
1 8¾-ounce can crushed
    pineapple
1 3-ounce package orange-
    flavored gelatin
1 12-ounce carton (1½ cups)
    cream-style cottage cheese
2 tablespoons all-purpose flour
2 tablespoons sugar
1 slightly beaten egg
1 tablespoon butter or margarine
1 cup frozen whipped dessert
    topping, thawed
⅓ cup shredded sharp process
    American cheese
3 bananas, peeled and bias-cut*
    Grape clusters

Drain apricots and pineapple, reserving ½ cup combined syrups. Dissolve gelatin in 1 cup boiling water; stir in 1 cup cold water. Chill till partially set. Fold in pineapple and cottage cheese. Pour into six ½-cup molds; chill till gelatin mixture is firm.

In small saucepan, combine flour and sugar. Stir in reserved syrup; blend in egg. Cook and stir till thickened. Remove from heat; stir in butter. Place clear plastic wrap or waxed paper directly on dressing; cool. Peel off covering. Fold in thawed dessert topping and American cheese.

At serving time, unmold gelatin salads in center of lettuce-lined plates. Arrange bananas and drained apricots around molds. Garnish with grape clusters. Pass cooked dressing. Makes 6 servings.

BERRY-PATCH SALAD

2 medium cantaloupes, chilled
1 12-ounce carton (1½ cups)
    cream-style cottage cheese
1 8¾-ounce can pineapple
    tidbits, chilled and drained
½ cup hulled and halved fresh
    strawberries
½ cup fresh red raspberries

Cut cantaloupes in half crosswise; remove seeds. Combine cottage cheese and pineapple. Spoon into melon halves. Top with strawberries and raspberries. Serves 4.

Any one of 3 cantaloupe-based salads makes a colorful mid-summer meal. Peaches and blueberries wreath lime sherbet for a Luncheon Cooler.

Coronado Salad boasts a liberally-garnished chicken salad. Red berries couched in a fruited cottage cheese bed spark the Berry-patch Salad.

CORONADO SALAD

    2 medium cantaloupes, chilled
    2 cups diced cooked chicken
    ½ cup chopped celery
    ½ cup halved seedless green
        grapes
    2 tablespoons sliced pimiento-
        stuffed green olives
    ½ teaspoon monosodium
        glutamate
    ½ cup whipping cream, whipped
    ¼ cup mayonnaise
    4 clusters seedless green grapes
        Hard-cooked egg slices
        Toasted sliced almonds

Cut cantaloupes in half crosswise; remove seeds. Combine next 5 ingredients and ½ teaspoon salt reserving a few olive slices, toss. Fold in mixture of whipped cream and mayonnaise. Spoon into melons. Garnish with remaining ingredients. Serves 4.

LUNCHEON COOLER

    2 medium cantaloupes, chilled
    2 medium peaches, peeled
    2 bananas, peeled and sliced*
    ½ cup fresh blueberries
    3 tablespoons honey
    2 to 3 teaspoons finely snipped
        candied ginger
        Lime sherbet

Cut cantaloupes in half crosswise; remove seeds. Slice *one* peach* and reserve for garnish. Dice remaining peach* into large bowl. Add next 4 ingredients and toss lightly; spoon into cantaloupe halves. Arrange reserved peaches around each cantaloupe rim; top with a scoop of lime sherbet. Garnish with extra blueberries, if desired. Serves 4.

  *To keep fruit attractive and bright, dip in ascorbic acid color keeper or dip in lemon juice mixed with a little water.

BUFFET SPECIALS

BUFFET FRUIT BOWL

  1 large banana
  2 fresh medium pears
  1 large apple
  1 medium pink grapefruit
  1 3-ounce package cream cheese,
     softened
  2 ounces (½ cup) blue cheese,
     softened
  ½ cup chopped pecans
  4 canned peach halves
    Green grape clusters
    Romaine
    Cranberry-orange relish
    Honey-lime Dressing
    Creamy Poppy Seed Dressing
    Chutney French Dressing

Peel banana and score lengthwise with tines of fork; cut diagonally into crosswise sections*. Halve pears*; remove cores. Cut apple into wedges*; remove core. Peel and section grapefruit. Blend cream cheese and blue cheese. Form into balls; roll in nuts.

Arrange fruits on bed of romaine in salad bowl. Top pears with cheese balls. Serve extra cheese balls on the side. Spoon relish into peaches. Serve with Honey-lime Dressing, Creamy Poppy Seed Dressing, and Chutney French Dressing. Makes 6 servings.

Honey-lime Dressing: In saucepan, combine 1 beaten egg, ½ cup honey, and ¼ cup lime juice. Cook and stir over low heat till mixture thickens. Blend in dash *each* salt and ground mace; cool. Fold in 1 cup dairy sour cream. Chill. Makes 1½ cups.

Creamy Poppy Seed Dressing: In mixing bowl, combine ½ cup mayonnaise or salad dressing, 2 tablespoons sugar, and 1 tablespoon lemon juice; blend thoroughly. Stir in 1 tablespoon poppy seed. Makes about ¾ cup.

Chutney French Dressing: In screw-top jar, combine 1 cup sweet French salad dressing, 2 tablespoons finely chopped chutney, and 1 teaspoon grated orange peel. Cover and shake well. Chill. Makes about 1 cup.

*To keep fruits bright, use ascorbic acid color keeper or dip in lemon juice mixed with a little water.

PINEAPPLE-TOP LAYERS

A colorful ribbon highlights a Christmas meal—

  1 3-ounce package lime-flavored
     gelatin
  1 cup boiling water
  1 13½-ounce can pineapple chunks
  2 tablespoons lemon juice
  1 3-ounce package lemon-flavored
     gelatin
  1 cup boiling water
  2 3-ounce packages cream cheese,
     softened
  ⅓ cup mayonnaise or salad
     dressing
  1 3-ounce package raspberry-
     flavored gelatin
  1 cup boiling water
  2 medium bananas, peeled and
     sliced (2 cups)

Dissolve lime-flavored gelatin in the *first* 1 cup boiling water. Drain pineapple, reserving syrup. Add lemon juice and enough water to syrup to make 1 cup; stir into gelatin mixture. Chill till partially set. Fold in pineapple chunks. Pour into one 10½-cup mold. Chill till *almost* firm.

Dissolve lemon-flavored gelatin in the *second* 1 cup boiling water. Chill till partially set. Whip gelatin mixture till light and the consistency of whipped cream. Beat cream cheese and mayonnaise together till smooth. Gradually fold whipped gelatin into cheese mixture. Pour over first layer. Chill lemon layer till *almost* firm.

Dissolve raspberry-flavored gelatin in the *third* 1 cup boiling water. Stir 1 cup cold water into gelatin mixture. Chill till partially set. Arrange banana slices over almost firm lemon layer; pour gelatin over. Chill till firm. Makes 10 to 12 servings.

Fruit arrangements make a flavorful addition → to a buffet dinner. Combining fresh and canned fruits, Buffet Fruit Bowl is served with a complementary dressing assortment to please any taste.

PREPARING FOR A CROWD

Use this table as a guide when planning and shopping for food for a large group. The size of *one serving* (serving unit) has been listed for each item. For hearty eaters, plan approximately 1½ servings per person. Add accordingly for second helpings.

Food	Number of Servings	Serving Unit	Amount Needed
Beverages			
Coffee	25	1 cup	½ to ¾ pound
Tea, hot	25	1 cup	1 ounce
Tea, iced	25	1 glass	3 ounces
Cream, coffee	25	1 tablespoon	1 pint
Milk	24	1 8-ounce glass	1½ gallons
Breads			
Biscuits	25	2 ounces	4½ dozen
Bread	25	1-ounce slice	1¼ pounds
Rolls	24	1	2 dozen
Casseroles	25	1 cup	6¼ quarts
Desserts			
Cake	24	1/12 cake	2 9-inch layer cakes
	24	2½-inch square	1 15½x10½x1-inch sheet
Ice Cream	24	½ cup or 1 slice	3 quarts
Pie	30	1/6 pie	5 9-inch pies
Fruit			
Canned	24	½ cup	1 6½- to 7¼-pound can
Relishes			
Carrot strips	25	2 to 3 strips	1 to 1¼ pounds
Cauliflowerets	25	2 ounces sliced, raw	7 pounds
Celery	25	1 2- to 3-inch piece	1 medium stalk
Olives	25	3 to 4	1 quart
Pickles	25	1 ounce	1 quart
Radishes	25	2	5 bunches
Tomatoes	25	3 ounces, sliced	5 to 6¼ pounds
Salads			
Side Dish:			
Cottage cheese	25	⅓ cup	5 pounds
Fruit	24	⅓ cup	2 quarts
Gelatin	25	½ cup liquid	3 quarts
Potato	24	½ cup	3 quarts
Tossed vegetable	25	¾ cup	1¼ gallons
Main Dish	25	1 cup	6¼ quarts
Vegetables			
Canned	25	½ cup	1 6½- to 7¼-pound can
Fresh:			
Potatoes	25	½ cup, mashed	6¾ pounds
	25	1 medium, baked	8½ pounds
Frozen:			
Beans	25	⅓ cup	5¼ pounds
Carrots or peas	25	⅓ cup	5 pounds
Potatoes, French-fried	25	10 pieces	3¼ pounds

DELLA ROBBIA WREATH

Named after Luca della Robbia, a 15th century artist famous for ornamental wreaths—

> 2 16-ounce cans pear halves
> 1 29-ounce can peach halves
> 1 20-ounce can pineapple slices, halved
> 1 16-ounce can peeled whole apricots
> 1 16-ounce jar spiced crab apples
>
> • • •
>
> Salad greens
> Seedless green grapes
> Dairy sour cream

Chill fruit. Drain canned fruit and crab apples thoroughly, reserving syrup for salad dressing. Put pear halves together and peach halves together to resemble whole fruit. (If desired, spread a little softened cream cheese on cut sides of pear and peach halves to make them hold together.)

Arrange bed of greens on large round platter. Around outer rim place 2 pineapple halves, standing with cut side down, between each whole pear and peach. Arrange apricots and crab apples alternately to form an inner circle. Place seedless green grapes in center of platter; if desired, garnish fruit with watercress. To prepare salad dressing, thin sour cream with a little of the reserved syrup. Serve with fruit. Makes 10 to 12 servings.

MELON BASKET

Chill 1 honeydew melon, fresh raspberries, seedless green grapes, red grapes, purple grapes, and fresh plums. Pare chilled *whole* honeydew melon. Leaving about a 2-inch circle uncut at top and bottom, mark melon with wooden picks in 10 to 12 equal wedges. Remove every other wedge with knife. Discard seeds. Cut thin slice from one end of melon to make it sit flat. Stand basket, on cut surface, in center of large platter. Arrange melon wedges spoke fashion on platter opposite openings in basket. Tuck lemon wedges between melon wedges.

Fill hollow of basket with raspberries and top basket with mint sprigs. Arrange small bunches of grapes and plums around melon. Offer a choice of salad dressings.

SUMMER FRUIT PLATTER

> Whole fresh pineapple
> Apples
> Fresh pears
> Fresh strawberries, sliced
> Oranges, sliced crosswise
> Cantaloupe wedges
> Stewed prunes, drained
> Lime Honey *or* Marshmallow Blizzard

Chill fruit. Halve pineapple lengthwise; remove hard core. Scoop out fruit and cut into chunks. Cube apples and pears; toss with pineapple and strawberries. Pile fruit mixture into pineapple shells. Arrange on a tray with orange slices, cantaloupe wedges, and prunes. If desired, garnish with sprigs of mint. Serve with Lime Honey or Marshmallow Blizzard Dressing.

Lime Honey: Blend together 1/4 cup honey with 2 tablespoons lime juice. Add dash salt.

Marshmallow Blizzard: To half of 7-ounce jar marshmallow creme, add 1 tablespoon *each* orange juice and lemon juice. With electric or rotary beater, beat till very fluffy. Fold in 1/4 cup mayonnaise or salad dressing.

PARADE OF FRUIT TRAY

> Pear Surprises
> Canned whole apricots
> Pineapple rings
> Stewed prunes
> Preserved kumquats
> Canned peach halves
> Cranberry-orange relish
> Frosted grapes (see Index)
> Spiced crab apples
> Salad greens

Pear Surprises: Drain chilled canned pear halves. Pat dry with paper toweling. Fill hollow of each with cream cheese. Put a red cherry, pitted date, or fig in between two pear halves. Seal halves of pears together with softened cream cheese. Using pastry tube, pipe cream-cheese ruffle along edges.

Chill all fruit, then drain canned and stewed fruit. On bed of salad greens, arrange pears, apricots, pineapple, prunes, kumquats, peach halves filled with cranberry-orange relish, grapes, and crab apples.

ROSY-WREATHED HONEYDEW

Each dainty raspberry mold hides a tasty cream cheese and nut ball—

    1 20½-ounce can pineapple slices
    1 16-ounce can fruit cocktail
    1 3-ounce package raspberry-
         flavored gelatin
    3 tablespoons lemon juice
    1 3-ounce package cream cheese
    ¼ cup finely chopped walnuts

        Honeydew Bowl
        Lettuce

Drain pineapple and fruit cocktail, reserving syrups. Add enough water to combined syrups to make 2 cups. Heat *1 cup* syrup mixture to boiling; add to gelatin and stir till gelatin is dissolved. Stir in remaining syrup mixture and lemon juice; chill gelatin mixture till partially set. Fold in drained fruit cocktail.

Form cream cheese into 8 balls; roll each in finely chopped nuts. Place 1 cheese ball in bottom of each of eight ½-cup molds. Carefully pour partially set gelatin over cheese balls in molds. Chill till firm.

Place Honeydew Bowl in center of large lettuce-lined platter. Arrange 8 pineapple slices on platter around Honeydew Bowl. Unmold individual raspberry molds on pineapple slices. Pass mayonnaise, if desired. Makes 8 servings.

Honeydew Bowl: Cut thin slice off bottom of 1 large honeydew, chilled, to make it sit flat. Cut top fourth off honeydew. Scoop out seeds and remove rind from entire melon. With round biscuit cutter, cut deep scallops around top edge of melon holding bottom of a custard cup or glass against inside of melon as each scallop is being cut.

Cube honeydew cut from scallops and top. Combine with drained canned peach and pear slices; remaining pineapple slices, cut in chunks; and seedless green grapes. Fill melon with fruit mixture. Trim with maraschino cherries and mint sprigs.

← **Lavishly displayed Fruited Watermelon** stars at an outdoor buffet. Heap juicy watermelon, cantaloupe, and honeydew balls in the cavity of the melon bowl and garnish with fresh fruit.

PEACH-PINEAPPLE RING

A fruit design arranged in the gelatin makes an impressive presentation—

    3 3-ounce packages lemon-flavored
         gelatin
    2 cups boiling water
    1 29-ounce can peach halves
    1 30-ounce can pineapple slices
    ½ cup drained maraschino
         cherries (20)

Dissolve gelatin in boiling water. Drain peaches and pineapple, reserving syrups. Combine syrups and add enough cold water to make 3 cups. Add syrup mixture to dissolved gelatin. Chill till partially set.

Alternate peaches, cut side up, and some of the cherries in bottom of 12½-cup ring mold. Gently pour *2 cups* partially set gelatin over; chill till *almost* firm. Keep remaining gelatin at room temperature. Halve pineapple slices; place, cut edge down, around outside and inside of mold to make "scalloped" design. Center remaining cherries in half rings. Carefully pour remaining gelatin over. Chill till firm. Makes 12 to 16 servings.

FRUITED WATERMELON

    1 large round watermelon
       Honeydew balls
       Cantaloupe balls
       Fresh blueberries
       Fresh raspberries
       Mint sprigs
       Red grape clusters
       Seedless green grape clusters
       Whole fresh plums
       Whole fresh pears

Cut slice off bottom of watermelon to make it sit flat. Cut top third off melon. Using a small bowl as guide, trace scallops around top edge. Carve out scallops following pattern; scoop out fruit. Place melon bowl on large platter. Cut watermelon fruit into balls with melon ball cutter. Chill all fruit.

Fill bowl with watermelon, honeydew, and cantaloupe balls. Top with blueberries and raspberries. Garnish with mint sprigs. Arrange grapes on platter around bottom of bowl. Fill in with plums and pears.

GARDEN-FRESH VEGETABLE SALADS

There is more to a good vegetable salad than lettuce and tomato. A myriad of greens and vegetables appear in salad bowls or gelatin molds.

For the tossed salad enthusiast there are ideas and recipes for basic and exotic combinations. And note, too, the Tips for Tossing that help the homemaker make the salad good to look at as well as good to eat.

There are many salad variations included in this chapter. Discover how gelatin, coleslaw, potato, macaroni, bean, and mixed vegetables build a salad recipe repertoire.

The chapter finale presents buffet salads with a vegetable twist—tossed, arranged, and molded.

The picturesque appeal of Superb Salad, a crackling-crisp tossed salad combination, is indicative of the tasteful and appealing recipes found in the following chapter.

48

GREEN SALAD
TOSS-UPS

SUPERB SALAD

    1 head romaine
    1 head Bibb lettuce
    1 small head lettuce
    ½ cup shredded Parmesan cheese
    2 ounces blue cheese,
        crumbled (½ cup)
    3 medium avocados
            . . .
    1 large cucumber, pared and
        sliced (1½ cups)
    18 cherry tomatoes, halved
    6 slices bacon, halved, crisp-
        cooked, and drained
        Red and green pepper slices
    ½ cup sliced pitted ripe olives
        Italian salad dressing

Tear salad greens into bite-size pieces; combine in large salad bowl. Sprinkle cheeses over greens. Halve avocados; remove seeds and peel. Slice avocado halves crosswise with fluted vegetable cutter. Arrange avocado slices, cucumber, tomatoes, bacon, pepper slices, and olives atop salad. To serve pour Italian salad dressing over vegetable mixture; toss lightly. Makes 12 to 14 servings.

DUTCH LETTUCE

    5 slices bacon, diced
    1 beaten egg
    ⅓ cup vinegar
    ¼ cup minced onion
    2 tablespoons sugar
    2 tablespoons water
    6 cups torn leaf lettuce

In skillet, cook bacon till crisp. Do *not* drain. Combine egg, vinegar, onion, sugar, water, and ½ teaspoon salt; add to bacon and drippings. Heat just to boiling, stirring constantly. Place lettuce in bowl. Pour hot dressing over and toss lightly. Makes 6 servings.

HEARTS-OF-PALM SALAD

        Pinch dried tarragon leaves,
            crushed
        Pinch dried thyme leaves,
            crushed
        Pinch dried basil leaves,
            crushed
    2 tablespoons vinegar
    ⅓ cup olive *or* salad oil
    1 tablespoon Dijon-style mustard
    1 clove garlic, crushed
    1 14-ounce can hearts of
        palm, drained
    3 cups watercress
    2 cups torn romaine
    1 cup torn lettuce

To prepare dressing, soak tarragon, thyme, and basil in vinegar for 1 hour in screw-top jar. Dissolve ½ teaspoon salt in vinegar mixture. Add oil, mustard, garlic, and ½ teaspoon pepper. Shake well.

Cut hearts of palm in serving-size pieces; combine with watercress, romaine, and lettuce in large salad bowl. Pour dressing over; toss lightly. Makes 6 to 8 servings.

SUMMER SALAD BOWL

The enticing salad on the cover—

        Leaf lettuce
    4 cups torn lettuce
    2 cups sliced raw cauliflower
    1 cup bias-cut celery
    1 cup sliced radishes
    1 green pepper, thinly sliced
    ⅓ cup crumbled blue cheese
        Italian salad dressing

Line salad bowl with leaf lettuce. Arrange lettuce, cauliflower, celery, radishes, and green pepper in bowl. Sprinkle cheese over. Serve with Italian dressing. Serves 8 to 10.

TOSSED ARTICHOKE SALAD

½ cup salad oil
⅓ cup vinegar
4 thin slices onion
1 tablespoon sugar
1 clove garlic, crushed
¼ teaspoon celery seed
1 9-ounce package frozen
    artichoke hearts
1 4-ounce can pimientos,
    drained and chopped
2 cups *each* torn lettuce, torn
    romaine, and torn spinach

In saucepan, combine oil, vinegar, 2 tablespoons water, onion, sugar, garlic, ½ teaspoon salt, celery seed, and dash pepper. Bring to boiling; add artichoke hearts. Cook till tender, 3 to 5 minutes; cool. Stir in pimiento. Chill. At serving time, drain reserving marinade. In bowl, add artichoke mixture to torn salad greens. Toss with enough of reserved marinade (about ¼ cup) to coat greens. Makes 8 to 10 servings.

FAMILY GREEN SALAD

LOW CALORIE · LOW CALORIE

2 cups torn lettuce
2 cups torn curly endive
2 medium tomatoes, cut in wedges
½ medium green pepper, sliced
½ cup sliced celery
¼ cup sliced radishes
2 tablespoons chopped green onion
    Low-calorie French-style salad
    dressing

Place lettuce and endive in salad bowl. Arrange next 5 ingredients over. Serve with low-calorie French-style dressing. Serves 6.

SPINACH-LETTUCE TOSS

In skillet, cook 5 slices bacon till crisp; drain, reserving drippings. Crumble bacon; combine with 3 cups *each* torn leaf lettuce and torn fresh spinach, ¼ cup diced celery, 2 tablespoons crumbled blue cheese, and 1 tablespoon chopped green onion. To drippings, add ¼ cup vinegar, 2 tablespoons sugar, and ½ teaspoon Worcestershire sauce; bring to boiling. Toss with salad. Serves 6.

SALATA

Means "mixed salad"—

6 cups shredded lettuce
3 tomatoes, peeled and chopped
1 large unpared cucumber,
    chopped
1 bunch watercress, chopped
1 medium green pepper, chopped
4 green onions, finely chopped
¼ cup sliced pitted Greek *or* ripe
    olives
3 tablespoons lemon juice
1 teaspoon salt
⅓ cup olive *or* salad oil

Combine first 6 ingredients. Add olives, lemon juice, and salt; toss. Mound salad on platter. Garnish with additional tomato wedges, cucumber slices, and olives, if desired. Pour oil over all. Let stand 15 minutes to blend flavors. Serves 8 to 10.

HARVEST TOSS

In screw-top jar, combine 3 tablespoons salad oil, 2 tablespoons vinegar, 1½ teaspoons sugar, ½ teaspoon salt, and dash pepper; shake well. In bowl, toss 6 cups torn leaf lettuce; 2 cups coarsely chopped unpared red apple; 1 cup thinly sliced unpared raw zucchini; and 1 small green pepper, cut in thin strips. Pour dressing over, toss. Serves 6.

CROUTONS FOR SALADS

Bread: Without removing crusts, cut white, whole wheat, or rye bread slices into small cubes. Toast cubes on baking sheet in slow oven (300°), stirring frequently, till dry and golden brown. In skillet, melt butter with 1 clove garlic. Remove garlic when it is golden brown. Add bread cubes; toss till they are butter coated.

Store a supply of croutons in a covered jar in the refrigerator. Heat them just before sprinkling over salads.

Walnut: In skillet, melt 2 tablespoons butter; add ½ teaspoon salt *or* garlic salt. Stir in ½ cup coarsely broken walnuts; brown over medium heat, stirring constantly. Add to salad dressing just before tossing.

BOSTON-COTTAGE TOSS

6 cups torn Boston *or* bibb
    lettuce
1 cup small curd cream-style
    cottage cheese
1 medium avocado, peeled and
    diced
⅓ cup coarsely chopped dill pickle
2 tablespoons sliced green onion
1 tablespoon salad oil
1 tablespoon wine vinegar
2 hard-cooked eggs, sliced

In large bowl season lettuce with salt and pepper; add next 4 ingredients. Toss in oil and vinegar; garnish with egg. Serves 4.

WILTED LETTUCE TOSS

4 slices bacon
4 cups torn leaf lettuce
1 large tomato, chopped
¼ cup sliced green onion
            • • •
2 tablespoons vinegar
½ teaspoon dried oregano leaves,
    crushed

Fry bacon in large skillet till crisp; drain, reserving 1 tablespoon bacon drippings. Crumble bacon and set aside. Meanwhile, combine lettuce, tomato, and onion.

In skillet, heat reserved drippings, vinegar, oregano, ¼ teaspoon salt, and dash pepper to boiling. Gradually add lettuce mixture, tossing just till leaves are coated and wilted slightly. Turn into serving bowl. Top with crumbled bacon. Serve immediately. Makes 4 or 5 servings.

CHIFFONADE SALAD

Place four 1-inch slices lettuce on salad plates. For each salad, top lettuce with 1 tablespoon low-calorie French-style salad dressing. Arrange down center 1 tablespoon finely chopped canned or cooked beets, chilled. Finely chop 2 chilled hard-cooked eggs. Sprinkle ½ egg on each salad arranging on both sides of beets. Border each salad with 1 tablespoon finely chopped celery. Season. Pass extra dressing. Serves 4.

MODERN CAESAR SALAD

½ cup salad oil
¼ cup red wine vinegar
1 large clove garlic, crushed
2 teaspoons Worcestershire sauce
¼ teaspoon salt
    Dash pepper
3 slices bread, cubed
½ cup shredded Parmesan cheese
1 ounce blue cheese,
    crumbled (¼ cup)
8 cups torn romaine (about
    1 medium head)
1 egg

For dressing, shake together salad oil, red wine vinegar, crushed garlic, Worcestershire sauce, salt, and pepper in screw-top jar. Refrigerate a few hours or overnight to blend flavors. Toast bread cubes in slow oven (225°) for 2 hours.

To serve, sprinkle cheeses over romaine in salad bowl; add toasted bread cubes. Shake egg well with dressing; toss lightly with salad. Makes 6 to 8 servings.

PEPPERONI SALAD

6 cups torn lettuce (about 1
    medium head)
2 tomatoes, cut in wedges
4 ounces mozzarella cheese, cubed
    (1 cup)
1 cup drained garbanzo beans
½ cup thinly sliced pepperoni
¼ cup sliced green onion
½ cup Italian salad dressing
    Salt
    Freshly ground black pepper

In large salad bowl, combine lettuce, tomato wedges, cheese, garbanzo beans, pepperoni, and green onion. Pour Italian salad dressing over. Toss lettuce mixture lightly with dressing. Sprinkle with salt and pepper to taste. Makes 8 or 9 servings.

A taste of Italy comes through Pepperoni Salad. → Sliced pepperoni, cubes of mozzarella cheese, garbanzo beans, and Italian dressing are tossed with crisp lettuce, juicy tomatoes, and green onion.

BACON AND TOMATO SALAD

A bacon-lettuce-tomato combo in a new form—

Toast 1 cup ½-inch bread cubes at 225° till dry, about 2 hours. Line salad bowl with romaine. Combine in salad bowl toasted bread cubes; 3 cups torn lettuce (½ medium head); 3 medium tomatoes, cut in wedges; 8 slices bacon, crisp-cooked and crumbled; and ½ cup mayonnaise or salad dressing. Toss lightly. Season to taste. Serves 4 or 5.

CHEF'S BOWL

1 clove garlic
1 medium head lettuce
. . .
1 to 2 cups fully-cooked ham cut in strips
1 8-ounce package process American cheese, cut in strips
1 pound fresh asparagus, cooked, drained, and chilled
1 10-ounce package frozen peas, cooked, drained, and chilled
¾ cup sliced radishes
Chef's French Dressing

Rub individual salad bowls with a cut end of garlic clove, then line with lettuce. Arrange next 5 ingredients in bowls. Season to taste with salt and pepper. Pass Chef's French Dressing. Makes 6 servings.

Chef's French Dressing: In screw-top jar, shake 2 tablespoons sugar and 1 teaspoon *each* salt, dry mustard, and paprika with ⅔ cup salad oil; ⅓ cup tarragon vinegar; 3 tablespoons lemon juice; and 2 teaspoons grated onion. Chill thoroughly.

CHUCK WAGON SALAD

For dressing, shake together ¼ cup salad oil; 2 tablespoons white wine vinegar; and 1 ounce blue cheese, crumbled (¼ cup), in screw-top jar. Chill thoroughly.

Rub bowl with cut end of 1 clove garlic. Add 4 cups torn lettuce; one 8½-ounce can (1 cup) limas, drained and chilled; 1 cup *each* sliced celery and sliced cucumber; and 2 medium tomatoes, cut in wedges. Season. Toss mixture with dressing. Serves 6.

WILTED SPINACH TOSS

A tang of orange penetrates throughout—

3 slices bacon
¼ cup vinegar
1 tablespoon salad oil
1½ teaspoons sugar
¼ teaspoon salt
⅛ teaspoon dried tarragon leaves, crushed
Dash freshly ground black pepper
. . .
¼ cup chopped celery
1 tablespoon sliced green onion
6 cups torn fresh spinach (about ½ pound)
2 medium oranges, peeled and cut in bite-size pieces

In large skillet, cook bacon till crisp; drain, reserving 2 tablespoons bacon drippings. Crumble bacon and set aside. Stir vinegar, oil, sugar, salt, tarragon, and pepper into reserved drippings; bring to boiling. Add chopped celery and sliced green onion.

Gradually add spinach, tossing just till leaves are coated and wilted slightly. Add oranges and crumbled bacon; toss lightly. Makes 6 to 8 servings.

ITALIAN ANCHOVY SALAD

1 2-ounce can anchovy fillets, drained
2 large tomatoes, peeled and cut in thin wedges
2 medium green peppers, cut in narrow strips
12 pitted ripe olives
8 green onions, chopped
. . .
¼ cup olive oil
2 tablespoons vinegar
Freshly ground black pepper
Shredded lettuce

Separate anchovy fillets into bowl; add tomatoes, green pepper, olives, and green onion. Combine oil and vinegar and drizzle over anchovy mixture. Sprinkle with pepper. Refrigerate about 1 hour. At serving time, spoon over shredded lettuce. Serves 4.

GREEN SALAD QUINTET

- ½ bunch watercress
- 6 romaine leaves
- 6 Boston lettuce leaves
- 4 escarole leaves
- 2 French endives

. . .

- 6 radishes, sliced
- 1 scallion, finely chopped
- 2 tablespoons olive oil
- 2 tablespoons wine vinegar
  Dash *each* garlic salt,
    monosodium glutamate,
    paprika, and freshly ground
    black pepper.

Rinse first 5 ingredients; drain. Tear leaves in bite-size pieces and slice endives. Combine greens with radishes and scallion. Combine remaining ingredients. Toss lightly with lettuce mixture. Makes 4 to 6 servings.

CURRY SALAD

- ½ teaspoon beef-flavored gravy
    base
- 1 cup mayonnaise or salad
    dressing
- 1 clove garlic, minced
- 1 tablespoon curry powder
- ¼ teaspoon Worcestershire sauce
- 6 to 8 drops bottled hot pepper
    sauce

. . .

- 6 cups torn mixed salad greens
- 4 cups torn fresh spinach
- 1 16-ounce can artichoke hearts,
    chilled, drained, and halved
- ¼ cup sliced radishes

For dressing, dissolve gravy base in ¼ cup hot water; blend into mayonnaise. Stir in garlic, curry, Worcestershire sauce, and hot pepper sauce. Chill. Combine remaining ingredients in large salad bowl. Toss lettuce mixture lightly with dressing. Serves 10.

"Spice of the East" dressing in Curry Salad flavors the meal with a nostalgia of India. Refrigerating the dressing several hours or overnight enhances the intriguing blend of ingredients.

TANGY SPINACH BOWL

Lemon and horseradish give it zip—

2 tablespoons sliced green
    onion
¼ cup butter or margarine
2 tablespoons all-purpose flour
¼ teaspoon salt
1 cup water
2 tablespoons lemon juice
1 tablespoon prepared horseradish
½ teaspoon Worcestershire sauce
2 hard-cooked eggs
1 pound fresh spinach, torn in
    bite-size pieces

In small saucepan, prepare dressing by cooking onion in butter about 1 minute; blend in
flour and salt. Add water, lemon juice, horseradish, and Worcestershire sauce; cook and
stir till mixture is boiling.

Dice 1 hard-cooked egg; add to dressing.
Pour hot dressing over spinach in salad
bowl; toss lightly. Slice remaining egg and
arrange over salad. Sprinkle with paprika, if
desired. Serve immediately. Serves 6 to 8.

FRUIT-VEGETABLE TOSS

An attractive salad for a special occasion—

12 cups torn lettuce
8 ounces sharp natural Cheddar
    cheese, cut in thin strips
½ cup sliced celery
⅔ cup salad oil
⅓ cup wine vinegar
½ cup sugar
1 tablespoon grated onion
1 teaspoon dry mustard
½ teaspoon salt
4 medium pared oranges, cut in
    bite-size pieces
2 medium nectarines, peeled and
    sliced

Combine lettuce, cheese, and celery in large
salad bowl. To prepare dressing, beat together oil, vinegar, sugar, onion, dry mustard, and salt. Pour enough dressing over lettuce to coat lightly; toss. Top with orange
pieces and nectarine slices. Toss again. Pass
remaining dressing. Makes 12 servings.

FOO YUNG TOSS

A Chinese version of tossed salad—

1 head romaine, torn in bite-
    size pieces
1 16-ounce can bean sprouts,
    rinsed and drained
1 5-ounce can water chestnuts,
    drained and sliced
5 slices bacon, crisp-cooked and
    crumbled
2 hard-cooked eggs, sliced
1 cup salad oil
½ cup sugar
⅓ cup catsup
¼ cup vinegar
2 tablespoons grated onion
2 teaspoons Worcestershire sauce

In salad bowl, combine romaine, bean
sprouts, water chestnuts, bacon, and eggs.
Season to taste with salt and pepper. To prepare dressing, combine remaining ingredients in screw-top jar. Shake well. Pour over
salad; toss lightly. Makes 6 to 8 servings.

CAMEMBERT SALAD

1 small head lettuce
4 ounces Camembert cheese, cubed
2 ounces sharp natural Cheddar
    cheese, shredded (½ cup)

Place 4 lettuce cups in salad bowl. Tear remaining lettuce into bite-size pieces (about
4 cups). Toss with cheeses and fill lettuce
cups. Serve with a vinegar-oil or Italian
salad dressing. Makes 4 servings.

SPINACH-AVOCADO BOWL

10 ounces fresh spinach, torn in
    bite-size pieces
2 medium avocados, peeled and
    sliced
½ pound bacon, crisp-cooked and
    crumbled
½ cup chopped peanuts

Place spinach in salad bowl. Arrange avocado slices, bacon, and nuts over. Serve with a
Russian salad dressing. Serves 8 to 10.

TOSSING TIPS

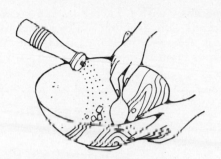

Try the Chef's flavor trick. Lightly sprinkle salt in a wooden salad bowl. Mash a clove of garlic into the salt with the back of a spoon. The fresh flavor of garlic will mingle pleasantly with that favorite tossed salad.

Roll-toss salads in a big bowl. Gently stroke downward to bottom with tool in one hand and up and over with tool in other hand. This down-and-over motion, with dressing delicately coating greens, assures the salad of superb taste.

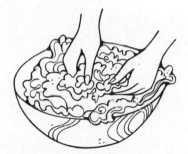

Tear salad greens into bite-size pieces rather than cutting them with a knife. Tearing exposes the juicy insides and allows the dressing to become absorbed by the greens. Besides tasting fresher, torn greens make a more attractive looking tossed salad.

Hold the juicy tomato wedges till last when tossing a bowl of salad greens. This prevents the dressing from becoming diluted. For delicious crunch, add a few crisp croutons or coarsely chopped walnuts that have been browned with butter in a skillet over medium heat.

Always shake an oil-vinegar dressing before using. Shaking emulsifies the oil and vinegar and blends those carefully chosen herbs and spices. Add just enough dressing to the salad so every leaf glistens. Toss together lightly.

Salad tossing delayed? Don't let greens wilt. For short delays, keep them fresh under damp paper toweling wrung out of ice water. For longer delays, place bowl covered with damp paper toweling on a refrigerator shelf.

TOSSED SALAD COMBINATION GUIDE

Venture into the realm of leafy greens and vegetables with a flavorful salad creation that will give each menu spark and variety. To prepare the winning combinations given below, tear salad greens in bite-size pieces unless otherwise indicated. Add remaining ingredients *except* garnish and toss lightly with your favorite dressing. Garnish with the ingredient in the last column; serve immediately.

To Go Along With	Add These	Garnish With
Bibb lettuce	Tomato, cut in wedges	Hard-cooked egg, sliced
	Unpared cucumber, sliced	
	Avocado, peeled and sliced	
Boston lettuce	Hard-cooked egg, chopped	Parsley sprigs
	Fresh mushrooms, sliced	
	Chives, snipped	
Boston lettuce	Watercress	Parmesan cheese, grated
	Anchovy fillets	
Chinese cabbage	Leaf lettuce	Water chestnuts, sliced
	Celery, bias-cut	
	Radishes, sliced	
	Chives, snipped	
Curly endive	Iceberg lettuce	Hard-cooked egg, sliced
	Bacon, crisp-cooked and crumbled	
	Tomato, cut in wedges	
	Celery, sliced	
	Radishes, sliced	
	Green onion, chopped	
Iceberg lettuce	Carrot, shredded	Raisins
	Celery, diced	
	Mandarin oranges, well-drained	

To Go Along With	Add These	Garnish With
Iceberg lettuce	Raw cauliflowerets, thinly sliced Onion, sliced and separated into rings Pimiento-stuffed green olives, sliced	Blue cheese, crumbled
Leaf lettuce	Chicory Watercress Tomato, cut in wedges Onion, thinly sliced Cucumber, sliced	Walnut halves
Leaf lettuce	Curly endive Tomato, finely diced Green onion, sliced	Cheddar cheese, cut in thin strips
Leaf lettuce	Watercress Raw spinach Carrot curls Pitted ripe olives, sliced	Almonds, toasted
Romaine	Tomato, diced Green pepper, chopped Romano cheese, grated	Artichoke hearts
Raw spinach	Bacon, crisp-cooked and crumbled Hard-cooked egg, chopped Carrot, thinly sliced	Canned French-fried onions
Raw spinach, shredded	Raw zucchini, sliced Radishes, sliced Green onion, sliced	Mushroom crowns

INVITING VEGETABLE MOLDS

CUCUMBER RING SUPREME

Cucumber-trim Layer
1 envelope (1 tablespoon)
    unflavored gelatin
2 tablespoons sugar
2 tablespoons lemon juice
1 8-ounce package cream cheese,
    cubed and softened
    About 6 medium pared
    cucumbers
1 cup mayonnaise or salad
    dressing
3 tablespoons finely chopped
    onion
¼ cup snipped parsley

Prepare *Cucumber-trim Layer:* Mix ½ envelope (1½ teaspoons) unflavored gelatin, 1 tablespoon sugar, and ½ teaspoon salt in small saucepan. Add ¾ cup water; heat and stir till gelatin and sugar are dissolved. Stir in 2 tablespoons lemon juice. Pour into 6½-cup ring mold. Chill till partially set. Overlay thin slices from ½ unpared cucumber in bottom of mold. Chill till *almost* firm.

Meanwhile, mix the 1 envelope unflavored gelatin, sugar, and ¾ teaspoon salt in saucepan. Add ⅔ cup water; stir over low heat till gelatin and sugar are dissolved. Stir in lemon juice. Gradually beat hot gelatin mixture into softened cream cheese with rotary beater till mixture is smooth.

Halve cucumbers and scrape out seeds; grind using fine blade, or finely shred. Measure 2 cups drained ground cucumber and add with remaining ingredients to cream cheese mixture. Pour over almost firm gelatin in mold. Chill till firm. Makes 8 servings.

←Cherry tomatoes and fresh watercress, both perky and bright, are decorative additions to Cucumber Ring Supreme. Enjoy the creamy richness and cucumber crunch in every bite.

CARROT-CABBAGE MOLD

Pickle perfection salad laced with vegetables—

2 3-ounce packages lemon-
    flavored gelatin
¼ cup lemon juice
1 cup shredded cabbage
½ cup shredded carrots
½ cup diced celery
¼ cup diced sweet pickle *or*
    pickle relish

Dissolve gelatin in 2 cups boiling water; stir in 1½ cups cold water, lemon juice, and ¼ teaspoon salt. Chill till partially set. Fold in remaining ingredients. Pour into 5½-cup mold. Chill till firm. Makes 8 to 10 servings.

CABBAGE ASPIC

2 envelopes (2 tablespoons)
    unflavored gelatin
4 cups tomato juice
½ medium onion, sliced
3 branches celery, 3 inches long
2 lemon slices
2 bay leaves
    Non-caloric liquid sweetener
    equal to 2 tablespoons sugar
2 teaspoons prepared horseradish
2 cups chopped cabbage *or* 1 cup
    chopped celery

Soften gelatin in ½ cup tomato juice; set aside. In saucepan, combine remaining tomato juice, onion, celery, lemon, and bay leaves. Bring to boiling; reduce heat and simmer, covered, for 10 minutes; strain. Add softened gelatin. Return to low heat and stir till gelatin is dissolved. Stir in non-caloric sweetener, horseradish, ½ teaspoon salt, and dash pepper. Chill till partially set. Fold in cabbage. Pour into eight ½-cup molds. Chill till firm. Makes 8 servings.

SPRING SALAD SOUFFLE

1 3-ounce package lime-flavored gelatin
1 10½-ounce can condensed cream of asparagus soup
½ cup mayonnaise or salad dressing
1 tablespoon vinegar
1 teaspoon grated onion
½ cup shredded unpared cucumber
¼ cup diced celery
1 tablespoon snipped parsley

In saucepan, mix gelatin and ½ cup water. Gradually blend in soup; heat and stir till gelatin is dissolved. Add next 3 ingredients and dash pepper to gelatin. Beat with rotary beater till mixture is smooth. Chill till gelatin mixture is partially set.

Pour gelatin into large chilled bowl; beat till thick and fluffy. Fold in remaining ingredients. Pour into 5½-cup ring mold; chill till firm. Makes 4 or 5 servings.

JELLIED POTATO SALAD

5 cups diced, peeled, cooked potatoes
1 tablespoon vinegar
1 cup chopped onion
1½ cups mayonnaise
1 tablespoon celery seed
2 3-ounce packages lemon-flavored gelatin
¼ cup vinegar
9 green pepper rings
9 red pepper rings or pimiento strips
1 cup diced cucumber

Sprinkle potatoes with the 1 tablespoon vinegar and 2 teaspoons salt. Toss with onion, mayonnaise, and celery seed; chill. Dissolve gelatin in 2½ cups boiling water; stir in the ¼ cup vinegar. To *half* the gelatin mixture add ¼ cup cold water. Pour into 9x 9x2-inch pan. Chill till partially set; arrange peppers atop gelatin. Chill till *almost* firm.

Meanwhile, chill remaining gelatin till partially set; beat till soft peaks form. Fold in potato mixture and cucumber. Spoon over gelatin in pan; chill till firm. Invert to unmold. Cut in squares. Makes 9 servings.

COLESLAW PARFAIT SALAD

Equally attractive made in individual molds—

1 3-ounce package lemon-flavored gelatin
½ cup mayonnaise or salad dressing
2 tablespoons vinegar
¼ teaspoon salt
. . .
1 cup finely shredded cabbage
½ cup diced celery
½ cup sliced radishes
2 tablespoons chopped green pepper
1 tablespoon chopped onion

Dissolve gelatin in 1 cup boiling water. Add ½ cup cold water, mayonnaise, vinegar, and salt; beat with rotary beater till smooth. Chill till partially set, then beat till light and fluffy. Fold in remaining ingredients. Pour into 3½-cup mold; chill till gelatin mixture is firm. Makes 5 or 6 servings.

EASY ASPIC

Dissolve two 3-ounce packages lemon-flavored gelatin in 1¾ cups boiling water. Stir in two 8-ounce cans (2 cups) tomato sauce, 2 tablespoons vinegar, ½ teaspoon salt, and ½ teaspoon seasoned salt. Pour into 4½-cup mold or eight ½-cup molds. Chill till firm. Makes 8 servings.

CREAMY BROCCOLI MOLD

Soften 1 envelope (1 tablespoon) unflavored gelatin in ¾ cup cold water. Cook one 10-ounce package frozen chopped broccoli following package directions, adding 2 chicken bouillon cubes, 1 tablespoon instant minced onion, and 1 teaspoon monosodium glutamate to cooking water. *Do not add salt. Do not drain.* Add softened gelatin and stir till gelatin is dissolved. Cool. Stir ½ cup dairy sour cream into broccoli mixture.

Fold in ½ cup chopped celery, ¼ cup chopped canned pimiento, 2 tablespoons snipped parsley, and 2 tablespoons lemon juice. Pour gelatin mixture into 5½-cup ring mold; chill till firm. Makes 6 to 8 servings.

VEGETABLE CREAM MOLDS

Dissolve one 3-ounce package lemon-flavored gelatin and 2 beef bouillon cubes in 1 cup boiling water; chill till partially set. Add 1 cup dairy sour cream and 2 tablespoons tarragon vinegar; beat with rotary beater till smooth. Fold in ½ cup *each* chopped celery, chopped radishes, and chopped unpared cucumber, and 2 tablespoons *each* chopped green pepper and chopped green onion. Pour into six ½-cup molds; chill till firm. Makes 6 servings.

BEET-PINEAPPLE MOLD

  1 **16-ounce can shoestring beets**
  1 **8¾-ounce can crushed pineapple**
  2 **3-ounce packages lemon-flavored**
    gelatin
  2 **cups boiling water**
  2 **tablespoons lemon juice**
    Dash salt

Drain beets and pineapple, reserving 1½ cups of the combined liquids. Dissolve gelatin in boiling water; stir in reserved liquid, lemon juice, and salt. Chill till partially set, then fold in drained beets and pineapple. Pour gelatin mixture into 6½-cup mold or eight to ten ½-cup molds. Chill till gelatin mixture is firm. Makes 8 to 10 servings.

VEGETABLE LIME RING

  1 **3-ounce package lime-flavored**
    gelatin
 ¾ **cup boiling water**
    • • •
 ¾ **cup shredded unpared cucumber**
 ¼ **cup finely sliced green onion**
  1 **8-ounce carton (1 cup)**
    cream-style cottage cheese
  1 **cup mayonnaise or salad**
    dressing
  1 **teaspoon prepared horseradish**
 ¼ **teaspoon salt**

Dissolve gelatin in boiling water; chill till partially set. Combine remaining ingredients and fold into gelatin. Pour gelatin mixture into 3½-cup ring mold. Chill till gelatin mixture is firm. Makes 5 or 6 servings.

PERFECTION SALAD

An all-time favorite—

  2 **envelopes (2 tablespoons)**
    unflavored gelatin
 ½ **cup sugar**
  1 **teaspoon salt**
 1½ **cups boiling water**
 1½ **cups cold water**
 ⅓ **cup white vinegar**
  2 **tablespoons lemon juice**
  2 **cups finely shredded cabbage**
  1 **cup chopped celery**
 ½ **cup chopped green pepper**
 ¼ **cup chopped canned pimiento**

Mix gelatin, sugar, and salt. Add boiling water and stir till gelatin, sugar, and salt are dissolved. Stir in cold water, vinegar, and lemon juice; chill till partially set. Fold cabbage, celery, green pepper, and pimiento into gelatin. Pour gelatin mixture into 5½-cup ring mold. Chill till firm. Serves 8 to 10.

CUCUMBER-CABBAGE MOLD

The center of the ring is an ideal spot for a small bowl of mayonnaise—

  2 **3-ounce packages lime-flavored**
    gelatin
  2 **cups boiling water**
 1¾ **cups cold water**
  2 **tablespoons vinegar**
  1 **teaspoon prepared horseradish**
 ½ **teaspoon salt**
    • • •
  1 **large unpared cucumber**
  1 **cup chopped cabbage**

Dissolve gelatin in boiling water. Stir cold water, vinegar, horseradish, and salt into dissolved gelatin. Chill till partially set. Pour ½ *cup* of the gelatin mixture into 5½-cup ring mold. Cut 10 to 15 paper-thin slices of unpared cucumber and arrange on gelatin in mold. Chill till *almost* firm.

Dice enough unpared cucumber to make 1 cup; fold cucumber and chopped cabbage into remaining partially set gelatin. Carefully pour cabbage mixture over almost firm gelatin layer. Chill till firm. Pass mayonnaise, if desired. Makes 8 to 10 servings.

Make-ahead salads like Calico Vegetable Molds ease last minute dinner duties. Premolded individual servings need only be placed on lettuce-lined plates and topped with a dollop of dressing.

CALICO VEGETABLE MOLDS

   1 3-ounce package lemon-flavored gelatin
   2 tablespoons vinegar
   1 8-ounce can peas and carrots, drained
  ¼ cup sliced radishes
   2 tablespoons sliced green onion

Dissolve gelatin in 1 cup boiling water; stir in ¾ cup cold water, vinegar, and ¼ teaspoon salt. Chill till partially set. Fold in peas and carrots, radishes, and green onion. Pour into six ½-cup molds. Chill till firm. Pass mayonnaise, if desired. Makes 6 servings.

"ONE CUP" COTTAGE RING

Dissolve one 3-ounce package lime-flavored gelatin in 1 cup boiling water. Add 1 cup mayonnaise or salad dressing and beat with rotary beater till smooth. Chill till partially set. Fold in one 8-ounce carton (1 cup) large curd cream-style cottage cheese, 1 cup chopped celery, and 1 cup diced green pepper. Pour into 4½-cup mold. Chill till firm. Makes 6 servings.

TOMATO ASPIC SOUFFLE

   1 6-ounce can (⅔ cup) evaporated milk
   3 cups tomato juice
   2 bay leaves
   4 black peppercorns
  ½ teaspoon onion salt
  ¼ teaspoon celery salt
  ¼ teaspoon dried oregano leaves, crushed
   2 envelopes (2 tablespoons) unflavored gelatin
   2 3-ounce packages cream cheese, softened

Pour milk into freezer tray. Freeze till soft ice crystals form around edges. In saucepan, blend *2 cups* of the tomato juice with the next 5 ingredients. Simmer, covered, for 5 minutes; strain. Soften gelatin in ½ *cup* cold tomato juice; stir into hot mixture till gelatin is dissolved. Cool. With rotary beater, gradually beat remaining juice into cream cheese; stir into gelatin mixture.

Chill till partially set. Whip icy cold evaporated milk till stiff peaks form; fold into gelatin mixture. Pour into 6½-cup mold; chill till firm. Makes 10 to 12 servings.

MOLDED ASPARAGUS SALAD

   1 envelope (1 tablespoon) unflavored gelatin
   1 10½-ounce can condensed cream of asparagus soup
   1 tablespoon lemon juice
  ¼ teaspoon salt
   1 8-ounce carton (1 cup) cream-style cottage cheese
  ½ cup dairy sour cream
   1 10½-ounce can asparagus spears, drained and cut
  ½ cup chopped celery
   2 tablespoons chopped canned pimiento

In saucepan, soften gelatin in ¼ cup cold water. Stir over low heat till gelatin is dissolved. Blend soup, lemon juice, and salt into gelatin; beat in cottage cheese and sour cream. Chill gelatin mixture till partially set, then fold in remaining ingredients. Pour into 4½-cup mold. Chill till firm. Serves 5 or 6.

PIMIENTO CHEESE MOLD

    1 3-ounce package lemon-flavored
        gelatin
    ½ teaspoon salt
    1 cup boiling water
    1 5-ounce jar process cheese
        spread with pimiento
    ¼ cup mayonnaise or salad
        dressing
    ¼ cup cold water
    2 to 3 teaspoons vinegar
        Dash bottled hot pepper sauce

          •   •   •

    ½ cup chopped celery
    2 tablespoons finely chopped
        onion
    2 tablespoons finely chopped
        green pepper

Dissolve gelatin and salt in boiling water. Add cheese spread and mayonnaise; beat with rotary beater till smooth. Stir in cold water, vinegar, and hot pepper sauce. Chill gelatin mixture till partially set.

Fold remaining ingredients into gelatin mixture. Pour into 3½-cup mold. Chill salad till firm. Makes 4 servings.

BLENDER CUCUMBER SALAD

An appliance does all the work—

    1 large cucumber, pared
    1 3-ounce package lemon-flavored
        gelatin
    Cottage Cheese Dressing

Slice cucumber into blender container. Cover and blend on high speed till pureed. Stop blender as needed to push cucumber down from sides. Measure cucumber; add water, if necessary, to make 1 cup.

Dissolve gelatin in 1¼ cups boiling water; stir in cucumber. Chill gelatin mixture till partially set, stirring occasionally. Pour into 3½-cup ring mold. Chill till firm. Serve with Cottage Cheese Dressing. Serves 4 to 6.

Cottage Cheese Dressing: In blender container, combine one 8-ounce carton (1 cup) cream-style cottage cheese; 2 tablespoons sugar; and 4 teaspoons lemon juice. Blend till creamy. Add 2 tablespoons milk, one at a time, till desired consistency.

BARBECUE BEAN MOLD

Soften 2 envelopes (2 tablespoons) unflavored gelatin in ½ cup tomato juice. Add 2 tablespoons brown sugar and 1 teaspoon prepared mustard; stir over low heat till gelatin and sugar are dissolved. Stir in 1 cup tomato juice and 2 tablespoons lemon juice. Chill till partially set.

Fold one 16-ounce can barbecue beans, ½ cup chopped celery, and 1 tablespoon finely chopped onion into gelatin mixture. Pour into 4½-cup mold. Chill till firm. Unmold on lettuce lined platter. Makes 8 servings.

HARVEST VEGETABLE MOLD

Dissolve two 3-ounce packages lemon-flavored gelatin in 2 cups boiling water; add 1½ cups cold water, 3 tablespoons vinegar, and ½ teaspoon salt. Chill till partially set. Place 1 cup cooked whole green beans crosswise in bottom of 8½x4½x2½-inch loaf dish. Pour *1 cup* gelatin slowly over beans. Chill till *almost* firm. Combine remaining gelatin with 1 cup coarsely chopped, cooked cauliflower; ½ cup cooked, sliced carrots; ¼ cup diced celery; ¼ cup sliced radishes; and 2 tablespoons sliced green onions. Pour over gelatin in pan; chill till firm. Serves 8 to 10.

CREAMY RICE MOLD

    2 envelopes (2 tablespoons)
        unflavored gelatin
    2 13¾-ounce cans (3½ cups)
        chicken broth
    ¾ cup mayonnaise or salad
        dressing
    2 tablespoons lemon juice
    1 cup whipping cream, whipped
    2½ cups cooked rice
    ¾ cup chopped celery
    ¼ cup sliced green onion

Soften gelatin in ½ cup cold water. Heat broth to boiling. Add softened gelatin and stir till dissolved. Add mayonnaise and lemon juice; beat with rotary beater till smooth. Chill mixture till partially set, then whip till light and fluffy. Fold in remaining ingredients. Pour into 8½-cup ring mold. Chill till firm. Makes 10 to 12 servings.

Make Tomato-celery Aspic the keynote for a summer patio supper. Pile spicy Swedish Pickled Shrimp or a favorite seafood or chicken salad in the center of the celery-dotted tomato ring. Trim plate with curly endive. The peppy shrimp can also double as appetizers or make a salad in themselves.

TOMATO-CELERY ASPIC

Soften 2 envelopes (2 tablespoons) unflavored gelatin in 1 cup cold tomato juice. In saucepan, mix 2 cups tomato juice with ⅓ cup chopped onion, ¼ cup snipped celery leaves, 2 tablespoons brown sugar, 1 teaspoon salt, 2 small bay leaves, and 4 whole cloves. Simmer, uncovered, 5 minutes. Strain to remove vegetables and seasonings.

Dissolve softened gelatin in seasoned hot tomato mixture. Add 1 cup tomato juice and 3 tablespoons lemon juice. Chill till gelatin mixture is partially set.

Fold in 1 cup chopped celery. Pour into 5½-cup ring mold. Chill till firm. Unmold and fill center of ring with Swedish Pickled Shrimp. Makes 8 to 10 servings.

SWEDISH PICKLED SHRIMP

In saucepan, cover 1½ pounds frozen shrimp in shells with boiling water. Add 4 celery tops, 2 tablespoons mixed pickling spices, and 1½ teaspoons salt. Cover and simmer 5 minutes. Drain, peel, and clean shrimp under cold water. Combine shrimp with 1 cup sliced onion, separated into rings; 4 bay leaves; and Pickling Marinade in shallow dish. Cover; chill at least 24 hours, spooning marinade over shrimp occasionally. Drain shrimp; spoon into center of aspic.

Pickling Marinade: Blend together 1½ cups salad oil, ¾ cup white vinegar, 3 tablespoons capers with liquid, 2 teaspoons celery seed, 1½ teaspoons salt, and few drops bottled hot pepper sauce. Pour over shrimp.

ASPARAGUS MOLD

2 tablespoons (2 envelopes)
  unflavored gelatin
½ cup sugar
¼ teaspoon salt
3½ cups cold water
⅓ cup white vinegar
3 tablespoons lemon juice
1 teaspoon grated onion
1 cup finely chopped celery
⅓ cup chopped canned
  pimiento
1 14½-ounce can asparagus cuts,
  drained
Mayonnaise or salad dressing

In saucepan, combine gelatin, sugar, and salt. Add 1½ *cups* of the cold water and vinegar; stir over low heat till gelatin and sugar are dissolved. Add lemon juice, onion, and remaining water. Chill till partially set.

Fold in celery and pimiento. Arrange *one-third* of the asparagus in bottom of 6½-cup mold. Carefully pour in *one-third* of the gelatin mixture. Repeat layers, ending with gelatin. Chill till firm. Serve with mayonnaise or salad dressing. Makes 10 to 12 servings.

POTATO SALAD MOLD

1 envelope (1 tablespoon)
  unflavored gelatin
2 tablespoons sugar
¼ cup lemon juice
4 cups diced, peeled, cooked
  potatoes
¾ cup chopped celery
3 hard-cooked eggs, chopped
¼ cup sliced pimiento-stuffed
  green olives
¼ cup chopped green pepper
¼ cup snipped parsley
1 cup mayonnaise
½ cup whipping cream, whipped

Mix gelatin, sugar, and ¾ teaspoon salt in saucepan. Add 1¼ cups water; stir over low heat till gelatin and sugar are dissolved. Add lemon juice. Cool to room temperature. Stir next 6 ingredients into gelatin mixture. Fold in mayonnaise and whipped cream. Spoon into 7½-cup mold or 9x9x2 inch pan. Chill till firm. Makes 8 or 9 servings.

RICE AND CARROT MOLD

1 3-ounce package lime-flavored
  gelatin
¼ teaspoon salt
1 cup boiling water
1 8¾-ounce can crushed
  pineapple
⅓ cup mayonnaise
1 cup cooked rice
½ cup grated carrot
¼ cup toasted slivered almonds

Dissolve gelatin and salt in boiling water. Drain pineapple, reserving syrup. Add enough water to syrup to make 1 cup; stir into gelatin. Chill till partially set. Add mayonnaise and beat with rotary beater till smooth. Fold in pineapple, rice, carrot, and nuts. Pour into 4½-cup mold. Chill till firm. Makes 5 or 6 servings.

CRAN-PERFECTION SALADS

1 envelope (1 tablespoon)
  unflavored gelatin
1 16-ounce can jellied cranberry
  sauce
1 cup shredded cabbage
½ cup diced celery
1 tablespoon vinegar

Soften gelatin in ½ cup cold water. Add ¼ teaspoon salt and stir over low heat till gelatin is dissolved. Beat cranberry sauce till smooth. Stir in gelatin mixture, cabbage, celery, and vinegar. Spoon into six ½-cup molds. Chill till firm. Makes 6 servings.

SPRINGTIME CALICO MOLD

1 4-serving envelope low-calorie
  lime-flavored gelatin
3 tablespoons lemon juice
½ cup shredded cucumber
¼ cup thinly sliced radishes
½ cup cubed Cheddar cheese

Dissolve gelatin in 1 cup boiling water. Stir in ¼ teaspoon salt, ¾ cup cold water, and lemon juice. Chill till partially set. Fold in cucumber, radishes, and cheese. Pour into 3½-cup mold. Chill till firm. Serves 6.

FROM CABBAGE TO COLESLAW

BEAN AND BACON SLAW

In skillet, fry 4 slices bacon till crisp. Drain bacon, reserving drippings; crumble and set aside. Cook ¼ cup chopped onion in reserved drippings in skillet till lightly browned. Stir in ⅓ cup wine vinegar, 1 teaspoon sugar, ½ teaspoon salt, and dash pepper; simmer several minutes. Pour over mixture of 2 cups shredded cabbage; one 17-ounce can baby limas, drained; and one 3-ounce can sliced mushrooms, drained. Toss. Sprinkle with bacon. Makes 6 servings.

COTTAGE CHEESE SLAW

Blend together ½ cup cream-style cottage cheese, ½ cup mayonnaise or salad dressing, 2 tablespoons vinegar, ½ teaspoon caraway seed, ½ teaspoon onion juice, and ¼ teaspoon Worcestershire sauce. (If stronger caraway flavor is desired, chill mayonnaise mixture several hours.) Just before serving, toss mayonnaise mixture lightly with 8 cups shredded cabbage, chilled. Serves 8 to 10.

COLESLAW VINAIGRETTE

  2 cups shredded cabbage
  ⅓ cup sliced green onion
  ¼ cup snipped parsley
  2 tablespoons sugar
  3 tablespoons vinegar
  2 tablespoons salad oil
  1 hard-cooked egg, chilled

Combine cabbage, onion, and parsley; chill. Blend together next 3 ingredients and 1 teaspoon salt, stirring till sugar is dissolved; chill. Pour vinegar mixture over vegetable mixture; toss lightly. Separate yolk from white of hard-cooked egg. Cut white into thin wedges. Arrange atop salad. Sieve yolk over. Makes 6 servings.

CHINESE CABBAGE TOSS

Delicately-flavored Oriental coleslaw—

  4 cups shredded Chinese cabbage
  1 3-ounce can sliced mushrooms, drained
  1 tablespoon chopped onion
  ½ cup mayonnaise
  1 tablespoon soy sauce
  ½ cup chow mein noodles

Combine cabbage, mushrooms, and onion. Blend together mayonnaise and soy; toss lightly with cabbage mixture. Just before serving, top with noodles. Serves 6 to 8.

TOMATO COLESLAW

Combine 2 cups shredded cabbage; 18 cherry tomatoes, halved; ¼ cup diced cucumber; and 2 teaspoons minced onion. Chill. Blend together ¼ cup mayonnaise or salad dressing, 2 tablespoons French salad dressing, 1½ teaspoons lemon juice, 1 teaspoon sugar, ½ teaspoon salt, and dash pepper; chill. Just before serving, toss mayonnaise mixture lightly with cabbage mixture. Makes 6 to 8 servings.

APPLE-PINEAPPLE SLAW

  3 cups shredded cabbage
  1 8¾-ounce can pineapple tidbits, drained (⅔ cup)
  1 cup diced unpared apple
  ½ cup chopped celery
  ½ cup mayonnaise
  1 cup miniature marshmallows

Combine all ingredients *except* marshmallows; toss lightly. Chill. Just before serving, fold in marshmallows. Trim with apple slices, if desired. Makes 10 to 12 servings.

Spark the meal in the American tradition with a bowl full of coleslaw. In Creamy Cabbage Slaw, a celery seed dressing lightly coats crisp shreds of cabbage and green onion rings. On another day, use all red or a combination of red and green cabbage for a pleasant change.

CREAMY CABBAGE SLAW

    6 cups shredded cabbage
    ¼ cup sliced green onion
        • • •
    1 cup mayonnaise or salad
        dressing
    2 tablespoons sugar
    2 tablespoons vinegar
    2 teaspoons celery seed
    1 teaspoon salt

Combine shredded cabbage and sliced green onion; chill. Blend together mayonnaise or salad dressing, sugar, vinegar, celery seed, and salt, stirring till sugar is dissolved; chill. Toss mayonnaise mixture lightly with cabbage mixture. Makes 10 servings.

SPRING GARDEN TOSS

    4 cups shredded cabbage
    ½ cup chopped celery
    ¼ cup chopped green pepper
    ¼ cup shredded carrot
    ¼ cup sliced radishes
    1 tablespoon chopped onion
    ½ cup dairy sour cream
    2 tablespoons tarragon vinegar
    1 tablespoon sugar
    ½ teaspoon salt

Combine cabbage, celery, green pepper, carrot, radishes, and onion; chill. Combine remaining ingredients; chill. Just before serving, toss sour cream mixture lightly with vegetable mixture. Makes 8 servings.

POLYNESIAN COLESLAW

  2 cups shredded lettuce
  2 cups shredded cabbage
  ½ cup chopped unpared cucumber
  2 tablespoons milk
  ¼ cup flaked coconut
  ⅔ cup mayonnaise or salad
     dressing
  ¼ teaspoon salt
    Dash pepper

Combine lettuce, cabbage, and cucumber; chill. Pour milk over coconut; let stand 10 minutes. To prepare dressing, blend together mayonnaise, salt, and pepper; stir in coconut mixture. Toss dressing lightly with cabbage mixture. Makes 5 or 6 servings.

BACON CURRY COLESLAW

  ½ cup mayonnaise or salad
     dressing
  2 tablespoons vinegar
  1 teaspoon sugar
  ¼ teaspoon salt
  ¼ teaspoon curry powder
  6 cups shredded cabbage, chilled
  5 to 6 slices bacon, crisp-cooked
     and crumbled

Combine mayonnaise, vinegar, sugar, salt, curry powder, and dash freshly ground black pepper. Chill. Combine cabbage and bacon. Toss dressing lightly with cabbage mixture. Serves 12 to 14.

PEANUTTY COLESLAW

  ½ cup mayonnaise or salad
     dressing
  ¼ cup dairy sour cream
  2 tablespoons sugar
  2 tablespoons vinegar
  ¼ teaspoon monosodium glutamate
  6 cups shredded cabbage, chilled
  ½ cup salted peanuts

To prepare dressing, blend together mayonnaise, sour cream, sugar, vinegar, and monosodium glutamate. Add to shredded cabbage and toss lightly. Mix in peanuts. Serve immediately. Makes 6 servings.

A sharp knife cuts even shreds of cabbage for coleslaw. Quarter the head; hold firmly to slice.

For fine, juicy slaw, shred cabbage with knife, then chop finely with a three-edged chopper.

A shredder makes fine, short shreds. Hold on board or over bowl; push quarter heads across.

BLUE CHEESE SLAW

    6 cups shredded cabbage
    2 tablespoons chopped canned
        pimiento
    2 tablespoons chopped green onion
        tops
            •   •   •
    ½ cup dairy sour cream
    2 tablespoons mayonnaise or
        salad dressing
    1 tablespoon lemon juice
    ½ teaspoon sugar
    4 ounces blue cheese,
        crumbled (1 cup)
    2 hard-cooked eggs, sliced

Combine first 3 ingredients; chill. To prepare
dressing, blend together sour cream, dash
salt, and remaining ingredients *except* eggs.
Toss dressing lightly with cabbage mixture.
Garnish with egg slices. Serves 10 to 12.

CABBAGE CUCUMBER SLAW

    3 cups shredded cabbage
    1 cup shredded red cabbage
    1 cup halved slices unpared
        cucumber
    ½ cup chopped celery
    2 tablespoons chopped onion
    2 tablespoons French salad
        dressing
    2 tablespoons mayonnaise or
        salad dressing

Combine first 5 ingredients; chill. Season to
taste with salt and pepper. At serving time,
blend French salad dressing and mayonnaise;
toss with cabbage mixture. Serves 8.

CABBAGE BOWLS

Loosen outer green leaves of large head of
cabbage but *do not* break off. Cut remainder
of head in 8 sections *halfway* down. Hollow
out center, leaving shell of 6 to 8 leaves.
Place upside down in ice water to crisp.
Drain. Shred center for slaw; refill bowl.

Or, make bowl by loosening outer leaves;
spread out petal fashion. Hollow out center
to within 1 inch of sides and bottom. Shred
center for slaw. Refill bowl with slaw.

KIDNEY BEAN COLESLAW

    3 cups shredded cabbage
    1 8-ounce can kidney beans,
        chilled and drained
    ¼ cup sweet pickle relish
    ¼ cup thinly sliced green onion
            •   •   •
    ¼ cup mayonnaise or salad
        dressing
    3 tablespoons chili sauce
    ¼ teaspoon celery seed
        Dash salt

Combine shredded cabbage, kidney beans,
sweet pickle relish, and green onion; chill. To
prepare dressing, blend together mayonnaise,
chili sauce, celery seed, and salt; toss with
cabbage mixture. Makes 10 servings.

BEET AND CABBAGE SLAW

    ½ 16-ounce jar pickled beets
    4 cups shredded cabbage
    2 tablespoons chopped green
        pepper
    ½ cup mayonnaise or salad
        dressing

Drain pickled beets, reserving 1½ tablespoons liquid; chop drained beets. Combine
beets, shredded cabbage, and chopped green
pepper; chill. At serving time, prepare dressing by blending mayonnaise and reserved
beet liquid; toss dressing lightly with cabbage mixture. Makes 8 servings.

SESAME SLAW

    2 cups shredded cabbage
    ¼ cup chopped green pepper
    2 tablespoons chopped onion
    3 tablespoons vinegar
        Non-caloric liquid sweetener
        equal to 8 teaspoons sugar
    ½ teaspoon salt
    ½ teaspoon toasted sesame seed

Combine shredded cabbage, chopped green
pepper, and chopped onion; chill. Combine
vinegar, non-caloric sweetener, salt, and
toasted sesame seed; toss lightly with cabbage mixture. Makes 8 servings.

YEAR 'ROUND POTATO AND MACARONI SALADS

GERMAN MACARONI SALAD

Pasta tossed in a hot dressing—

    1 3-ounce can sliced mushrooms
    5 slices bacon
    ½ cup sugar
    3 tablespoons all-purpose flour
    ⅓ cup vinegar
         • • •
    ½ 7-ounce package uncooked elbow
        macaroni
    ½ cup chopped green onion
    ½ cup chopped celery

Drain mushrooms, reserving liquid; add enough water to reserved liquid to make 1 cup. In 3-quart saucepan, fry bacon till crisp; drain, reserving drippings. Crumble bacon; set aside. Combine sugar, flour, ½ teaspoon salt, and ⅛ teaspoon pepper; blend into reserved drippings in saucepan. Combine vinegar and reserved 1 cup liquid. Add to flour mixture; cook and stir till thickened and bubbly.

Meanwhile, cook macaroni following package directions; drain. In saucepan, lightly toss macaroni with dressing, mushrooms, bacon, onion, and celery. Spoon into serving dish. Garnish with radishes and parsley, if desired. Serve immediately. Serves 8 to 10.

HOT DILL POTATO SALAD

In saucepan, melt 1 tablespoon butter or margarine over low heat. Stir in 1 tablespoon all-purpose flour, 1 teaspoon salt, ¼ teaspoon dried dillweed, and ⅛ teaspoon pepper. Add 1 cup milk all at once; cook and stir till thickened and bubbly. Blend in ½ cup mayonnaise or salad dressing and 2 tablespoons finely chopped onion; fold in 4 cups diced, peeled, cooked potatoes. Spoon into serving dish; sprinkle with paprika. Serve immediately. Serves 4 to 6.

SWEET POTATO SALAD

Featuring fall foods—

Combine 2 cups cooked sweet potatoes cut in chunks; 1 medium apple, diced; ½ cup diced celery; ½ cup chopped walnuts; ¼ cup chopped dates; and ½ teaspoon salt. Blend together ¼ cup dairy sour cream, ¼ cup mayonnaise or salad dressing, and 2 tablespoons milk. Fold sour cream mixture into potato mixture. Chill. Serve potato salad on lettuce-lined plates. Serves 8.

CALICO POTATO SALAD

    6 cups diced cooked potatoes
    ½ cup diced cucumber
    ½ cup chopped onion
    ¼ cup chopped green pepper
    3 tablespoons chopped canned
        pimiento
 1½ teaspoons salt
    ¾ teaspoon celery seed
    ¼ teaspoon pepper
    2 hard-cooked eggs
    ½ cup whipping cream, whipped
    ½ cup mayonnaise
    2 tablespoons vinegar
    1 tablespoon prepared mustard

Combine first 8 ingredients. Coarsely chop eggs, reserving 1 whole egg yolk. Add chopped eggs to potato mixture. Chill. Combine remaining ingredients, *except* yolk; toss with potato mixture ½ hour before serving. To serve, spoon into lettuce-lined bowl. Sieve reserved yolk over. Serves 10 to 12.

Calico Potato Salad describes this tangy-dressed → salad dotted with green pepper and pimiento. Serve it with roll-ups made by rolling green onions with tops in slices of ham and cheese.

PATIO POTATO SALAD

An ideal outdoor barbecue dish—

  ⅓ cup sugar
  1 tablespoon cornstarch
  ½ cup milk
  ¼ cup vinegar
  1 egg
  4 tablespoons butter or margarine
  ¾ teaspoon celery seed
  ¼ teaspoon dry mustard
  ¼ cup chopped onion
  ¼ cup mayonnaise or salad
    dressing
  7 medium potatoes, cooked,
    peeled, and diced
  3 hard-cooked eggs, chopped
    Paprika

In saucepan, combine sugar and cornstarch; add next 6 ingredients and ¾ teaspoon salt. Cook and stir over low heat till bubbly. Remove from heat; add onion and mayonnaise. Cool. Combine potatoes and hard-cooked eggs; gently fold in dressing. Chill. Just before serving, sprinkle with paprika. Serves 6.

PARSLEYED POTATO SALAD

Molding in a loaf dish adds interest—

  4 cups diced, peeled, cooked
    potatoes
  ¼ cup sliced celery
  3 tablespoons snipped parsley
  2 tablespoons chopped green
    pepper
  2 tablespoons chopped green onion
  2 tablespoons chopped dill pickle
  ¾ cup mayonnaise or salad
    dressing
  2 tablespoons clear French salad
    dressing with herbs and
    spices
  ¾ teaspoon seasoned salt
  ¼ teaspoon dry mustard

Combine first 6 ingredients; toss lightly. Blend together remaining ingredients and dash pepper; gently fold into potato mixture. Pack into 8½x4½x2½-inch loaf dish; chill. Unmold on lettuce-lined plate; trim with additional parsley, if desired. Serves 4 or 5.

CAROUSEL SALAD

  ½ 7-ounce package spaghetti,
    broken, cooked, drained, and
    cooled (about 2 cups)
  1 cup shredded carrots
  ½ cup diced celery
  ½ cup mayonnaise or salad
    dressing
  2 tablespoons chopped dill pickle
  1 teaspoon dill pickle juice
  ¼ teaspoon dried basil
    leaves, crushed

Combine cooked spaghetti, carrots, and celery. Blend together remaining ingredients and ½ teaspoon salt. Toss with spaghetti mixture. Chill. Makes 6 to 8 servings.

CHEDDAR POTATO SALAD

To 8 warm medium potatoes, cooked, peeled, and cubed, add 2 tablespoons snipped parsley, 2 tablespoons salad oil, 1 tablespoon grated onion, 1 teaspoon salt, and ¼ teaspoon pepper. Combine 1 cup chicken broth and 1 tablespoon white wine vinegar. Pour over potato mixture; toss lightly.

Chill mixture 1 hour, stirring occasionally. Before serving, fold in 1 cup shredded natural Cheddar cheese. Makes 8 servings.

BLUE CHEESE-SPUD SALAD

  5 cups cubed, peeled, cooked
    potatoes
  1 cup chopped celery
  4 hard-cooked eggs, chopped
  ½ cup sliced green onion
  ¼ cup chopped green pepper
  1 cup dairy sour cream
  ⅓ cup evaporated milk
  1 ounce blue cheese, crumbled
    (¼ cup)
  2 tablespoons vinegar
  ¼ teaspoon dry mustard
  ⅛ teaspoon pepper

Sprinkle cooked potatoes with 1 teaspoon salt. Combine potatoes, celery, eggs, onion, and green pepper. Blend together remaining ingredients. Pour over potato mixture; toss lightly. Chill. Makes 10 to 12 servings.

COUNTRY POTATO SALAD

New potatoes and lettuce pair up—

> 1 pound (8 to 10) small new
>   potatoes, cooked and peeled
> 3 cups torn lettuce
> 2 hard-cooked eggs, diced
> 3 tablespoons thinly sliced green
>   onion
> 6 slices bacon
> ¼ cup vinegar
> 1 teaspoon seasoned salt
> ¼ teaspoon celery seed
> ⅛ teaspoon pepper

Leave very small potatoes whole; halve or quarter larger ones. In bowl, combine potatoes, lettuce, eggs, and onion. In skillet, cook bacon till crisp; drain, reserving ¼ cup drippings. Crumble bacon; add to salad.

To reserved drippings in skillet, add vinegar, seasoned salt, celery seed, and pepper. Heat mixture to boiling then pour over potato mixture. Toss quickly; serve immediately. Makes 4 to 6 servings.

GINGERY MACARONI SALAD

Salad suitable for a "Sultan"—

> ½ 7-ounce package elbow
>   macaroni, cooked and drained
>   (about 2 cups)
> ¼ cup golden raisins
> ¼ cup chopped celery
>   . . .
> ½ cup mayonnaise or salad
>   dressing
> 1 tablespoon chopped onion
> 1 teaspoon chopped candied ginger
> ¼ teaspoon salt
> ¼ teaspoon curry powder
>   Dash garlic salt
>   Dash pepper
> 2 tablespoons coarsely chopped
>   peanuts

Combine macaroni, raisins, and celery. Blend together mayonnaise, onion, candied ginger, salt, curry, garlic salt, and pepper. Toss mayonnaise mixture lightly with macaroni mixture. Chill. Serve in lettuce cups; garnish with peanuts. Makes 4 to 6 servings.

SKILLET POTATO SALAD

An easy version of old-fashioned German potato salad makes a hit when served with a cheese and sausage assortment—

> 6 medium potatoes, cooked,
>   peeled, and diced
> 8 slices bacon
> ½ cup chopped onion
> 1 10½-ounce can condensed cream
>   of celery soup
> ⅓ cup milk
> 2 tablespoons sweet pickle relish
> 2 tablespoons vinegar
> ½ teaspoon salt
>   . . .
>   Parsley sprigs
> 1 hard-cooked egg, cut in wedges

Keep potatoes warm. In large skillet, cook bacon till crisp; drain, reserving ¼ cup drippings. Crumble bacon and set aside. Add chopped onion to drippings in skillet and cook just till tender. Blend in condensed soup, milk, pickle relish, vinegar, and salt. Heat to boiling, stirring constantly.

Gently stir in warm diced potatoes and crumbled bacon, reserving 1 tablespoon bacon for topping. Heat through. Sprinkle remaining bacon over top of potato salad; garnish with sprigs of parsley and hard-cooked egg wedges. Makes 4 to 6 servings.

For a casual supper, prepare and serve garnished Skillet Potato Salad in an electric skillet.

Look what's in a new dress. An old-time pasta favorite is now Macaroni-cheese Salad. Celery and carrot add color and crunch to shell macaroni.

Serve this hearty flavorful salad often—perfect for brunch, a satisfying main dish for supper, and a favorite to round out the barbecue picnic.

MACARONI-CHEESE SALAD

    6 ounces uncooked shell macaroni
        (about 1½ cups)
    1 cup sliced celery
    1 cup shredded carrots
    ¼ cup chopped onion
    1 10¾-ounce can condensed
        Cheddar cheese soup
    ¼ cup salad oil
    2 tablespoons vinegar
    1 teaspoon sugar
    1 teaspoon prepared mustard
    1 teaspoon Worcestershire sauce

Cook macaroni following package directions; drain and cool. Combine macaroni, celery, carrots, and onion. In small bowl, beat together soup, remaining ingredients, ½ teaspoon salt, and dash pepper. Spoon atop macaroni mixture; toss. Chill. Serves 4 to 6.

POTATO-APPLE SALAD

Combine 4 cups cubed, peeled, cooked potatoes; 2 cups chopped unpared apple; and 2 tablespoons thinly sliced green onion. Blend together 1 cup dairy sour cream, 2 tablespoons lemon juice, ½ teaspoon salt, ¼ teaspoon dillweed, and dash pepper; toss lightly with potato mixture. Chill. Serves 10 to 12.

COTTAGE SHELL SALAD

Cook 2 cups shell macaroni following package directions; drain. Stir in 2 cups cottage cheese, ¼ cup *each* diced canned pimiento, snipped chives, and sliced radishes. Blend 1 cup dairy sour cream, ¼ cup French salad dressing, 2 tablespoons lemon juice, ½ teaspoon *each* salt and dry mustard. Toss with macaroni. Chill. Serves 10.

DEVILED POTATO SALAD

Cut 8 hard-cooked eggs in half. Remove yolks and mash; blend with 3 tablespoons vinegar and 3 tablespoons prepared mustard. Stir in 1 cup mayonnaise or salad dressing, ½ cup dairy sour cream, 1 teaspoon salt, and ½ teaspoon celery salt; mix well.

Chop egg whites; combine with 6 medium potatoes, cooked, peeled, and cubed, and 2 tablespoons chopped onion. Fold in egg yolk mixture; chill. Garnish with tomato wedges and cucumber slices. Serves 6 to 8.

SWISS POTATO SALAD

4 cups cubed, peeled, cooked
    potatoes
1 teaspoon salt
4 slices (4 ounces) Swiss cheese,
    cut in narrow strips
1 cup dairy sour cream
3 tablespoons milk
2 tablespoons snipped chives *or*
    chopped green onion
½ teaspoon dry mustard

Sprinkle salt over potatoes; combine with cheese strips. Blend remaining ingredients; pour over potato mixture. Toss lightly. Serve at room temperature. Serves 4 or 5.

MASHED POTATO SALAD

4 medium potatoes, pared
¾ cup mayonnaise or salad
    dressing
2 tablespoons vinegar
1½ teaspoons celery salt
⅓ cup chopped sweet pickle
¼ cup chopped celery
¼ cup finely chopped onion
4 hard-cooked eggs, sliced
2 tablespoons chopped canned
    pimiento

In medium saucepan, cook potatoes in boiling salted water till tender. Drain and mash. Combine mayonnaise, vinegar, celery salt, and dash pepper; stir into hot mashed potatoes. Add pickle, celery, and onion; mix well. Fold in hard-cooked eggs and pimiento. Serve warm or chilled. Serves 8 to 10.

EASY POTATO SALAD

2 9-ounce packages frozen French-
    fried potatoes
1½ teaspoons salt
⅔ cup coarsely grated unpared
    cucumber
½ cup sliced radishes
½ cup diced celery
2 tablespoons sliced green onion
2 tablespoons snipped parsley
1 cup mayonnaise or salad
    dressing
1 to 2 tablespoons vinegar
     • • •
2 hard-cooked eggs, sliced
Paprika

Pour 4 cups water into large saucepan; bring to rapid boil. Carefully drop frozen potatoes into water. Remove from heat immediately; cover and let stand 4 to 5 minutes. Drain potatoes at once, and spread onto paper toweling. Sprinkle with salt; cool. Blend together remaining ingredients *except* eggs and paprika. Add potatoes and toss. Chill. Garnish with eggs and paprika. Serves 10 to 12.

MACARONI-BEAN SALAD

Cook ½ of 7-ounce package elbow macaroni (about 1 cup) following package directions. Drain well and cool. Combine cooked macaroni; one 8-ounce can kidney beans, drained; 2 hard-cooked eggs, chopped; and ¼ cup pickle relish.

Blend together ½ cup mayonnaise or salad dressing, ½ teaspoon salt, and 3 drops bottled hot pepper sauce; toss lightly with macaroni mixture. Chill. Serves 6 to 8.

POTATO SALAD CUPS

Combine 6 cups cubed, peeled, cooked potatoes; 1 medium unpared cucumber, diced (2 cups); 1 cup chopped celery; 3 hard-cooked eggs, sliced; ½ cup chopped onion; 1½ teaspoons salt; and ¼ teaspoon paprika. Pour ¼ cup French salad dressing with herbs and spices over. Chill. Combine ½ cup mayonnaise and 1 teaspoon celery seed. Add to potato mixture; toss lightly. Pack into custard cups; unmold on lettuce. Serves 8.

WAYS WITH BEANS

ONE BEAN TOSS

½ cup sliced pitted ripe olives
¼ cup sliced pimiento-stuffed
    green olives
1 16-ounce can peas, drained
1 16-ounce can limas, drained
½ cup mayonnaise
2 tablespoons grated onion
1 tablespoon lemon juice
1 tablespoon drained capers
2 teaspoons liquid from capers
    Herbed Carrots
    Parsley

Set aside a few olive slices for garnish; combine remaining olive slices, peas, and limas in bowl. Combine next 5 ingredients, ½ teaspoon salt, and dash pepper; pour over bean mixture and toss lightly. Cover; chill several hours, stirring occasionally. To serve, mound salad in center of lettuce-lined platter. Top with reserved olives and additional mayonnaise, if desired. Arrange Herbed Carrots and parsley around. Serves 8.

Herbed Carrots: Place one 16-ounce can whole small carrots, drained, in a deep bowl. Combine ⅓ cup salad oil; 2 tablespoons tarragon vinegar; 2 tablespoons finely snipped parsley; ¼ teaspoon salt; ¼ teaspoon dried thyme leaves, crushed, *or* dried marjoram leaves, crushed; and dash pepper. Pour over carrots. Cover; chill 3 hours, spooning dressing over occasionally. Drain.

HOT FIVE BEAN SALAD

In large skillet, cook 8 slices bacon till crisp; drain, reserving ¼ cup drippings. Crumble bacon; set aside. In skillet, combine ⅔ cup sugar, 2 tablespoons cornstarch, 1½ teaspoons salt, and dash pepper with reserved drippings. Stir in ¾ cup vinegar and ½ cup water; heat to boiling, stirring constantly. Add one 16-ounce can *each* kidney beans, cut green beans, limas, cut wax beans, and garbanzo beans, *all drained.* Reduce heat. Cover; simmer 15 to 20 minutes. Turn into dish. Top with bacon. Serves 10 to 12.

FOUR BEAN SALAD

Want applauds and cheers for a good-tasting salad? Try this delicious combination—

Romaine leaves
. . .
1 16-ounce can red kidney beans,
    drained
1 16-ounce can cut wax
    beans, drained
1 16-ounce can black-eyed peas
    or limas, drained
1 16-ounce can cut green beans,
    drained
1 medium green pepper, thinly
    sliced into rings
1 medium onion, thinly sliced
    and separated into rings
. . .
½ cup sugar
½ cup wine vinegar
½ cup salad oil
2 tablespoons snipped parsley
1 teaspoon salt
½ teaspoon dry mustard
½ teaspoon dried tarragon
    leaves, crushed, *or* 2
    teaspoons finely snipped
    fresh tarragon
½ teaspoon dried basil leaves,
    crushed, *or* 2 teaspoons
    finely snipped fresh basil

Line large salad bowl with romaine. Layer drained red kidney beans, wax beans, black-eyed peas, green beans, and pepper rings in order given. Top with onion rings. Thoroughly combine sugar, vinegar, oil, parsley, salt, dry mustard, tarragon, and basil. Drizzle over vegetables. Cover; chill thoroughly, stirring occasionally. Just before serving, stir; then drain. Makes 12 servings.

Surprise and please bean lovers with these →
salads. Herbed Carrots add tempting appeal to One Bean Toss. Hot Five Bean Salad and Four Bean Salad are hearty main dish selections.

ITALIAN BEAN TOSS

Sprightly seasoned with Parmesan and curry—

- 2 9-ounce packages frozen Italian green beans
- ½ cup mayonnaise or salad dressing
- 2 tablespoons grated Parmesan cheese
- 1 tablespoon finely chopped canned pimiento
- ¼ teaspoon curry powder

Cook beans following package directions; drain and chill. Blend together mayonnaise, Parmesan, pimiento, curry, and 1 teaspoon salt. Add beans and toss; chill. If desired, sprinkle with additional Parmesan cheese before serving. Makes 6 to 8 servings.

KIDNEY BEAN CLASSIC

Hard cook 3 eggs; chop 2 eggs and slice remaining for garnish. Combine one 16-ounce can kidney beans, drained; ¾ cup chopped celery; ¼ cup chopped sweet pickle; the 2 chopped eggs; and 1 tablespoon chopped onion. Blend ½ cup mayonnaise, 2 teaspoons prepared mustard, and ½ teaspoon salt. Add mayonnaise mixture to bean mixture and toss. Arrange the sliced hard-cooked egg atop salad. Chill. Makes 6 servings.

EGG AND BEAN SALAD

- 1 16-ounce can barbecue beans, drained
- 6 hard-cooked eggs, coarsely chopped
- ¼ cup chopped onion
- 1 tablespoon mayonnaise or salad dressing
- 1 teaspoon prepared mustard
- ¼ teaspoon salt
- 3 slices bacon, crisp-cooked and crumbled

Combine beans, eggs, and onion. Chill. Blend together mayonnaise, mustard, salt, and dash pepper. Add to egg mixture and toss. Spoon into lettuce-lined salad bowl. Sprinkle bacon over top. Makes 6 to 8 servings.

CREAMY LIMA CUPS

Cook one 10-ounce package frozen baby limas following package directions; drain and chill well. Blend together ¼ cup dairy sour cream; 1 tablespoon vinegar; 1 tablespoon salad oil; 1 small clove garlic, minced; ½ teaspoon sugar; ¼ teaspoon salt; and dash paprika. Add chilled beans and toss. Spoon into 4 lettuce cups. Sprinkle with additional paprika. Makes 4 servings.

HOT BEAN SALAD

- 1 16-ounce can kidney beans, drained
- 1 cup thinly sliced celery
- 3 ounces sharp process American cheese, diced (¾ cup)
- ⅓ cup chopped sweet pickle
- ¼ cup thinly sliced green onion
- ½ cup mayonnaise or salad dressing
- ⅓ cup finely crushed rich round cracker crumbs

Combine first 6 ingredients and ¼ teaspoon salt; toss. Spoon into four 8-ounce bakers or six 5-ounce custard cups. Top with crumbs. Bake in very hot oven (450°) for 10 minutes or till bubbly. Makes 4 to 6 servings.

CHILI-BEAN SALAD

Zestful salad from the Southwest—

- 2 16-ounce cans green beans, drained and chilled
- ¾ cup diced celery
- ¼ cup small white onion rings
- 2 tablespoons pickle relish
- Chili Salad Dressing

Combine first 4 ingredients and ½ teaspoon salt. Add Chili Salad Dressing; toss. Cover and chill at least 1 hour. Serves 6 to 8.

Chili Salad Dressing: Combine 2 tablespoons salad oil, ½ small clove garlic, ¼ teaspoon chili powder, ⅛ teaspoon salt, and dash pepper. Let stand 1 hour. Remove and discard garlic. Add 1 tablespoon vinegar and 1½ teaspoons lemon juice; beat with rotary beater. Chill thoroughly.

"Make-ahead" recipes end the last minute mealtime rush. Tomato-bean Combo not only falls into this category but also takes little preparation time. The vegetable mixture is evenly coated with a tingling sour cream and Italian dressing blend. Tomato wedges are the colorful garnish.

TOMATO-BEAN COMBO

  1 16-ounce can cut green beans, drained
  2 medium tomatoes, peeled, chopped, and drained (about 1½ cups)
  ¼ cup finely chopped onion
  ½ cup dairy sour cream
  ¼ cup Italian salad dressing
    Romaine leaves
    Tomato wedges

Combine cut green beans, chopped tomato, and chopped onion. Blend together sour cream and Italian salad dressing; add to bean mixture and toss lightly. Chill at least 2 to 3 hours. At serving time, spoon salad into romaine-lined salad bowl. Garnish with tomato wedges. Makes 6 servings.

MARINATED BEAN SALAD

  1 16-ounce can cut green beans
  1 16-ounce can cut yellow wax beans
  ⅔ cup vinegar
  1 teaspoon mixed pickling spices
    Non-caloric liquid sweetener equal to ¼ cup sugar
  ½ cup chopped celery
  2 slices bacon, crisp-cooked and crumbled

Drain beans, reserving ½ cup liquid. Heat bean liquid with vinegar, ⅓ cup water, and spices. Boil 2 to 3 minutes. Cool and strain. Stir in sweetener. Combine beans and celery; add dressing. Cover and chill 6 hours or overnight, stirring occasionally. Before serving, top with bacon. Makes 8 servings.

LOW CALORIE · LOW CALORIE

VARIATIONS WITH VEGETABLES

ASPARAGUS-TOMATO SALAD

      2 pounds fresh asparagus spears,
         cooked and drained
    1/3 cup mayonnaise
    1 1/4 teaspoons lemon juice
      1 medium tomato, peeled and
         diced

Keep asparagus hot. In small saucepan, combine mayonnaise, lemon juice, 1/4 teaspoon salt, and 1/8 teaspoon pepper. Stir over low heat till heated through. Stir in tomato; heat through. Serve over asparagus. Serves 6.

MEDITERRANEAN SALAD

      1 10-ounce package frozen
         Italian green beans
      2 tablespoons butter or margarine
      3 slices bread, cut in cubes
         (2 cups)
      1 12-ounce can whole kernel corn,
         drained
    1/2 cup mayonnaise or salad
         dressing
      2 tablespoons chopped canned
         pimiento
      1 teaspoon dried basil leaves,
         crushed

Cook beans following package directions; drain and cool. In skillet, melt butter. Add bread cubes and cook till crisp, turning occasionally. Combine beans, corn, mayonnaise, pimiento, basil, and 1/4 teaspoon salt; chill. Before serving, add toasted bread cubes to bean mixture; toss. Serves 8.

← **A magnificent vegetable mixture** awaiting all salad lovers—that's Mediterranean Salad. Italian beans, corn, and pimiento team up with crunchy toasted bread cubes in this savory special.

CALICO RICE SALAD

      3 cups cooked rice
      6 hard-cooked eggs, coarsely
         chopped
    1/2 cup chopped onion
    1/4 cup chopped canned pimiento
    1/4 cup chopped green pepper
    1/4 cup chopped celery
    1/4 cup chopped dill pickle
    1/3 cup mayonnaise or salad
         dressing
    1/4 cup French salad dressing
      2 tablespoons prepared mustard

Combine rice, eggs, onion, pimiento, green pepper, celery, dill pickle, 1 teaspoon salt, and dash pepper. Blend together mayonnaise, French salad dressing, and mustard; add to rice mixture and toss. Chill thoroughly. Lightly pack rice mixture into five 5-ounce custard cups; immediately turn out on lettuce-lined plates. Makes 5 servings.

ENDIVE-AVOCADO SALAD

      8 French endives
      1 avocado, halved, peeled, and
         sliced
      4 scallions *or* green onions,
         chopped
    1/4 cup salad oil
      1 tablespoon wine vinegar
      2 tablespoons snipped parsley

Chill endive in ice water to crisp. Dry gently with paper toweling. Remove a few outer leaves and set aside. Cut endive stalks into large crosswise slices. In salad bowl, combine endive slices, avocado, and scallions. Season to taste with salt and pepper.

Combine salad oil and vinegar; pour over endive mixture and toss lightly. Top with parsley. Arrange reserved endive leaves around edge of bowl. Makes 6 servings.

PIQUANT CAULIFLOWER

A creative treatment of a vinaigrette—

1 medium head cauliflower
2/3 cup salad oil
1/3 cup white vinegar
1 large tomato, chopped
2 tablespoons chopped pimiento-
   stuffed green olives
1 tablespoon pickle relish
1 teaspoon sugar
1 teaspoon salt
1 teaspoon paprika
1/8 teaspoon pepper

Separate cauliflower into flowerets. Cook, covered, in small amount of boiling salted water just till crisp-tender, about 10 minutes; drain. Place cauliflowerets in deep bowl. Combine remaining ingredients. Pour over cauliflower and chill 2 to 3 hours, stirring occasionally. At serving time, drain off excess oil-vinegar mixture. Serve in lettuce-lined bowl. Makes 8 servings.

SWEDISH VEGETABLES

1 10-ounce package frozen
   cauliflower
1 16-ounce can *each* shoestring
   carrots, drained; cut green
   beans, drained; and peas,
   drained
1 15-ounce can artichoke hearts,
   drained and halved
1 cup chopped celery
1/2 cup low-calorie French-style
   salad dressing
1 tablespoon instant minced onion
   Chili-dill Dressing

Cook cauliflower according to package directions; drain well. Cool and separate into flowerets. Arrange vegetables in large salad bowl. Combine French-style salad dressing and onion. Drizzle over vegetables; chill 1 hour. Serve with Chili-dill Dressing. Makes 10 to 12 servings.

Chili-dill Dressing: Blend 3/4 cup low-calorie mayonnaise-type dressing with 1/4 cup chili sauce, 2 teaspoons dried dillweed, 1 teaspoon salt, dash pepper, and 1 tablespoon lemon juice. Chill thoroughly.

VEGETABLE COMBO

For a speedy salad, use canned vegetables—

1/2 cup peas, cooked and drained
1/2 cup baby limas, cooked and
   drained
1/2 cup finely diced carrot
1/2 cup bias-cut celery
1/2 cup paper-thin onion slices
   Dairy sour cream
10 to 20 capers

Combine all ingredients *except* sour cream and capers. Chill thoroughly. Serve on lettuce-lined plates. Spoon sour cream over. Garnish with capers. Makes 6 servings.

PANAMA RADISH SALAD

1 1/2 cups sliced radishes
1 cup finely diced tomato
1/4 cup thinly sliced onion rings
   . . .
2 tablespoons salad oil
2 tablespoons lemon juice
2 teaspoons snipped parsley
1/2 teaspoon salt
1/8 teaspoon garlic salt
1/8 teaspoon black pepper

Combine radishes, tomato, and onion. In screw-top jar, shake together remaining ingredients. Pour over radish mixture; toss. Chill 1 hour. Makes 4 or 5 servings.

HERBED PEA SALAD

Dill is the fragrant herb used—

2 10-ounce packages frozen peas
1/3 cup clear French salad dressing
   with herbs and spices
1/2 teaspoon dried dillweed
1 cup thinly sliced celery
1 hard-cooked egg, sliced

Cook peas according to package directions; drain. Combine clear French salad dressing with dillweed; pour over peas and celery. Chill several hours or overnight, stirring occasionally. Serve in lettuce-lined bowl. Top with hard-cooked egg slices. Serves 6 to 8.

VEGETABLE MARINADE

1 medium head cauliflower
1 16-ounce can whole green beans, drained
⅔ cup salad oil
⅓ cup vinegar
1 envelope onion salad dressing mix

Separate cauliflower into small flowerets. Cook, covered, in small amount of boiling salted water till crisp-tender, about 10 minutes; drain well. Place hot cauliflower and beans in bowl. In screw-top jar, combine oil, vinegar, and salad dressing mix; cover and shake well. Pour dressing over vegetables; chill several hours or overnight, stirring occasionally. Drain; serve vegetables on lettuce-lined plates. Makes 4 to 6 servings.

ZUCCHINI VINAIGRETTE

The zucchini tastes like Italian pickles—

¼ cup sauterne
1 envelope Italian salad dressing mix
½ cup salad *or* olive oil
¼ cup white wine vinegar
3 to 4 tablespoons finely sliced green onion
3 tablespoons drained pickle relish
2 tablespoons finely snipped parsley
2 tablespoons finely chopped green pepper
5 or 6 medium zucchini
3 or 4 medium tomatoes, chilled and sliced

For dressing, combine wine and dressing mix in screw-top jar; cover and shake. Add salad oil and next 5 ingredients.

Slice each zucchini in 6 lengthwise strips. Cook in boiling salted water just till tender, about 3 to 5 minutes. Drain; arrange in shallow dish. Shake dressing and pour over zucchini. Cover and refrigerate several hours or overnight, spooning dressing over occasionally. To serve, drain zucchini and arrange on lettuce-lined platter with tomatoes. Makes 8 or 9 servings.

MEXICAN SALAD

2 medium tomatoes, cut in chunks
1 large green pepper, cut in ½-inch chunks
¼ cup chopped celery
2 tablespoons sliced green onion
2 slices bacon, crisp-cooked and crumbled
2 hard-cooked eggs, sliced
. . .
¼ cup vinegar
¼ teaspoon salt
¼ teaspoon chili powder

Combine first 6 ingredients. Heat vinegar, salt, and chili powder to boiling. Pour over vegetable mixture; toss. Makes 4 servings.

VEGETABLE MEDLEY

Combine 2 cups chopped cucumbers, 1 cup sliced radishes, and 1 cup sliced green onions with tops. Blend together ½ cup dairy sour cream, 1 tablespoon lemon juice, ½ teaspoon salt, and ⅛ teaspoon dry mustard; toss lightly with vegetable mixture. Chill. Serve on lettuce-lined plate. Serves 4 to 6.

Cucumber Medley: Prepare recipe for Vegetable Medley *except* use 1½ cups sliced cucumbers in place of chopped cucumbers, radishes, and green onions.

FILLED TOMATO ROSETTES

4 medium tomatoes
¼ teaspoon salt
1 avocado, peeled and diced
1 8-ounce carton (1 cup) cream-style cottage cheese, drained
¼ cup dairy sour cream
1 tablespoon snipped chives *or* chopped green onion tops

With stem end down, cut each tomato into 6 wedges, *cutting to, but not through,* base of tomato. Spread wedges apart slightly. Sprinkle with salt; chill. In small mixing bowl, blend avocado and next 2 ingredients together. Fill each tomato with about ⅓ cup avocado mixture. Top with chives or green onion tops. Makes 4 servings.

VEGETABLES TO BRIGHTEN BUFFETS

VEGETABLE SALAD TRAY

> Sour Cream Potato Toss (see below)
> Fresh or frozen asparagus spears, cooked, drained, and chilled
> Tomatoes, cut in wedges
> Raw zucchini, bias-cut

Mound Sour Cream Potato Toss in center of large lettuce-lined tray. Sieve reserved egg yolk over. Arrange asparagus, tomatoes, and zucchini on tray around potato salad.

SOUR CREAM POTATO TOSS

> 6 cups diced, peeled, cooked potatoes
> 1/4 cup chopped green onions with tops
> 1 1/2 teaspoons salt
> 1 teaspoon celery seed
> 4 hard-cooked eggs
> 1 cup dairy sour cream
> 1/2 cup mayonnaise
> 2 tablespoons vinegar
> 1 teaspoon prepared mustard
> 3/4 cup diced pared cucumber

Combine first 4 ingredients and 1/8 teaspoon pepper. Separate whites of hard-cooked eggs from yolks; chop whites and add to potato mixture. Chill thoroughly.

Reserve 1 hard-cooked yolk. To prepare dressing, mash remaining yolks; blend in sour cream, mayonnaise, vinegar, and mustard. Pour dressing over potato mixture; toss lightly. Let stand 20 minutes. Just before serving, fold in cucumber. Sieve reserved hard-cooked yolk over. Serves 10 to 12.

Curried Potato Toss: Prepare Sour Cream Potato Toss omitting mustard; add 1/2 to 1 teaspoon curry powder to dressing mixture.

COLESLAW HAWAIIAN

Is a pleasing balance of sweet and sassy—

In very large bowl, dissolve six 3-ounce packages lemon-flavored gelatin in 7 cups boiling water. Stir in 3 tablespoons lemon juice. Chill till partially set. Beat in 1 1/2 cups dairy sour cream till smooth.

Fold in 2 quarts (8 cups) chopped cabbage, two 20 1/2-ounce cans undrained crushed pineapple, and 1/3 cup chopped green pepper. Pour into 18x12x2-inch pan. Chill till firm. Makes 30 (1/2 cup) servings.

AVOCADO-VEGETABLE TOSS

Lots of hearty distinction—

> 2 12-ounce cans whole kernel corn, drained and chilled
> 2 medium avocados, peeled and diced
> 6 hard-cooked eggs, diced and chilled
> 2 tablespoons chopped onion
> 1 cup mayonnaise or salad dressing
> 1 tablespoon lemon juice
> 1/2 teaspoon chili powder
> 1/4 teaspoon ground cumin
> 1/8 teaspoon ground nutmeg

Combine corn, avocados, eggs, and onion. Blend together remaining ingredients. Toss mayonnaise mixture lightly with avocado mixture. Garnish with sliced pitted ripe olives, if desired. Makes 8 to 10 servings.

Guests will return to the buffet table for sec-→ ond helpings of Vegetable Salad Tray. A colorful splash of asparagus, tomato, and zucchini encompasses a mound of zippy Sour Cream Potato Toss.

VEGETABLE SALAD WREATH

Arrange salad greens on large platter. Set Starlight Molds around rim; tuck two 10-ounce packages frozen asparagus spears, cooked, drained, and chilled, in between molds. Break 1 small head raw cauliflower into flowerets; slice and arrange with two 16-ounce cans small whole carrots, drained and chilled, in inner circle. Place cherry tomatoes and greens in center. Serve with French salad dressing. Makes 14 servings.

Starlight Molds: Dissolve two 3-ounce packages lemon-flavored gelatin in 2 cups boiling water. Add 2 cups cold water and 2 tablespoons lemon juice. Chill *1 cup* gelatin till partially set; fold in 1 cup shredded cabbage and 1 tablespoon chopped canned pimiento. Divide among six ½-cup molds. Chill till *almost* firm.

Chill remaining gelatin till partially set; fold in 2 cups shredded carrots. Fill eight ½-cup molds. Spoon remaining gelatin over partially-filled molds. Chill till firm. Unmold; top with pimiento stars. Makes 14.

MEAL-ON-A-PLATTER

    3 cups whole green beans, cooked
        and drained
 1½ cups peas, cooked and drained
    1 cup garlic salad dressing
    1 12-ounce carton (1½ cups)
        cream-style cottage cheese
      Snipped chives
    4 large lettuce cups
   12 celery strips
   12 carrot curls
    1 12-ounce can luncheon meat,
        cut in thin strips
      Canned pimiento strips

Place beans and peas in separate dishes; pour dressing over. Chill 2 hours, spooning dressing over occasionally; drain. Center bowl of chive-topped cottage cheese on platter. Arrange lettuce cups around bowl; fill one with peas, one with celery, one with carrots, and one with meat. Arrange beans between cups; top with pimiento. Pass extra dressing. Makes 6 servings.

Decorate the party buffet table with a Vegetable Salad Wreath. The platter, lined with perky salad greens, is centered with an array of vege-tables. Individual serving-size molds around the outside are filled with crisp shredded cabbage and carrot and garnished with colorful pimiento stars.

THREE SALAD ENSEMBLE

Arrange 3 large lettuce cups in shallow bowl. Fill one with Herbed Tomato Slices, one with Relish Cottage Cheese, and one with Oriental Relish. Garnish with parsley sprigs and cucumber slices.

HERBED TOMATO SLICES

⅓ cup salad oil
2 tablespoons tarragon vinegar
½ teaspoon salt
¼ teaspoon dried thyme leaves, crushed
¼ teaspoon dried marjoram leaves, crushed
3 tomatoes, peeled and sliced

Combine first 5 ingredients and dash pepper. Pour over tomatoes in shallow bowl. Chill 2 to 3 hours, spooning dressing over tomatoes occasionally; drain. Makes 4 cups.

RELISH COTTAGE CHEESE

1 12-ounce carton (1½ cups) cream-style cottage cheese, drained
2 tablespoons chopped canned pimiento
1 to 2 tablespoons chopped green onions *or* chives
1 to 2 tablespoons chopped green pepper
1 teaspoon prepared horseradish
¼ teaspoon salt

Combine ingredients; chill. Makes 2 cups.

ORIENTAL RELISH

Sprinkle 2 cups paper-thin cucumber slices with ½ teaspoon salt; chill. Drain in sieve, pressing with paper towels to remove excess moisture. Sprinkle 2 cups shredded carrots with ¼ teaspoon salt.

Dissolve ¼ cup sugar in ½ cup white vinegar. Place cucumber slices and carrots in separate dishes. Pour vinegar mixture over. Chill at least 1 hour. Before serving, drain. Heap cucumber in center of lettuce cup; circle with carrots. Makes 3½ cups.

TOSSED GREEN SALAD

3 heads (1½ to 2 pounds each) lettuce
1 bunch romaine (½ pound)
2 bunches radishes, sliced
2 large cucumbers, thinly sliced (4 cups)
2 large green peppers, chopped
1 large onion, chopped (optional)
1 pint French salad dressing
⅔ cup sweet pickle relish
⅓ cup vinegar

Tear lettuce and romaine in bite-size pieces and layer in several large salad bowls with next 4 ingredients; chill. Combine remaining ingredients; before serving, toss with vegetables. Makes 25 (about 1 cup) servings.

SALAD WHEEL

1 bunch leaf lettuce
Pitted green and ripe olives
4 large tomatoes, sliced
2 raw turnips, sliced
1 medium unpared cucumber, sliced
10 radish roses
Green onions with tops
Whole sweet pickles
Parsley sprigs
Green pepper rings

Arrange lettuce leaves on serving platter. Place olives in center of platter. Form 6 vegetable "spokes" by alternating slices of tomato, turnip, and cucumber. Arrange groupings of radishes, onions, and pickles between spokes. Garnish with sprigs of parsley and green pepper rings.

CABBAGE SLAW

Combine 2¼ pounds cabbage, shredded (15 cups); ¾ pound carrots, shredded (3 cups); and ¾ cup diced green pepper; chill. Blend 3 cups mayonnaise or salad dressing, ⅓ cup sugar, ⅓ cup vinegar, 1 tablespoon prepared mustard, 3 teaspoons celery seed, and 2 teaspoons salt. Just before serving, toss vegetables and mayonnaise mixture lightly. Makes 25 (½ cup) servings.

SALAD ENTREES

Looking for a menu for that next luncheon or late evening supper? Plan the meal around a salad. All that needs to be added is a bread, beverage, and luscious dessert.

Lightly tossed salad bowls head the list of this idea-packed chapter. To keep salad bowls cool, place the bowl in a bed of crushed ice (as seen at left). Or, prepare individual salad bowls and serve in icers.

If one fancies gelatin salads that are made ahead, choose a molded main dish salad. It will eliminate much of the last-minute fuss. Then, when the serving hour arrives, just unmold on a lettuce-lined plate.

Suggestions abound for presenting main dish salads attractively. Impressive meals are easy to plan around these delightful entrees.

When the temperature soars and appetites are on the wane, serve Ham and Cheese Medley. Two "old-favorites" are teamed with fruit, then capped with sour cream.

MEALS IN A BOWL

HAM AND CHEESE MEDLEY

1 8¾-ounce can pineapple tidbits
1 small head lettuce, torn in
    bite-size pieces (4 cups)
1 cup cubed fully-cooked ham
1 cup halved seedless green grapes
2 ounces natural Swiss cheese,
    cut in strips
    Bibb lettuce
1 cup dairy sour cream

Drain pineapple, reserving ¼ cup syrup. Toss together pineapple and next 4 ingredients. Line salad bowl with Bibb lettuce; spoon in salad mixture. Chill. For dressing, stir reserved syrup into sour cream till well blended; chill. To serve, spoon a little dressing atop salad. Garnish with additional green grapes and Bibb lettuce, if desired. Pass remaining dressing. Makes 6 servings.

DEVILED BEEF TOSS

1 head romaine, torn in bite-size
    pieces
3 cups torn lettuce
1½ cups cooked roast beef cut
    in strips
12 cherry tomatoes
½ medium onion, sliced and
    separated into rings
1 2-ounce can rolled anchovy
    fillets, drained
    Mustard-horseradish Dressing

In large bowl, toss greens together. Arrange beef strips, cherry tomatoes, onion rings, and anchovies on greens. Serve with Mustard-horseradish Dressing. Makes 6 servings.

Mustard-horseradish Dressing: In small bowl, combine 1 tablespoon sugar, 1 teaspoon salt, 1 teaspoon dry mustard, ¼ teaspoon white pepper, and dash paprika. Add 1 tablespoon horseradish and ½ teaspoon grated onion. With electric mixer at medium speed, slowly add ⅔ cup salad oil, a little at a time, alternately with ⅓ cup white wine vinegar. Chill thoroughly.

SALAMI-CHEESE SALAD

6 cups torn lettuce
1 cup sliced salami cut in
    quarters
4 ounces natural Swiss cheese,
    cut in strips
½ cup sliced pitted ripe olives
3 tablespoons chopped canned
    pimiento
1 2-ounce can anchovy fillets,
    drained and chopped
⅓ cup salad oil
3 tablespoons wine vinegar
½ clove garlic, crushed

Combine lettuce, salami, cheese, olives, pimiento, and anchovies. In screw-top jar, combine oil, vinegar, and garlic for dressing. Cover; shake well. Pour dressing over salad and toss lightly. Makes 8 servings.

HAM-CHICKEN SUPREME

6 cups torn lettuce
1 cup diced cucumber
1 medium green pepper, cut in
    narrow strips
1 cup fully-cooked ham cut
    in strips
1 cup cooked chicken cut
    in strips
3 hard-cooked eggs, sliced
2 medium tomatoes, cut in wedges
    . . .
½ cup salad oil
3 tablespoons vinegar
1 tablespoon prepared horseradish
½ teaspoon Worcestershire sauce
2 drops bottled hot pepper sauce
½ teaspoon salt
⅛ teaspoon pepper

Line individual salad bowls with lettuce. Arrange cucumber, green pepper, ham, chicken, eggs, and tomatoes in each. In screw-top jar, combine remaining ingredients for dressing. Cover and shake well. Pass dressing with salads. Makes 8 to 10 servings.

TUNA-CREAM PUFF BOWL

    4 hard-cooked eggs
    1 9¼-ounce can tuna, drained
    1 tablespoon lemon juice
    1 cup sliced celery
    ¼ cup sliced pimiento-stuffed
        green olives
    ¼ cup finely chopped onion
    ½ cup mayonnaise
        Cream Puff Bowl
    2 cups shredded lettuce

Sieve 1 egg yolk and slice 1 whole egg; reserve for garnish. Coarsely chop remaining eggs and white. Break tuna in chunks; sprinkle with lemon juice. Add next 3 ingredients, ¼ teaspoon salt, and dash pepper. Fold in mayonnaise and chopped eggs; chill. Just before serving, cover bottom of Cream Puff Bowl with lettuce; fill with tuna salad. Garnish with egg slices and sieved yolk. Serves 6.

CREAM PUFF BOWL

    ¼ cup butter or margarine
    ½ cup boiling water
    ½ cup sifted all-purpose flour
    ¼ teaspoon celery seed
    2 eggs

In 1-quart saucepan, melt butter in boiling water. Add flour, celery seed, and dash salt all at once; stir vigorously. Cook, stirring constantly, over low heat till mixture forms a ball that doesn't separate. Remove from heat and cool slightly. Add eggs, one at a time, beating vigorously after each till smooth. Spread batter evenly over bottom and sides of greased 9-inch pie plate. Bake in very hot oven (450°) 15 minutes; reduce oven temperature to 325° and bake 30 minutes longer. Turn oven off (keep oven door closed) and let puff dry out, about 20 minutes. Remove from oven and cool on rack.

Fascinate guests and family alike with Tuna-cream Puff Bowl. A baked salad bowl to be eaten along with the crunchy salad adds to the fun. Since the ingredients are usually right at hand, there's no need to wait for a special occasion. The compliments make it worth any extra preparation time.

LEMON CAPER CRAB SALAD

2 6-ounce packages frozen crab
   meat, thawed
1 10-ounce package frozen
   asparagus spears, cooked,
   drained, and chilled
        . . .
½ cup low-calorie mayonnaise-
   type dressing
1 tablespoon lemon juice
1 teaspoon drained capers
½ teaspoon prepared mustard
½ teaspoon Worcestershire sauce
3 hard-cooked eggs, sliced

Break crab into chunks, removing cartilage.
Place 3 asparagus spears on each of 6 lettuce-
lined plates and ⅓ cup crab meat over asparagus. Blend together remaining ingredients
except eggs. Spoon 1 tablespoon mayonnaise
mixture atop crab. Trim with hard-cooked
egg slices. Makes 6 servings.

MEAT AND BEAN SALAD

1 cup cubed cooked meat
1 8-ounce can kidney beans,
   drained
½ cup sliced celery
1 hard-cooked egg, chopped
3 tablespoons chopped onion
1 tablespoon sweet pickle relish
⅓ cup mayonnaise
1 tablespoon chili sauce

Combine first 6 ingredients. To prepare
dressing, blend together mayonnaise, chili
sauce, and ¼ teaspoon salt. Toss dressing
with meat mixture; chill. Serves 3 or 4.

TUNA-MELON DINNER SALAD

Combine 4 cups torn lettuce (about ½
large head); 2 cups cubed cantaloupe; one
11-ounce can mandarin oranges, drained;
one 6½- or 7-ounce can tuna, drained and
flaked; ¾ cup sliced process American cheese
cut in strips; ½ cup chopped celery; ¼ cup
sliced green onion; and ¼ cup sliced pitted
ripe olives. Blend ½ cup mayonnaise or salad
dressing and 1 tablespoon lemon juice; add
to tuna mixture and toss lightly. Serves 8.

MACARONI SALMON SALAD

¾ cup uncooked elbow macaroni
1 7¾-ounce can salmon, drained
   and flaked
¾ cup chopped celery
2 tablespoons chopped onion
¾ cup mayonnaise or salad
   dressing
¼ teaspoon liquid smoke
   Parsley

Cook macaroni following package directions;
drain. Combine macaroni, salmon, celery,
and onion. Blend mayonnaise, liquid smoke,
and ¼ teaspoon salt; toss lightly with salmon mixture. Chill. Garnish with parsley.
Makes 3 or 4 servings.

DUBLIN POTATO SALAD

2 tablespoons vinegar
1 teaspoon celery seed
1 teaspoon mustard seed
3 medium-large potatoes
2 teaspoons sugar
2 cups finely shredded cabbage
1 12-ounce can corned beef,
   chilled and cubed
¼ cup sliced green onion
¼ cup finely chopped dill pickle
1 cup mayonnaise or salad
   dressing
¼ cup milk

Combine vinegar, celery seed, and mustard
seed; set aside. Meanwhile, pare and cook
potatoes in enough boiling salted water to
cover for 30 to 40 minutes or till done; drain
and cube. While potatoes are still warm,
drizzle with vinegar mixture. Sprinkle with
sugar and ½ teaspoon salt; chill.

Before serving, add cabbage, corned beef,
onion, and pickle to potatoes. Combine mayonnaise, milk, and ½ teaspoon salt. Pour
mayonnaise mixture over corned beef mixture and toss lightly. Serves 6 to 8.

It's the luck o' the Irish when portions of →
Dublin Potato Salad are served. The familiar
corned beef and cabbage combination with
potato welcomes a peppy sweet-tart dressing.

Think "fast and easy" when preparing Skillet Chef's Salad. Strips of hearty ham and cheese, hard-cooked egg slices, lettuce, and an assortment of vegetables are heated in a sassy sweet-sour dressing. The menu is complete when served with piping-hot muffins, jam or jelly, and beverage.

SKILLET CHEF'S SALAD

In medium skillet, blend 2 tablespoons salad oil, 1 tablespoon all-purpose flour, 1 tablespoon sugar, 1 teaspoon instant minced onion, ½ teaspoon garlic salt, ½ teaspoon prepared mustard, and dash pepper. Add ½ cup water and ¼ cup vinegar; cook over medium heat to boiling, stirring constantly.

Layer the following in the hot sauce: 2 cups fully-cooked ham cut in thin strips; 3 hard-cooked eggs, sliced; ½ cup sliced celery; 3 cups torn lettuce (½ medium head); ½ cup thinly sliced cucumber; 4 ounces natural Cheddar cheese, cut in strips (1 cup); and 1 large tomato, cut in thin wedges.

Cook, covered, over medium heat 4 to 5 minutes, or till heated through. Remove from heat; toss mixture together lightly. Serve immediately. Makes 4 to 6 servings.

FIESTA SALAD BOWL

An imaginative combination for the corned beef and cabbage lover—

Cook ½ of 7-ounce package (1 cup) elbow macaroni and one 10-ounce package frozen Brussels sprouts in separate saucepans following package directions; drain. Halve Brussels sprouts. Combine cooked macaroni; halved Brussels sprouts; one 4-ounce package cooked corned beef, cut in julienne strips; 2 tablespoons chopped onion; and 2 tablespoons chopped green pepper.

Gradually stir 2 tablespoons vinegar into ½ cup mayonnaise or salad dressing. Add 1 tablespoon sugar, ½ teaspoon salt, and ½ teaspoon prepared horseradish. Pour mayonnaise mixture over macaroni mixture; toss lightly. Chill. Makes 5 or 6 servings.

BEAN AND TONGUE SALAD

Combine one 16-ounce can kidney beans, drained; 1 cup cooked tongue cut in julienne strips; ½ cup chopped celery; ¼ cup chopped candied dill pickle; 2 tablespoons chopped green pepper; and 2 tablespoons chopped canned pimiento. Blend together ½ cup mayonnaise or salad dressing, ½ teaspoon salt, and dash pepper. Toss mayonnaise with tongue mixture; chill. Makes 4 servings.

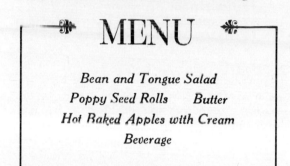

MENU

Bean and Tongue Salad

Poppy Seed Rolls   Butter

Hot Baked Apples with Cream

Beverage

CRAB-WILD RICE SALAD

A salad with gourmet elegance—

- 1 6-ounce package long-grain and wild rice mix
- 1 7½-ounce can crab meat, drained, flaked, and cartilage removed
- 1 tablespoon lemon juice
- ¼ cup chopped green pepper
- ¼ cup chopped canned pimiento
- 2 tablespoons snipped parsley
- ½ cup mayonnaise or salad dressing
- 2 tablespoons Russian salad dressing
- ½ teaspoon salt
- 2 medium avocados, peeled and sliced*

Cook rice following package directions; cool. Mix together crab meat and lemon juice. Combine rice, crab, green pepper, pimiento, and parsley. Blend together mayonnaise, Russian salad dressing, and salt. Add mayonnaise mixture to vegetable-crab mixture and toss lightly. Chill. Serve with avocado slices. Makes 4 or 5 servings.

*To keep avocado slices bright, dip in lemon juice mixed with a little water.

FISH SLAW

- 1 pound frozen halibut fillets, thawed
- ¾ cup mayonnaise or salad dressing
- 2 tablespoons chopped sweet pickle
- 2 tablespoons chopped onion
- 1 tablespoon vinegar
- 2 cups shredded cabbage, chilled

Place fillets in 1 quart boiling water with 1 tablespoon salt. Simmer, covered, 10 minutes, or till fish flakes easily with fork; drain. Remove skin and bones; flake fish. Combine fish with next 4 ingredients and 1 teaspoon salt. Chill 1 hour. Add cabbage; toss lightly. Sprinkle with paprika, if desired. Makes 6 servings.

CHICKEN SALAD PIE

A richly frosted salad pie—

- 1 cup sifted all-purpose flour
- ⅓ cup shortening
- ⅓ cup shredded sharp process American cheese
- 1½ cups cubed cooked chicken
- 1 8¾-ounce can pineapple tidbits, drained (⅔ cup)
- ½ cup sliced celery
- ½ cup chopped walnuts
- ¾ cup dairy sour cream
- ½ cup mayonnaise

Sift flour and ¼ teaspoon salt together; cut in shortening and ¼ cup cheese till pieces are size of small peas. Sprinkle 3 to 4 tablespoons cold water over, 1 tablespoon at a time, gently tossing with fork till all the mixture is moistened. Form into ball. Roll on lightly floured surface to ⅛ inch thickness. Fit into 8-inch pie plate. Bake in hot oven (450°) for 8 to 10 minutes. Cool.

Combine chicken, pineapple, celery, and nuts. Blend together sour cream and mayonnaise. Add ⅔ cup sour cream mixture to chicken mixture; mix well. Spoon into pastry shell. Spread remaining sour cream mixture over. Sprinkle with remaining cheese. Chill. Trim with sliced pitted ripe olives, if desired. Makes 6 servings.

LOW-CAL SCALLOP SALAD

1½ pounds frozen scallops, thawed
1 10-ounce package frozen green
  beans, cooked and drained
1 cup sliced celery
2 tablespoons chopped green onion
2 tablespoons chopped green
  pepper
2 tablespoons chopped
  canned pimiento
½ cup vinegar
1 tablespoon salad oil
  Non-caloric liquid sweetener
    equal to 1 tablespoon sugar
¼ teaspoon dried tarragon leaves,
    crushed

Place scallops and 2 tablespoons salt in 1 quart boiling water. Cover; return to boiling. Reduce heat; simmer 3 to 4 minutes. Drain and cool; slice. Combine scallops and next 5 ingredients. In screw-top jar, combine vinegar, salad oil, liquid sweetener, ¼ teaspoon salt, tarragon, and dash pepper. Cover and shake. Pour vinegar mixture over scallop mixture. Cover; chill at least 1 hour, stirring occasionally. Drain before serving. Spoon into lettuce cups. Makes 6 servings.

❧ MENU ☙

Tomato Juice
Low-cal Scallop Salad
Saltine Crackers
Fresh Blueberries   Dessert Topping
Skim Milk

BEEF 'N MUSHROOM SALAD

Also doubles as an appetizer—

Combine 4 cups cooked beef cut in julienne strips, 1 cup sliced fresh mushrooms, and ¼ cup thinly sliced green onion. Blend together ½ cup mayonnaise or salad dressing, ½ cup dairy sour cream, 1 tablespoon milk, ½ teaspoon salt, and dash pepper; toss with meat mixture. Chill. Serve in lettuce cups; sprinkle with paprika. Makes 5 or 6 servings.

TURKEY-POTATO SALAD

2 cups cubed cooked turkey
2 cups cubed, peeled,
  cooked potatoes
1 cup diced celery
4 hard-cooked eggs, coarsely
  chopped
2 tablespoons finely chopped
  onion
1 cup mayonnaise
1 tablespoon vinegar
1 teaspoon prepared horseradish
¼ teaspoon dried rosemary leaves,
  crushed

Combine first 5 ingredients. Blend together mayonnaise, vinegar, 1 teaspoon salt, horseradish, rosemary, and dash white pepper. Toss mayonnaise mixture lightly with potato mixture. Cover and chill. Serves 6 to 8.

CHEF'S SUPPER BOWL

4 cups cubed, peeled,
  cooked potatoes
1 cup sliced celery
½ cup chopped onion
½ cup Caraway Cheese Dressing
½ cup mayonnaise
½ cup chopped dill pickle
4 cups shredded lettuce
2 medium tomatoes, cut in wedges
4 slices (4 ounces) bologna,
  cut in thin strips
2 slices process American cheese,
  cut in thin strips
2 slices process Swiss cheese,
  cut in thin strips

Sprinkle potatoes with ½ teaspoon salt. Combine potatoes, celery, and onion. Blend together Caraway Cheese Dressing, mayonnaise, and pickle. Pour *half* the dressing mixture over potato mixture; toss lightly. Cover and chill. Place shredded lettuce in bottom of large bowl. Mound potato salad in center. Arrange tomatoes, bologna, and cheeses over. Pass remaining dressing. Serves 6 to 8.

Caraway Cheese Dressing: Gradually stir 2 tablespoons vinegar into one 6-ounce can evaporated milk. Add 3 tablespoons grated Parmesan cheese, ½ teaspoon salt, and ½ teaspoon caraway seed. Makes about 1 cup.

"Two's company, but three's not a crowd" when it's three servings of Jacques' Chicken Salad. Colorful extras, such as juicy tomato slices, ripe olives, and wedges of hard-cooked egg, garnish the salad. Peppy green beans, marinated with Italian dressing, complete this elegant luncheon plate.

JACQUES' CHICKEN SALAD

  1 10-ounce package frozen French-style green beans, cooked and drained, or 1 16-ounce can green beans, drained
¼ cup Italian salad dressing
  3 large chicken breasts, cooked and chilled
½ cup mayonnaise
¼ cup whipping cream, whipped
  1 cup diced celery
  3 lettuce cups
      Mayonnaise or salad dressing
  2 teaspoons drained capers
  6 tomato slices
  6 ripe olives
  2 hard-cooked eggs, quartered

In small bowl, combine green beans and Italian salad dressing. Chill several hours, stirring occasionally. Cut 3 thin slices of meat from chicken breasts and reserve for garnish. Cube remaining chicken. Gently fold the ½ cup mayonnaise into whipped cream. Fold cubed chicken, celery, ½ teaspoon salt, and dash pepper into mayonnaise-whipped cream mixture. Chill thoroughly.

Place lettuce cups on serving platter. To assemble salads, spoon chilled chicken mixture into lettuce cups. Arrange reserved chicken slices and a dollop of mayonnaise atop salad mixture; sprinkle with drained capers. Drain green beans; arrange on platter between filled lettuce cups. Garnish with tomato slices, ripe olives, and hard-cooked egg wedges. Makes 3 servings.

APPLE AND HAM SALAD

Lend a subtle flavor variation to an apple and ham toss with blue cheese—

3 cups sliced tart apples
1 cup cubed fully-cooked ham
½ cup diced celery
¼ cup mayonnaise or salad dressing
2 tablespoons light cream
2 tablespoons crumbled blue cheese
1 tablespoon lemon juice

Combine apple slices, cubed ham, and diced celery. Blend together mayonnaise, cream, blue cheese, and lemon juice. Toss mayonnaise mixture lightly with apple-ham mixture. If desired, garnish salad with a star of unpared apple wedges. Serves 5 or 6.

GULF SHRIMP-RICE SALAD

12 ounces shrimp, cooked, peeled, and cleaned *or* 3 4½-ounce cans shrimp, drained
2 cups cooked rice
1 cup chopped celery
½ cup shredded carrots
¼ cup snipped parsley
¾ cup mayonnaise or salad dressing
2 tablespoons French salad dressing
1 tablespoon lemon juice
½ teaspoon salt

Cut large shrimp in half; combine with rice, celery, carrot, and parsley. Blend together remaining ingredients; toss with shrimp mixture. Chill. Makes 6 servings.

PICNIC BEAN SALAD

Easy to tote to picnic site—

Cut 4 ounces salami in thin strips (1 cup). Combine with one 16-ounce can baked beans, drained; ¼ cup chopped sweet pickles; ¼ cup mayonnaise; and 2 tablespoons finely chopped onion. Season to taste. Chill several hours. Serves 3.

HOT TUNA-MACARONI TOSS

Try a hot salad for a change—

½ 7-ounce package (1 cup) elbow macaroni
¼ cup Italian salad dressing
¾ teaspoon dry mustard
½ teaspoon celery seed
½ teaspoon salt
Dash pepper
1 6½- or 7-ounce can tuna, drained and flaked
½ cup diced celery
¼ cup chopped green pepper
¼ cup mayonnaise or salad dressing
Green pepper rings

Cook macaroni in boiling salted water till tender following package directions; drain. In skillet, mix Italian salad dressing, mustard, celery seed, salt and pepper. Heat just to boiling. Add drained macaroni, tuna, celery, and green pepper. Toss and heat through. Stir in mayonnaise. Top with green pepper rings; serve hot. Serves 4.

MENU

Pineapple Juice
Hot Tuna-macaroni Toss
Green Beans with Parmesan Cheese
Bread Sticks   Butter
Applesauce a la Mode

CUTTING SIZE GUIDE

Terms used in recipes refer to the size of the cut-up pieces. From largest to smallest they are as follows:
Julienne—To cut food in long, thin strips.
Cube—To cut food in pieces of uniform size and shape, such as 1 inch or ½ inch.
Dice—To cut food in small cubes of uniform shape and size.
Chop—To cut food in small pieces about the size of peas.
Mince—To cut or finely chop food into very small pieces.

PORK SALAD JAMBOREE

1 cup cubed unpared apple
1 tablespoon lemon juice

. . .

2 cups cubed cooked pork
1 cup halved and seeded
   red grapes
½ cup chopped celery
½ cup mayonnaise
½ teaspoon salt

Sprinkle apple with lemon juice. Toss with remaining ingredients. Chill. Serves 4 or 5.

MENU

Pork Salad Jamboree
Buttered Broccoli
Cloverleaf Rolls   *Butter*
Gingerbread with Orange Sauce
Beverage

RICE AND HAM SALAD

Includes the familiar ham and cheese blend—

¾ cup uncooked rice
1½ cups water
¼ cup finely chopped onion
2 tablespoons soy sauce
1 medium clove garlic, minced

. . .

2 cups diced fully-cooked ham
½ cup chopped celery
½ cup mayonnaise or salad
   dressing
1 tablespoon vinegar
⅛ teaspoon cayenne
4 ounces process Swiss cheese,
   shredded (1 cup)

In skillet, cook rice over low heat till lightly browned. Add water, onion, soy sauce, and garlic; mix well. Cover; cook 20 minutes or till rice is tender and liquid is absorbed. Add ham and celery; heat through. Stir in mayonnaise, vinegar, cayenne, and cheese. To serve, top with additional Swiss cheese, if desired. Makes 4 to 6 servings.

BASIC CHICKEN SALAD

3 cups cubed cooked chicken
1 cup chopped celery
¼ cup chopped sweet pickle

. . .

½ cup mayonnaise or salad
   dressing
1 tablespoon lemon juice
½ teaspoon seasoned salt
   Dash pepper
   Pitted ripe olive slices *or*
   hard-cooked egg slices

Combine chicken, celery, and pickle. Blend together mayonnaise, lemon juice, seasoned salt, and pepper; toss lightly with chicken mixture. Chill. Serve in lettuce cups. Trim with slices of ripe olive or hard-cooked egg. Makes 4 servings.

CHICKEN-BEAN SALAD

1 16-ounce can cut green beans,
   chilled and drained
2 tablespoons Italian salad
   dressing
2 cups cubed cooked chicken
¼ cup sliced radishes
¼ cup mayonnaise or salad
   dressing
1 tablespoon lemon juice
   Whole radishes

Combine beans and Italian salad dressing; chill at least 1 hour. Add chicken, sliced radishes, mayonnaise, and lemon juice; toss lightly. Serve in lettuce cups; garnish with whole radishes. Makes 4 servings.

HOLIDAY TURKEY SALAD

2 cups cubed cooked turkey
1 cup sliced celery
1 8¾-ounce can pineapple
   tidbits, drained (⅔ cup)
½ cup pomegranate seeds
½ cup mayonnaise or salad
   dressing
¼ cup toasted slivered almonds

Combine all ingredients; toss. Chill. Serve on lettuce-lined plates. Serves 4 or 5.

ZIPPY SHRIMP SALAD

¼ cup dairy sour cream
¼ cup chili sauce
2 teaspoons prepared horseradish
1 pound shrimp, cooked, peeled, cleaned, and coarsely chopped
1 cup chopped celery

Blend together first 3 ingredients and ¼ teaspoon salt; stir in shrimp and celery. Chill thoroughly. Makes 4 servings.

HAM AND EGG SALAD

1½ cups cubed fully-cooked ham
6 hard-cooked eggs, coarsely diced
½ cup chopped celery
½ cup chopped sweet pickle
⅓ cup mayonnaise or salad dressing
2 tablespoons prepared mustard

Combine first 4 ingredients. Blend together mayonnaise and mustard. Add to ham mixture; toss lightly. Chill. Makes 4 servings.

TURKEY-MUSHROOM SALAD

2½ cups cubed cooked turkey
1½ cups sliced fresh mushrooms
1 cup chopped celery
2 tablespoons sliced pimiento-stuffed green olives
⅓ cup mayonnaise or salad dressing
1 tablespoon lemon juice
1 teaspoon finely chopped onion
Romaine leaves

Combine first 4 ingredients. Blend together mayonnaise, lemon juice, onion, and ½ teaspoon salt. Add to turkey mixture; toss lightly. Chill. Line salad bowl with romaine. Spoon in turkey salad. Makes 6 servings.

←**Fresh mushrooms** give Turkey-mushroom Salad a sophisticated touch. Use canned sliced mushrooms if the fresh are not available. Fill in with pert pimiento-stuffed olive slices and celery.

ALADDIN'S SALAD BOWL

4 cups torn lettuce
2 cups torn endive
1 4-ounce package sliced jellied beef loaf, cut in strips
1 4-ounce package sliced salami, cut in strips
6 ounces sliced natural Muenster cheese, cut in strips
2 hard-cooked eggs, sliced
½ cup mayonnaise or salad dressing
¼ cup Russian salad dressing

Combine lettuce and endive in salad bowl. Arrange beef, salami, cheese, and egg slices atop greens. Season to taste with salt and pepper. Combine mayonnaise and Russian dressing. Serve with salad. Serves 4 to 6.

CURRY CHICKEN SALAD

2 cups cubed cooked chicken
¾ cup diced celery
2 tablespoons raisins
½ cup mayonnaise or salad dressing
1 tablespoon lemon juice
¼ teaspoon curry powder
¼ cup whole cashew nuts

Combine chicken, celery, and raisins in large bowl. Blend together mayonnaise, lemon juice, ¼ teaspoon salt, curry powder, and dash pepper; toss lightly with chicken mixture. Chill. Just before serving, add cashew nuts and toss. Makes 4 servings.

STEWING CHICKEN FOR SALADS

Place one 5- to 6-pound ready-to-cook stewing chicken, cut up, *or* 2 large broiler-fryer chickens, cut up, in Dutch oven with water to cover (about 2 quarts). Add 2 sprigs parsley; 4 cut-up celery branches with leaves; 1 carrot, pared and sliced; 1 small onion, cut up; 2 teaspoons salt; and ¼ teaspoon pepper. Cover; bring to boiling. Reduce heat, then cook over low heat about 2½ hours till tender. Remove meat from bones. Makes about 5 cups diced cooked chicken.

TUNA-SPINACH TOSS

A perky, eye-catching salad bright with cheese strips and onion rings—

      2 cups torn spinach
      1 cup torn lettuce
    ½ small red onion, thinly sliced
         and separated into rings
         (about ½ cup)
      1 6½- or 7-ounce can tuna,
         drained and flaked
      4 ounces Swiss cheese, cut into
         narrow 2-inch strips (about
         1 cup)
    ¼ cup olive *or* salad oil
      1 tablespoon vinegar
      1 tablespoon lemon juice
    ½ teaspoon salt
    ¼ teaspoon dried tarragon
         leaves, crushed

Toss spinach and lettuce in large bowl. Place onion rings around sides of bowl. Heap tuna in center; surround with cheese. Combine remaining ingredients and dash pepper in screw-top jar; shake. Just before serving, toss dressing mixture with salad. Serves 4.

LOBSTER-ORANGE CUPS

Delicately flavored mounds of lobster with orange sections in creamy dressing—

      1 5-ounce can lobster, drained
         and cartilage removed
      3 large oranges, peeled and
         sectioned
      2 tablespoons mayonnaise or
         salad dressing
    ¼ teaspoon grated orange peel
      2 tablespoons orange juice
    ¼ teaspoon prepared horseradish
    ½ cup whipping cream, whipped

Break lobster into ½-inch pieces; sprinkle with ¼ teaspoon salt. Toss with orange sections. Chill. To prepare dressing, combine mayonnaise, orange peel, orange juice, and horseradish. Gently fold in whipped cream. Heap chilled lobster mixture in individual lettuce-lined bowls or sherbet glasses. Pass whipped cream dressing. Top with dash of nutmeg, if desired. Makes 3 or 4 servings.

HAM AND FRUIT SALAD

Ham's good flavor is highlighted with the addition of cherries and oranges—

      2 cups cubed fully-cooked ham
      1 16-ounce can pitted dark
         sweet cherries, drained
      1 11-ounce can mandarin
         oranges, drained
      1 cup chopped celery
    ½ cup mayonnaise
      1 tablespoon milk
      1 tablespoon vinegar

Combine ham, cherries, oranges, and celery. Blend together mayonnaise, milk, vinegar, and dash pepper; toss with ham mixture. Chill thoroughly. Makes 6 servings.

TURKEY-APPLE TOSS

First-class way to use leftover turkey. A hearty salad with apples and celery—

      2 cups cubed cooked turkey
    ½ cup cubed apple
      1 tablespoon lemon juice
    ¾ cup diced celery
      2 hard-cooked eggs, chopped
    ½ cup mayonnaise
    ½ teaspoon salt
    ¼ teaspoon dried basil
         leaves, crushed
         Dash pepper
    ¼ cup toasted slivered
         almonds

Toss turkey and apple with lemon juice. Add celery and eggs. Blend together next 4 ingredients; toss lightly with turkey mixture. Chill. Before serving, fold in nuts. Serve in lettuce cups. Makes 4 servings.

THURINGER SALAD

   Combine 4 ounces thuringer, cubed (about 1 cup); 2 hard-cooked eggs, chopped; ½ cup chopped celery; ¼ cup cubed natural Swiss cheese; ¼ cup sliced pitted ripe olives; and ¼ cup mayonnaise or salad dressing. Toss together lightly and thoroughly. Chill well. Makes 2 or 3 servings.

HAM AND POTATO SALAD

Meat, potatoes, vegetables—all in one salad—

  2 cups cubed cooked potatoes
  1 tablespoon Italian
       salad dressing

  . . .

1½ cups cubed fully-cooked ham
  2 hard-cooked eggs, chopped
  ½ cup diced unpared cucumber
  ¼ cup sliced radishes
  ¼ cup chopped celery
  2 tablespoons chopped onion
  2 tablespoons chopped
       green pepper
  ¼ teaspoon salt
  ⅛ teaspoon paprika
  ½ cup mayonnaise
       or salad dressing

Sprinkle cubed potatoes with Italian dressing. Let stand ½ hour. Add remaining ingredients to potatoes *except* mayonnaise. Chill thoroughly. Before serving, gently fold in mayonnaise. Makes 5 servings.

```
┌──────────────────────────────────┐
│   ❧   MENU   ☙                    │
│                                   │
│      Ham and Potato Salad         │
│        Grilled Tomatoes           │
│   Brown and Serve Rolls   Butter  │
│   Lemon Sherbet  Chocolate Cookies│
│           Beverage                │
│                                   │
└──────────────────────────────────┘
```

TUNA-MACARONI SALAD

Cook 1 cup shell macaroni following package directions. Drain thoroughly.

In large bowl, break two 6½- or 7-ounce cans tuna, drained, into large pieces. Combine tuna with drained macaroni, 1 cup sliced celery, and ¼ cup drained pickle relish.

In another bowl, blend together ¾ cup mayonnaise or salad dressing, ¼ cup Russian salad dressing, 1 tablespoon lemon juice, ½ teaspoon salt, ⅛ teaspoon pepper, and few drops onion juice. Add to tuna mixture; toss lightly. Garnish with slices from 1 hard-cooked egg. Makes 6 servings.

Fish adds a different twist to Tuna Potato Salad. Cheese and olives are also a surprise.

TUNA-POTATO SALAD

  2 medium potatoes, pared
  2 tablespoons Italian salad
       dressing
  1 tablespoon snipped parsley
  3 cups torn lettuce (about ½
       medium head)
  1 9¼-ounce can tuna, drained
       and flaked
  3 hard-cooked eggs, quartered
  ¾ cup Swiss cheese cut in strips
  ½ cup sliced pitted ripe olives
  ¼ cup chopped onion
  ½ cup Italian salad dressing

Cook potatoes in small amount of water for 20 to 25 minutes, till tender. Slice into salad bowl. Sprinkle with 2 tablespoons dressing and parsley. Chill. Layer remaining ingredients on top *except* ½ cup Italian dressing. Before serving, pour dressing over salad and toss lightly. Makes 4 servings.

CHOP SUEY SALAD

Combine 1½ cups cubed cooked beef *or* pork; 1 cup chopped celery; 2 hard-cooked eggs, chopped; ¼ cup diced sweet pickle; and 2 tablespoons finely chopped onion.

Blend together ½ cup mayonnaise or salad dressing, ½ teaspoon Worcestershire sauce, and ½ teaspoon salt; toss with meat mixture. Chill thoroughly. At serving time, fold in ½ cup chow mein noodles; top with additional noodles, if desired. Makes 3 or 4 servings.

CHICKEN SALAD ORIENTAL

    3 cups diced cooked chicken
    1 13½-ounce can pineapple tidbits,
       drained (1 cup)
    1 5-ounce can water chestnuts,
       drained and sliced
    2 tablespoons sliced green onion
    ¾ cup dairy sour cream
    1 teaspoon ground ginger
    ¼ cup toasted slivered almonds

Combine first 4 ingredients; chill. Blend sour cream, ginger, ½ teaspoon salt, and dash pepper; add to chicken mixture and toss lightly. Serve on crisp greens. Sprinkle with almonds. Makes 4 to 6 servings.

TOSSED TUNA SALAD

Break one 9¼-ounce can tuna, chilled and drained, into large pieces. In salad bowl, combine tuna; 3 cups torn fresh spinach *or* lettuce; one 16-ounce can bean sprouts, drained and rinsed; one 5-ounce can water chestnuts, drained and sliced; 2 tablespoons sliced green onion, separated into rings; and ½ cup Italian salad dressing. Toss lightly. Garnish with 1 medium tomato, cut in wedges. Makes 6 servings.

HAM AND TURKEY TOSS

    1 small head lettuce
    2 heads Bibb lettuce
    ½ bunch curly endive
    2 cups fully-cooked ham cut in
       thin strips
    1½ cups cooked turkey cut in thin
       strips
    2 slices natural Swiss cheese,
       cut in strips
    1 medium avocado, peeled and
       sliced
    1 2-ounce can anchovy fillets,
       drained
       Chili French Dressing (see Index)

In bowl, tear greens in bite-size pieces. Arrange remaining ingredients *except* dressing atop greens. Toss salad lightly with dressing at table. Pass additional dressing. Serves 8.

GUACAMOLE SALAD BOWL

In bowl, combine 3 cups torn lettuce (½ medium head); one 6½-, 7-, or 9¼-ounce can tuna, chilled and drained; 2 tomatoes, cut in wedges; ½ cup sliced pitted ripe olives; ¼ cup chopped green onion; and 1 cup corn chips.

Combine ½ cup mashed ripe avocado; 1 tablespoon lemon juice; ½ cup dairy sour cream; ⅓ cup salad oil; 1 clove garlic, crushed; ½ teaspoon sugar; ½ teaspoon chili powder; and ¼ teaspoon *each* salt and bottled hot pepper sauce. Beat with electric mixer or blender till smooth.

Toss lettuce-tuna mixture lightly with avocado dressing. Top with ½ cup shredded Cheddar cheese. Makes 4 servings.

CRAB LOUIS

    4 Bibb lettuce cups
    8 cups shredded lettuce (1 large
       head)
    2 to 3 cups cooked crab meat *or*
       2 7½-ounce cans crab meat,
       chilled and drained
          • • •
    2 large tomatoes, cut in wedges
    2 hard-cooked eggs, sliced
       Louis Dressing
       Pitted ripe olives

Line 4 salad plates with Bibb lettuce cups. Place shredded lettuce atop cups. If necessary, remove cartilage from crab meat. Reserve claw meat; leave remainder in chunks and arrange atop lettuce.

Circle with tomato and egg. Sprinkle with salt. Top with claw meat. Pour ¼ *cup* Louis Dressing atop each salad. Top with olives. Pass remaining dressing. Serves 4.

Louis Dressing: Fold 1 cup mayonnaise or salad dressing, ¼ cup chili sauce, ¼ cup chopped green pepper, 2 tablespoons sliced green onion with tops, and 1 teaspoon lemon juice into ¼ cup whipping cream, whipped. Season to taste; chill thoroughly.

An international dinner salad—Crab Louis. →
Chunks of crab meat, tomato wedges, and hard-cooked egg slices bask in the matchless Louis Dressing. Offer breadsticks on the side.

MOLDED MAIN DISH SALADS

SALMON AVOCADO MOLD

In saucepan, soften 1 envelope (1 tablespoon) unflavored gelatin in 1 cup cold water. Stir over low heat until all gelatin is completely dissolved.

Add 2 tablespoons sugar, 1 tablespoon lemon juice, 1 tablespoon vinegar, 2 teaspoons grated onion, ½ teaspoon salt, and ½ teaspoon prepared horseradish. Chill till gelatin mixture is partially set.

Fold in one 16-ounce can salmon, drained, flaked, and small bones removed; ½ cup mayonnaise or salad dressing; ⅓ cup sliced pitted ripe olives; and ¼ cup finely chopped celery. Spoon into 3½-cup mold; chill till gelatin mixture is firm.

To prepare avocado dressing, peel and mash 1 large avocado. Blend together mashed avocado (about ⅔ cup), ½ cup dairy sour cream, and ½ teaspoon salt. Chill. Unmold salmon salad onto serving platter; spread avocado dressing mixture evenly over outside of salad. Garnish with curly endive and a lemon twist. Makes 4 servings.

MENU

Salmon Avocado Mold

Sliced Tomatoes

Hard Rolls   Butter

Lemon-filled Jelly Roll

Beverage

← **A spectacular salad for a foursome** is the Salmon Avocado Mold. Frosted with an avocado dressing, cut wedges are pretty on the plates. It's a do-ahead beauty to make the hostess' job easier.

CORNED BEEF LOAF

Flavorful corned beef in a delicate pink mold—

> 2 envelopes (2 tablespoons) unflavored gelatin
> 2 cups tomato juice
> 1 cup mayonnaise or salad dressing
> 2 teaspoons lemon juice
> ½ teaspoon salt
>   • • •
> 1 12-ounce can corned beef, crumbled (2 cups)
> ½ cup chopped celery
> ½ cup chopped unpared cucumber
> 1 tablespoon chopped onion

In saucepan, soften gelatin in *1 cup* tomato juice; stir over low heat till gelatin is dissolved. Add remaining tomato juice, mayonnaise, lemon juice, and salt; beat smooth with rotary beater. Chill till partially set. Fold in corned beef, celery, cucumber, and onion. Pour into 8½x4½x2½-inch loaf dish; chill till firm. Makes 4 to 6 servings.

TUNA MOUSSE SQUARES

In saucepan, soften 2 envelopes (2 tablespoons) unflavored gelatin in 1½ cups cold chicken broth; stir over low heat till gelatin is dissolved. Cool. With rotary beater, beat 1 cup mayonnaise or salad dressing into gelatin mixture. Chill till partially set.

Fold in two 6½- or 7-ounce cans tuna, drained and flaked; ½ cup diced celery; 2 tablespoons chopped pimiento-stuffed green olives; 1 tablespoon finely chopped onion; 1 tablespoon lemon juice; 1 teaspoon prepared horseradish; and ¼ teaspoon paprika.

Fold in ½ cup whipping cream, whipped. Pour into 10x6x1½-inch dish. Chill till firm. Cut into squares; serve on lettuce-lined salad plates. Makes 6 servings.

SHRIMP RING SMOOTHY

A pleasing pastel gel—

2 envelopes (2 tablespoons)
   unflavored gelatin
2 cups cold water
2 cups dairy sour cream
¼ cup catsup
2 tablespoons lemon juice
1 tablespoon prepared horseradish
1 teaspoon salt
1 pound shrimp, cooked, cleaned,
   and cut up
1 cup chopped celery
¼ cup chopped green pepper

In saucepan, soften gelatin in cold water. Stir over low heat till gelatin is dissolved; cool slightly. Blend together sour cream, catsup, lemon juice, horseradish, and salt; add to dissolved gelatin and beat with rotary beater till smooth. Chill gelatin mixture till partially set; fold in shrimp, celery, and green pepper. Pour into 6½-cup ring mold. Chill till firm. Makes 6 servings.

Ham slices surround Potato Salad Loaf. Luncheon meat cornucopias dress up the platter.

TUNA GUMBO MOLD

1 3-ounce package lemon-flavored
   gelatin
1 cup boiling water
½ cup mayonnaise or salad
   dressing
1 10½-ounce can condensed
   chicken gumbo soup
1 6½- or 7-ounce can tuna,
   drained and flaked
½ cup chopped celery
1 tablespoon minced onion

Dissolve gelatin in boiling water; cool. Beat in mayonnaise with rotary beater till smooth; stir in soup. Chill till partially set. Fold in tuna, celery, and onion. Pour into 4½-cup mold. Chill till firm. Serves 4.

POTATO SALAD LOAF

1 8-ounce package sliced chopped
   ham (8 slices)
1 envelope (1 tablespoon)
   unflavored gelatin
½ cup cold water
1 cup mayonnaise or salad
   dressing
¼ cup chopped celery
2 tablespoons chopped onion
1 tablespoon snipped parsley
1 tablespoon chopped canned
   pimiento
1 teaspoon prepared mustard
1 teaspoon salt
6 cups diced, peeled, cooked
   potatoes
1 8-ounce package pickle and
   pimiento loaf, diced

Line 9x5x3-inch loaf pan with waxed paper, extending paper up over sides. Line bottom and sides of pan with slices of chopped ham. In saucepan, soften gelatin in cold water; stir over low heat till dissolved; cool.

Combine mayonnaise, celery, onion, parsley, pimiento, mustard, and salt. Stir in dissolved gelatin. Fold in potatoes and diced pickle and pimiento loaf. Spoon evenly into ham-lined pan; press down lightly. Chill till firm. Unmold onto platter; remove paper. Garnish with luncheon meat cornucopias, if desired. Makes 6 to 8 servings.

PARTY HAM RING

- 1 envelope (1 tablespoon) unflavored gelatin
- 1 cup dairy sour cream
- ½ cup mayonnaise or salad dressing
- 2 tablespoons white vinegar
- ¼ teaspoon salt
- 1½ cups diced fully-cooked ham
- 1 cup sliced celery
- 2 tablespoons chopped green onion

In saucepan, soften gelatin in 1 cup cold water; stir over low heat till gelatin is dissolved. Cool slightly. Beat in sour cream, mayonnaise, vinegar, and salt with rotary beater till smooth. Chill till partially set; then whip till fluffy. Fold in remaining ingredients. Pour into 5½-cup ring mold. Chill till firm. Makes 4 or 5 servings.

HAM AND POTATO SQUARES

- 1½ cups diced fully-cooked ham
- ¼ cup chili sauce
- 1 tablespoon finely chopped onion
- 2 teaspoons prepared mustard
- 1 teaspoon prepared horseradish
- 1 envelope (1 tablespoon) unflavored gelatin
- 1 cup mayonnaise
- 2 cups diced, peeled, cooked potatoes
- ½ cup diced celery
- 2 tablespoons finely chopped green pepper
- 1 tablespoon finely chopped onion
- 2 teaspoons vinegar
- 1 teaspoon salt

Combine first 5 ingredients. In saucepan, soften gelatin in ½ cup cold water; stir over low heat till gelatin is dissolved. Stir gelatin mixture into mayonnaise; fold *half* the gelatin mixture into ham mixture. Pour into 10x6x1½-inch dish; chill till *almost* firm. Keep remaining gelatin-mayonnaise mixture at room temperature.

Combine potatoes, celery, green pepper, onion, vinegar, salt, and ⅛ teaspoon pepper. Fold remaining gelatin-mayonnaise mixture into potato mixture. Spoon over ham layer; chill till firm. Makes 8 to 10 servings.

SNOWY CHICKEN SALAD

The gelatin mixture doubles as the dressing—

- 2 envelopes (2 tablespoons) unflavored gelatin
- ½ cup cold water
- 1 13¾-ounce can chicken broth
- 2½ cups cubed cooked chicken
- 1 cup mayonnaise or salad dressing
- ½ cup diced celery
- ¼ cup diced green pepper
- 3 tablespoons sliced pimiento-stuffed green olives
- 2 tablespoons lemon juice
- 1 cup whipping cream, whipped

In saucepan, soften gelatin in cold water. Stir over low heat till gelatin is dissolved. Stir in chicken broth. Chill gelatin mixture till partially set.

Fold in chicken, mayonnaise, celery, green pepper, olives, and lemon juice. Fold in whipped cream. Pour into 6½-cup mold. Chill till firm. Makes 6 servings.

Two favorites come together in a superb meal-in-one salad—Ham and Potato Squares.

SEAFOOD SOUFFLE PIE

    1 stick piecrust mix
    2 3-ounce packages lime–flavored
        gelatin
    1 cup mayonnaise or salad
        dressing
    2 tablespoons lemon juice
1½ cups diced, cleaned, peeled,
        cooked shrimp
    2 cups diced avocado
  ½ cup diced celery
    2 tablespoons finely chopped
        onion

Using piecrust mix, prepare and bake one 9-inch pastry shell following package directions. Dissolve gelatin and ½ teaspoon salt in 2 cups boiling water. Stir in 1 cup cold water, mayonnaise, and lemon juice; beat till smooth. Chill till partially set. Whip till fluffy. Fold in remaining ingredients. Chill till mixture mounds when spooned. Pour into baked pastry shell. Chill 4 or 5 hours or till firm. Garnish with additional cooked shrimp, if desired. Makes 6 servings.

HAM SALAD SUPREME

    2 3-ounce packages lemon–flavored
        gelatin
  ½ cup dairy sour cream
1½ teaspoons prepared horseradish
1½ teaspoons prepared mustard
    2 3-ounce packages smoked sliced
        ham, snipped
  ½ cup diced celery

Dissolve gelatin in 2 cups boiling water. Stir in 1 cup cold water. To ⅓ cup gelatin, add next 3 ingredients and ¼ teaspoon salt; beat just till smooth with rotary beater. Pour into 5½-cup mold. Chill till *almost* firm.

Meanwhile, chill remaining gelatin till partially set. Fold in ham and celery. Carefully pour over almost firm sour cream layer. Chill till firm. Makes 5 servings.

← **Leaf lettuce and meat flowers** spruce up Ham Salad Supreme. To make flowers, gather each ham slice at center. Secure at gathered point with halved wooden pick. Turn back outside edge.

TURKEY LIME MOLD

    2 3-ounce packages lime–flavored
        gelatin
    1 7-ounce bottle (about 1 cup)
        ginger ale, chilled
    2 cups diced cooked turkey
        . . .
    1 cup dairy sour cream
  ¼ teaspoon ground ginger
    1 16-ounce can pears, drained and
        diced

Dissolve gelatin and ¼ teaspoon salt in 2 cups boiling water; cool. To *half* the gelatin mixture, slowly add ginger ale and ½ cup cold water. Chill till partially set. Fold in turkey. Pour gelatin mixture into 6½-cup mold; chill till *almost* firm.

Meanwhile, beat sour cream and ginger into remaining gelatin till smooth. Chill till partially set. Fold in pears. Pour over almost firm layer. Chill till firm. Serves 4.

❊ **MENU** ❊

Apple Cider
Turkey Lime Mold
Popovers   Whipped Butter
Hot Fudge Sundaes   Nut Topping
Beverage

HAM AND PINEAPPLE MOLD

    2 3-ounce packages lemon–flavored
        gelatin
    1 13½-ounce can pineapple tidbits
  ¼ cup salad oil
        . . .
    2 cups chopped fully-cooked ham
    1 cup finely shredded cabbage
  ¼ cup chopped green pepper

Dissolve gelatin in 2 cups boiling water. Drain pineapple, reserving syrup. Add enough water to syrup to make 1 cup; stir into gelatin mixture. Add salad oil. Chill till partially set. Fold in pineapple tidbits and remaining ingredients. Pour into 7½-cup mold; chill till firm. Makes 6 servings.

Enchant guests with crunchy Ham-cabbage Molds. They're sure to ask for the recipe.

Entertaining? Creamy Tuna Mold is the perfect choice for a distinctive salad.

HAM-CABBAGE MOLDS

Arrange with ham slices and deviled eggs—

1 3-ounce package lemon-
    flavored gelatin
½ teaspoon salt
1 cup boiling water
½ cup cold water
1½ tablespoons vinegar
¾ cup mayonnaise or salad
    dressing
1 teaspoon prepared mustard

• • •

1½ cups finely diced fully-
    cooked ham
1 cup finely shredded cabbage
2 tablespoons minced onion

Dissolve gelatin and salt in boiling water. Stir in cold water and vinegar. Cool mixture to room temperature. Blend in mayonnaise and mustard. Chill till partially set. Fold in ham, shredded cabbage, and onion. Pour into 5 or 6 custard cups or individual molds. Chill till firm. Unmold on lettuce-lined plates. Makes 5 or 6 servings.

CREAMY TUNA MOLD

1 envelope (1 tablespoon)
    unflavored gelatin
¼ cup cold water
2 6½- or 7-ounce cans tuna,
    drained and flaked
½ cup mayonnaise or salad
    dressing
2 tablespoons lemon juice
2 tablespoons finely chopped
    onion
1 cup dairy sour cream
2 tablespoons drained capers
  Unpared cucumber slices
  Cherry tomatoes

In small saucepan, soften gelatin in cold water; stir over low heat till gelatin is dissolved. In small bowl, combine tuna, mayonnaise, lemon juice, and finely chopped onion; beat till smooth. Blend in dissolved gelatin, sour cream, and capers. Spoon into 3½-cup mold; chill till firm. Unmold on lettuce-lined platter; garnish with cucumber slices and cherry tomatoes. Makes 4 or 5 servings.

SALMON FRUIT MOLD

An unusual but tasty combination—

2 envelopes (2 tablespoons)
    unflavored gelatin
2 tablespoons sugar
¼ cup lemon juice
1 cup mayonnaise or salad
    dressing
1 cup dairy sour cream
1 7¾-ounce can salmon, drained,
    flaked, and bones removed
1 8¾-ounce can undrained
    crushed pineapple
1 medium banana, thinly
    sliced (1 cup)
¾ cup chopped celery

In saucepan, soften gelatin in 1 cup cold water; stir in sugar. Stir over low heat till gelatin and sugar are dissolved. Cool. Add lemon juice. Combine mayonnaise and sour cream; beat into cooled mixture till smooth. Fold in remaining ingredients. Pour into 5½-cup mold; chill till firm. Makes 8 to 10 servings.

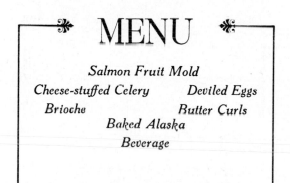

MENU

Salmon Fruit Mold

Cheese-stuffed Celery   *Deviled Eggs*

Brioche   *Butter Curls*

Baked Alaska

Beverage

CURRIED CHICKEN SALAD

In saucepan, soften 2 envelopes (2 tablespoons) unflavored gelatin in 1½ cups cold water; stir over low heat till gelatin is dissolved. Remove from heat. Blend in one 10½-ounce can *condensed* chicken broth, 1 cup mayonnaise or salad dressing, 2 tablespoons lemon juice, 2 tablespoons chopped onion, and 1½ to 2 teaspoons curry powder. Beat till smooth. Chill till partially set.

Fold 2 cups diced cooked chicken and 1 cup diced celery into partially set gelatin mixture. Pour into 9x9x2-inch dish. Chill till firm. Cut into squares to serve. Serves 9.

CHEF'S MOLD

A popular salad combination made in a mold—

Dissolve one 3-ounce package lime-flavored gelatin in 1 cup boiling water; stir in ¾ cup cold water and 2 tablespoons lemon juice. Chill till partially set.

Fold in 1 cup finely shredded lettuce; ½ cup cubed fully-cooked ham; 2 ounces sharp process American cheese cut in julienne strips (½ cup); 2 tablespoons thinly sliced radishes; and 2 teaspoons finely chopped onion. Pour gelatin mixture into 3½-cup mold. Chill till firm. Unmold onto lettuce-lined platter. Makes 3 or 4 servings.

BEEF-MACARONI MOLD

2 3-ounce packages lemon-
    flavored gelatin
2 tablespoons vinegar
¾ cup mayonnaise
1 cup uncooked elbow macaroni
1 12-ounce can corned beef,
    flaked
½ cup diced celery
2 tablespoons chopped onion

Dissolve gelatin in 2 cups boiling water; stir in 1 cup cold water and vinegar. Add mayonnaise; beat with rotary beater till smooth. Chill till partially set. Meanwhile, cook macaroni following package directions; drain. Fold drained macaroni, corned beef, celery, and onion into gelatin mixture. Pour into 7½-cup mold. Chill till firm. Serves 8.

LOBSTER RING MOLD

In saucepan, soften 1 envelope (1 tablespoon) unflavored gelatin in ¾ cup cold milk; stir over low heat till gelatin is completely dissolved. Cool.

Beat in 1 cup dairy sour cream, 2 tablespoons tarragon vinegar, ½ teaspoon onion salt, and ¼ teaspoon salt till smooth. Chill till partially set. Fold in one 5-ounce can lobster, drained, flaked, and cartilage removed; one 8-ounce carton cream-style cottage cheese; ½ cup diced pared cucumber; and ⅓ cup sliced celery. Pour into 4½-cup ring mold. Chill till firm. Serves 4.

MORE MAIN DISHES

HOT EGG SALAD DELUXE

Prepare 1½ cups finely crushed saltine cracker crumbs. Blend together *1 cup* of the crumbs; 6 hard-cooked eggs, chopped; 1 cup mayonnaise or salad dressing; 3 slices bacon, crisp-cooked and crumbled; ½ cup diced celery; 2 tablespoons diced canned pimiento; ¼ cup milk; ¼ teaspoon salt; and dash pepper. Turn into 9-inch pie plate. Blend remaining cracker crumbs with 2 tablespoons butter or margarine, melted, sprinkle over casserole. Bake at 400° about 25 minutes, or till golden. Makes 4 servings.

SHRIMP RICE SALAD

    6 large tomatoes
    2 cups cleaned, peeled, cooked
        shrimp, cut up
 1½ cups cooked rice
    ⅓ cup chopped celery
    ¼ cup sliced pitted ripe olives
    1 tablespoon snipped parsley
    ¼ cup salad oil
    2 tablespoons red wine vinegar
    1 small clove garlic, minced
    ¼ teaspoon dry mustard
    ¼ teaspoon paprika

With stem ends down, cut tomatoes into 6 wedges, *cutting to, but not through,* bases. Spread wedges apart slightly. Carefully scoop out pulp; dice and drain pulp. Chill tomato shells. Combine diced tomato, shrimp, rice, celery, olives, and parsley.

Blend together remaining ingredients and ½ teaspoon salt; toss with shrimp mixture. Season with salt and pepper to taste. Chill. Just before serving, spoon shrimp salad into shells. If desired, trim with watercress and additional shrimp. Makes 6 servings.

←— **Tomato stars,** brim full of a shrimp salad special, will highlight that springtime luncheon. Shrimp Rice Salad can be prepared in advance then spooned into the tomato shells just before serving.

QUICK TUNA SALAD

    1 16-ounce can (2 cups) macaroni
        and cheese
    1 6½- or 7-ounce can tuna,
        drained and flaked
    1 8-ounce can peas, drained
    ⅓ cup mayonnaise or salad
        dressing
    2 hard-cooked eggs, chopped
    1 tablespoon chopped green pepper
    1 teaspoon instant minced onion
    ¼ teaspoon salt
    6 medium tomatoes

Combine first 8 ingredients and dash pepper; chill. With stem ends down, cut tomatoes into 6 wedges, *cutting to, but not through,* bases. Spread wedges apart slightly. Chill tomatoes. Season insides with salt; fill with tuna mixture. Makes 6 servings.

MACARONI-CHEESE CUPS

    ½ 7-ounce package (1 cup)
        uncooked elbow macaroni
    8 medium green peppers
    2 cups cubed fully-cooked ham
    4 ounces sharp process American
        cheese, diced (1 cup)
    ¼ cup diced sweet pickle
    2 tablespoons chopped canned
        pimiento
    2 tablespoons finely chopped
        onion
    ½ cup mayonnaise
    2 teaspoons prepared mustard

Cook macaroni following package directions; drain and cool. Cut off pepper tops; remove seeds and membrane. Cook peppers in boiling salted water 5 minutes; plunge immediately in cold water. Combine macaroni, ham, cheese, pickle, pimiento, and onion.

Blend together mayonnaise, mustard, and ¼ teaspoon salt; toss lightly with macaroni mixture. Season inside of peppers with salt; fill with macaroni mixture. Chill. Serve on lettuce-lined plates. Makes 8 servings.

SALMON-FILLED TOMATOES

Scoop out centers of 6 medium tomatoes. Invert and chill tomatoes. Break one 16-ounce can salmon, drained, into small chunks, removing bones and skin. Combine salmon, 1½ cups diced pared cucumber, ½ cup mayonnaise or salad dressing, 1 tablespoon chopped onion, 1 tablespoon chopped canned pimiento, ¼ teaspoon salt, and dash pepper; chill salad mixture thoroughly.

Just before serving, sprinkle insides of tomatoes with salt. Spoon chilled salmon mixture into cavities. Serve on lettuce-lined plates. Trim with cucumber slices, if desired. Makes 6 servings.

HARD-COOKED EGGS

Place eggs in saucepan and cover with cold water at least 1 inch above eggs; rapidly bring to boiling. When water boils, reduce heat at once to keep water just *below simmering*. Cover and cook eggs 15 to 20 minutes. Cool immediately in cold water to prevent yolk darkening. To shell, crack shell all over. Roll gently between palms of hands to loosen. Start to peel from large end.

EGG SALAD ACCORDIONS

 4 medium tomatoes
 6 hard-cooked eggs, chopped
¼ cup finely chopped celery
¼ cup chopped green pepper
 2 tablespoons thinly sliced green onion
 2 tablespoons prepared mustard
½ teaspoon salt
 Dash pepper
¼ cup mayonnaise or salad dressing
 Parsley sprigs

With stem ends down, cut tomatoes into 6 slices, *cutting to, but not through*, bases. Spread slices apart slightly. Chill tomatoes. Combine eggs, celery, green pepper, onion, mustard, salt, and pepper. Stir in mayonnaise; chill. Sprinkle cut surfaces of tomatoes with salt. Fill in between slices with egg mixture. Arrange on lettuce-lined plates. Garnish with parsley. Makes 4 servings.

SHRIMP COCKTAIL SALAD

 6 medium tomatoes
 1 cup mayonnaise or salad dressing
 2 tablespoons minced onion
 2 tablespoons prepared horseradish
 4 drops bottled hot pepper sauce
1½ cups cleaned, peeled, and cooked shrimp

Cut thin slices off bottoms of tomatoes to make them sit flat. Scoop out centers halfway down, reserving pulp. Invert and chill.

Finely chop reserved tomato pulp; drain well. Combine ⅓ cup chopped tomato, next 4 ingredients, and dash salt; chill. Before serving, sprinkle insides of tomatoes with salt. Hook shrimp over edges. Spoon mayonnaise mixture into cavities. Serve on shredded lettuce. Makes 6 servings.

Egg Salad Accordions, served with tumblers of iced tea, tempt appetites on a sizzling summer day.

HOT FRANK-POTATO SALAD

Dress up franks and canned potatoes—

4 or 5 frankfurters (½ pound),
  cut in ½-inch slices
1 tablespoon butter or margarine
½ envelope dry onion soup mix
1 tablespoon all-purpose flour
1 tablespoon sugar
½ cup water
2 tablespoons vinegar
2 16-ounce cans sliced
  white potatoes, drained
½ cup dairy sour cream

In skillet, brown frankfurters in butter; remove from heat. Stir in soup mix, flour, sugar, and dash pepper; add water and vinegar. Return to heat; cook and stir till boiling. Reduce heat; cover and simmer gently for 10 minutes. Stir in potatoes and sour cream; heat just to boiling. Makes 6 servings.

MENU

Hot Frank-potato Salad

Buttered Carrots

Dill Pickles   Bread and Butter Pickles

Strawberry Shortcake

Beverage

HAM-STUFFED TOMATOES

Asparagus lends an unusual touch—

With stem ends down, cut 8 medium tomatoes into 6 wedges, *cutting to, but not through*, bases. Spread wedges apart slightly. Chill. Cook ½ cup macaroni following package directions; drain. Combine macaroni; 1½ cups cubed fully-cooked ham; ½ of 10-ounce package frozen asparagus tips, cooked and drained; and ⅓ cup chopped celery.

Blend together ½ cup mayonnaise or salad dressing, ¼ teaspoon salt, ¼ teaspoon onion salt, and ⅛ teaspoon pepper. Add mayonnaise mixture to macaroni mixture; toss lightly. Chill. Just before serving, fill tomatoes with ham mixture. Makes 8 servings.

SHRIMP IN CHEESE RING

2 3-ounce packages lime-flavored
  gelatin
2 12-ounce cartons (3 cups) large
  curd cream-style cottage
  cheese, drained
2 tablespoons mayonnaise or salad
  dressing
1 tablespoon vinegar or lemon
  juice
1 tablespoon chopped onion
2 teaspoons prepared horseradish
2 cups cleaned, peeled, and
  cooked shrimp
  Watercress

Dissolve gelatin in 2 cups boiling water. Add 1 cup cold water. Chill till partially set; then beat with rotary beater till fluffy. Fold in cottage cheese and next 4 ingredients. Pour into 6½-cup ring mold. Chill till firm. Unmold. Fill center with shrimp and watercress. Makes 6 to 8 servings.

THOUSAND ISLAND MOLD

In saucepan, soften 1 envelope (1 tablespoon) unflavored gelatin in ⅓ cup cold water. Stir over low heat till gelatin is dissolved. Cool. Combine ¾ cup mayonnaise or salad dressing, ½ cup chili sauce, ¼ cup catsup, 1½ teaspoons Worcestershire sauce, few drops bottled hot pepper sauce, and dash salt. Stir in gelatin mixture. Chill gelatin mixture till partially set.

Fold in 2 hard-cooked eggs, sliced and quartered; ½ cup diced celery; and 2 tablespoons chopped canned pimiento. Pour into 4½-cup mold. Chill till firm. Unmold onto serving platter. Around mold alternate halved French endives *or* lettuce wedges and Stuffed Shrimp. Makes 6 servings.

Stuffed Shrimp: Cook about 2 dozen large peeled and deveined frozen shrimp following package directions. Drain and chill thoroughly. Split shrimp part way down along vein side. Meanwhile, blend together one 3-ounce package cream cheese, softened; 1 ounce blue cheese, crumbled (¼ cup); ½ teaspoon prepared mustard; and dash garlic salt. Using pastry tube, stuff shrimp in groove split along back. Roll shrimp, cheese side down, in ½ cup finely snipped parsley.

SALAD SANDWICHES

The Earl of Sandwich, originator of that world famous item, would have delighted in an opportunity to savor salad sandwiches. He might have chosen one of the many interesting and tantalizing variations found on the pages that follow.

The salad sandwich "boat" is a good example. A delicately-dressed salad nestles in the hollow of an un-sliced loaf of bread which acts as the serving bowl. Fit for a king or an earl.

Or, he might have tried tempting individual salad sandwiches made by using different kinds of breads—pumpernickel, rye, or whole wheat. Rolls and English muffins also make ideal bases for meaty mixtures.

Whichever sandwich is favored, lettuce frills and decorative garnishes give it extra eye-appeal.

Prepare all three salad sandwiches—Rocky Mountain Loaf, Golden Gate Salad Loaf, and Polynesian Salad Loaf—when expecting the crowd for a buffet snack.

GOLDEN GATE SALAD LOAF

1 unsliced loaf French bread
   Butter or margarine, softened
1 ½-pound piece bologna, cut in
   ½-inch cubes (2 cups)
½ cup sliced radishes

. . .

⅓ cup mayonnaise or salad
   dressing
¼ cup pickle relish
   Dash pepper
2 cups shredded lettuce

Cut French bread in half lengthwise; wrap top half and store for later use. Cut thin slice off bottom of remaining half to make it sit flat. Scoop out center to make slight hollow; spread inside with butter.

Combine bologna cubes and radish slices. Blend together mayonnaise, pickle relish, and pepper. Add to bologna mixture; toss lightly. Place shredded lettuce in bottom of hollow; spoon bologna mixture over. Garnish with radishes and sweet pickle slices, if desired. Makes 6 servings.

ROCKY MOUNTAIN LOAF

An electric carving knife makes serving easy—

1 unsliced loaf French bread
   Butter or margarine, softened
   Leaf lettuce
6 slices boiled ham
4 slices process Swiss cheese,
   halved diagonally
1 16-ounce can peach halves,
   well-drained
½ cup mayonnaise or salad
   dressing
2 tablespoons chili sauce
1 tablespoon pickle relish

Cut French bread in half lengthwise; wrap top half and store for later use. Cut thin slice off bottom of remaining half to make it sit flat; spread inside with butter. Arrange lettuce and ham atop bread; top with cheese triangles and peach halves.

Blend together mayonnaise, chili sauce, and pickle relish; drizzle over salad loaf. Garnish with sprigs of watercress, if desired. Makes 6 servings.

DILLY BEEF CARTWHEEL

1 cup dairy sour cream
4 teaspoons dry onion soup mix
1 tablespoon prepared horseradish
4 slices large round rye bread
1½ cups shredded lettuce
1½ cups shredded endive *or* spinach
1 medium tomato, sliced
6 thin slices roast beef
6 dill pickle strips
1 medium tomato, cut in wedges
   Milk
   Ripe olives

Combine first 3 ingredients and dash pepper. Lay 2 slices bread, bottom to bottom, to form circle; spread with ⅓ *cup* sour cream mixture. Top with *1 cup each* lettuce and endive. Place tomato slices over. Lay remaining bread atop tomato; spread with ⅓ *cup* sour cream mixture. Top with remaining lettuce and endive.

Make 6 cornucopias of beef with pickle strip in center of each; arrange with tomato wedges atop sandwich. Thin remaining sour cream mixture with a little milk; drizzle over top. Garnish with ripe olives. Cut in wedges to serve. Makes 6 servings.

AVOCADO-BACON SANDWICH

¼ cup buttermilk
½ cup mayonnaise
2 tablespoons chopped onion
½ teaspoon Worcestershire sauce
   Dash garlic salt
2 ounces blue cheese, crumbled
   (½ cup)
6 slices rye bread, toasted
   Leaf lettuce
12 slices bacon, crisp-cooked
   and drained
3 medium avocados, peeled and
   sliced
1 lemon, cut in 6 wedges

Put first 5 ingredients in blender container; add *half* the cheese. Cover and run on high speed till smooth. Stir in remaining cheese. Spread each toast slice generously with dressing. Top each with lettuce, 2 slices bacon, and avocado slices. Drizzle remaining dressing over. Garnish with lemon. Serves 6.

TUNA TUGS

Break one 6½-, 7-, or 9¼-ounce can tuna, drained, into chunks; sprinkle with 1 tablespoon lemon juice. Combine tuna; 2 hard-cooked eggs, coarsely chopped; ¼ cup thinly sliced dill pickle; 2 tablespoons thinly sliced green onion; ¼ teaspoon salt; and dash pepper. Toss lightly and chill thoroughly.

Split 3 English muffins in half; toast, then spread with softened butter or margarine. Thinly slice 3 medium tomatoes into 18 slices. Top each buttered muffin half with Boston *or* Bibb lettuce, 3 tomato slices, and tuna-egg mixture. Garnish each sandwich with dollop of mayonnaise or salad dressing. Makes 6 servings.

TURKEY SALAD-WICHES

2½ **cups diced cooked turkey**
¾ **cup finely chopped celery**
¼ **cup toasted chopped almonds**
2 **tablespoons** *each* **chopped onion, chopped green pepper, and chopped canned pimiento**
2 **tablespoons lemon juice**
⅔ **cup mayonnaise**
8 **hard rolls, halved lengthwise**

In large bowl, combine first 7 ingredients and ½ teaspoon salt. Blend in mayonnaise; chill. Scoop out center of roll halves to make slight hollow; toast. Fill each half with about ½ cup turkey mixture. Makes 8 servings.

Transform this sandwich into a low-calorie luncheon. Prepare the standard recipe for Tuna Tugs, substituting one 6½-ounce can dietetic-pack tuna for regular tuna and using 4 unbuttered toasted English muffin halves. Spoon 2 tablespoons low-calorie mayonnaise-type dressing over.

POLYNESIAN SALAD LOAF

Equally delicious served warm—

2 cups cubed cooked chicken
1 5-ounce can bamboo shoots,
  drained
½ cup sliced celery
2 tablespoons chopped green onion
1 hard-cooked egg, chopped
½ cup mayonnaise or salad
  dressing
2 tablespoons frozen orange juice
  concentrate, thawed
½ teaspoon salt
1 unsliced loaf French bread
  Butter or margarine, softened
  Bibb lettuce
  Mandarin oranges
  Green pepper slices
¼ cup toasted slivered almonds

Combine first 8 ingredients; chill. Cut thin slice from bottom of loaf to make it sit flat. Cut loaf in half lengthwise; wrap top half of loaf for later use.

Scoop out center of bottom half of loaf to make a slight hollow. Spread with butter. Arrange Bibb lettuce on bread. Top with chicken salad. Garnish with mandarin oranges, green pepper slices, and almonds. Serves 6.

CHEF'S SALAD IN A ROLL

4 French rolls
  Butter or margarine, softened
  Romaine
4 ounces sharp process American
  cheese, cut in julienne
  strips
4 slices pressed ham
4 slices salami
2 hard-cooked eggs, sliced
  French salad dressing

Split rolls lengthwise, *cutting to, but not through,* crust at side. Spread cut surfaces with butter. For each sandwich, layer bottom half of roll with romaine, cheese, and ham and salami slices folded to fit roll. Place egg slices atop meat. Drizzle each sandwich with about 1 tablespoon French salad dressing. Anchor tops with wooden picks, if necessary. Makes 4 servings.

OLIVE-EGG SALAD BAKE

1 unsliced loaf Vienna bread
8 hard-cooked eggs,
  coarsely diced
1 cup diced celery
½ cup chopped pimiento-stuffed
  green olives
¼ cup chopped onion
1 clove garlic, minced
¼ teaspoon salt
  Dash pepper
½ cup mayonnaise or salad
  dressing
2 tablespoons prepared mustard
2 tablespoons butter or
  margarine, melted

Cut lengthwise slice from top of bread; set aside. Scoop out loaf to within 1 inch of bottom and sides. Crumble bread cut out of loaf (about 2 cups); combine with eggs and next 6 ingredients. Blend together mayonnaise and mustard; toss with egg mixture.

Spoon egg mixture into hollow loaf; replace reserved top. Brush loaf with butter; wrap in foil. Bake at 425° for 25 to 30 minutes, or till heated through. Cut loaf in 8 slices; serve immediately. Makes 8 servings.

TUNA OPEN-FACER

1 6½-ounce can dietetic-pack
  tuna, drained
½ cup coarsely grated cabbage
¼ cup coarsely grated carrot
1 tablespoon sliced green onion
⅓ cup low-calorie mayonnaise-
  type dressing
1 tablespoon catsup
1 tablespoon lemon juice
½ teaspoon seasoned salt
  Dash pepper
4 lettuce leaves
2 hamburger buns, split and
  toasted

Break tuna in chunks; combine with cabbage, carrot, and onion. Blend together low-calorie mayonnaise, catsup, lemon juice, seasoned salt, and pepper; add to tuna mixture and toss lightly. Place 1 lettuce leaf on each toasted bun half; spoon tuna salad mixture on top. Makes 4 servings.

HAM-EGG SALAD RIBBON

**1 unsliced loaf white sandwich
  bread
  Butter or margarine, softened
  Ham Filling
  Egg Filling**
**3 3-ounce packages cream cheese,
  softened**
¼ cup light cream

Trim crusts from loaf; cut in 4 equal lengthwise slices. Spread butter on one side of *three* slices. Spread remaining unbuttered slice with *half* the Ham Filling; top with second slice, buttered side down. Spread Egg Filling atop second slice; top with third slice, buttered side down. Spread remaining Ham Filling atop third slice; top with remaining bread slice, buttered side down.

Wrap loaf in foil, clear plastic wrap, or waxed paper; chill several hours. Meanwhile, beat cream cheese till smooth. Gradually add cream and beat till fluffy; frost loaf. Sprinkle with snipped parsley, if desired. Cover; chill 1 hour longer. Makes 8 to 10 servings.

Ham Filling: Combine 2½ cups ground fully-cooked ham; ½ cup mayonnaise or salad dressing; ¼ cup finely chopped celery; ¼ cup pickle relish, drained; and 1 teaspoon prepared horseradish.

Egg Filling: Combine 3 hard-cooked eggs, chopped; 2 tablespoons *each* chopped pimiento-stuffed green olives, snipped parsley, and mayonnaise; 1 teaspoon prepared mustard; and ½ teaspoon grated onion.

CORNED BEEF CAPTAINS

1 12-ounce can corned beef
4 cups finely shredded cabbage
¼ cup chopped green onion
½ cup mayonnaise
2 teaspoons prepared mustard
**4 or 5 slices whole wheat bread
  Butter or margarine, softened**

Chill corned beef; cut into 8 to 10 slices. Combine cabbage and onion. Blend together mayonnaise and mustard; toss lightly with cabbage mixture. Toast bread; spread with butter. Spoon cabbage mixture onto each slice; arrange 2 slices corned beef atop cabbage mixture. Makes 4 or 5 servings.

CRAB SANDWICH BROIL

Top hot apple-crab salad open-face sandwiches with a slice of melted cheese—

**1 7½-ounce can crab meat,
  drained, flaked,
  and cartilage removed**
½ cup chopped unpared apple
¼ cup chopped celery
½ cup mayonnaise
1 tablespoon lemon juice
**3 hamburger buns, split and
  toasted**
**3 tablespoons butter or
  margarine, softened**
**6 slices sharp process American
  cheese**

Combine first 5 ingredients. Spread buns with butter; top each half with ⅙ cup crab mixture. Broil 4 inches from heat for 3 to 4 minutes. Top each with slice of cheese; broil till cheese is slightly melted, about 1 to 2 minutes. Makes 6 servings.

FRANKFURTER SALAD LOAF

The "in" snack for teen get-togethers—

**1 unsliced loaf French bread,
  18 to 20 inches long**
**4 tablespoons butter or margarine,
  softened**
1 cup dairy sour cream
2 tablespoons dry onion soup mix
**2 tablespoons mustard-style hot
  dog relish**
**4 or 5 frankfurters, thinly
  sliced (½ pound)**
¾ cup chopped celery

Cut lengthwise slice from top of bread; set top aside. Scoop out loaf to within ¾ inch of bottom and sides. Spread inside of loaf and cut side of top with butter. Wrap loaf in foil, leaving cavity uncovered. Combine sour cream, onion soup mix, and relish; stir in frankfurter slices and celery. Spoon frankfurter mixture into hollow of loaf.

Bake at 375° for 25 minutes. During last 5 minutes of baking, place reserved top of loaf in oven to toast. To serve, place top on loaf; cut loaf into 1½-inch slices. Serves 12.

SALAD DRESSINGS

Salads rely on their dressings to tempt the flavor seeker beyond the first bite. Whether tart or tangy, spicy or sweet, rich or creamy—the dressing determines the success of the salad. For the simplest of recipes, salad dressings often involve little more than measuring and shaking to create gourmet fare.

Learn the difference between various types of dressings and salads which they complement best. Follow the tips for using herbs and spices to create exciting flavor variations in everyday dressings.

Look through the next few pages to inspire a new taste blend for the popular tossed salad, to discover the perfect touch for an elegant fruit salad, or to blend a hearty dressing with a favorite main dish salad.

Add tantalizing flavor to popular salads by preparing a simple Italian Dressing, a tangy Tomato Soup Dressing, or a tart and fluffy Lemonade Dressing.

CLEAR AND CREAMY DRESSINGS

FRENCH DRESSING

A top-notch basic with many variations—

- ½ cup salad oil
- 2 tablespoons vinegar
- 2 tablespoons lemon juice
- 2 teaspoons sugar
- ½ teaspoon salt
- ½ teaspoon dry mustard
- ½ teaspoon paprika
  Dash cayenne

Combine all ingredients in screw-top jar; cover and shake. Chill. Shake again just before serving. Makes ¾ cup.

Chiffonade Dressing: Prepare French Dressing adding 1 hard-cooked egg, chopped; ¼ cup chopped cooked beets; 2 tablespoons snipped parsley; and 1 tablespoon chopped onion to other ingredients. Serve with vegetable salads. Makes 1 cup.

Chili Dressing: To ½ *cup* French Dressing, add 2 tablespoons catsup, 2 teaspoons grated onion, ¾ teaspoon chili powder, and few drops bottled hot pepper sauce. Serve with vegetable salads. Makes ⅔ cup.

CREAMY FRENCH DRESSING

Combine 1 tablespoon paprika, 2 teaspoons sugar, 1 teaspoon salt, and dash cayenne. Add ⅓ cup vinegar and 1 egg; beat well. Add 1 cup salad oil in slow stream, beating constantly with electric or rotary beater till thick. Chill. Makes 1⅔ cups.

Cottage Cheese French Dressing: To *1 cup* Creamy French Dressing, add ⅓ cup cream-style cottage cheese, 1 tablespoon chopped sweet pickle, and 1 tablespoon snipped parsley. Mix well. Serve with vegetable salads. Makes 1¼ cups dressing.

FRUIT FRENCH DRESSING

- 1 cup salad oil
- ¼ cup pineapple juice
- ¼ cup lime juice
- 1 tablespoon vinegar
- ⅓ cup sugar
- 1½ teaspoons paprika

Combine all ingredients and 1 teaspoon salt in screw-top jar; cover and shake. Chill. Shake again just before serving. Serve with fresh or canned fruit. Makes 1¾ cups.

HERB DRESSING

LOW CALORIE · LOW CALORIE

- ¾ cup wine vinegar
  Non-caloric liquid sweetener equal to 2 teaspoons sugar
- 1½ teaspoons dried basil leaves, crushed
  Dash coarsely ground black pepper

Combine all ingredients and ¼ teaspoon salt in screw-top jar; cover and shake. Chill. Shake again just before serving. Serve with meat salad bowls. Makes ¾ cup.

For salad variety, keep a selection of bottled dressings and dressing ingredients on hand.

Celery Seed Dressing with its sweet-sour balance has long been a classical accompaniment with fruit. Combine such choice fresh fruits as watermelon, pineapple, strawberries, and grapes with canned favorites. At another meal, substitute poppy seed for celery seed and serve with a vegetable salad.

CELERY SEED DRESSING

 ½ cup sugar
 ⅓ cup lemon juice
 1 teaspoon each celery seed, dry
   mustard, and paprika
 ¾ cup salad oil

Combine first 5 ingredients and ½ teaspoon salt. Slowly add oil, beating with electric or rotary beater till thick. Makes 1⅓ cups.

FRENCH PICKLE SAUCE

 Combine ¾ cup bottled creamy French salad dressing and ¼ cup mustard-style hot dog relish. Chill. Makes about 1 cup.

GLOSSY FRUIT DRESSING

Good with vegetable salads, too—

 ½ cup sugar
 ¼ cup vinegar
 1 teaspoon celery salt
 1 teaspoon paprika
 1 teaspoon dry mustard
 ½ teaspoon grated onion
 1 cup salad oil

In small saucepan, combine sugar and vinegar; heat and stir just till sugar is dissolved. Cool. Add next 4 ingredients and ½ teaspoon salt. Add oil in slow stream, beating with electric mixer or rotary beater till thick. Makes 1½ cups.

SNAPPY GARLIC DRESSING

The garlic is subtle—mustard adds the pep—

In screw-top jar, combine ⅔ cup salad oil; ¼ cup vinegar; 1 small clove garlic, minced; 1 teaspoon sugar; ¾ teaspoon salt; ¾ teaspoon dry mustard; and dash freshly ground black pepper. Cover and chill several hours. Shake well before serving with salad greens or shredded cabbage. Makes 1 cup.

ITALIAN DRESSING

For those who like mild seasoning—

1 cup salad oil
¼ cup vinegar
1 clove garlic, minced
1 teaspoon salt
½ teaspoon white pepper
½ teaspoon celery salt
¼ teaspoon cayenne
¼ teaspoon dry mustard
Dash bottled hot pepper sauce

Combine all ingredients in screw-top jar. Cover and shake well. Chill thoroughly. Shake again just before serving. Serve with vegetable salads. Makes 1¼ cups.

DRESSING DICTIONARY

French Dressing: Both clear and creamy French dressings are a mixture of oil, vinegar or lemon juice and seasonings. Clear dressings separate and must be continually shaken. Creamy dressings are homogenized and do not separate.

Mayonnaise: This creamy dressing is made by beating oil very slowly into egg, vinegar or lemon juice, and seasonings. The egg emulsifies and prevents separation.

Salad Dressing: Oil and egg are used in lower proportions than in mayonnaise. Starch pastes may be used as thickening agents and emulsifiers are sometimes added. The flavor is more tangy than mayonnaise.

Cooked Dressing: Also called boiled dressing, this type is high in egg and low in fat. It is made by cooking a white sauce-egg base to which vinegar, butter or margarine, and seasonings are added.

SESAME DRESSING

⅔ cup sugar
⅓ cup vinegar
2 tablespoons finely chopped onion
½ teaspoon salt
½ teaspoon Worcestershire sauce
¼ teaspoon dry mustard
¼ teaspoon paprika
4 to 5 drops bottled hot pepper sauce
1 cup salad oil
2 to 3 tablespoons sesame seed, toasted

Combine sugar and vinegar; blend in onion, salt, Worcestershire, mustard, paprika, and hot pepper sauce. Gradually add salad oil, beating constantly with rotary beater or electric mixer till thick; chill. Stir in sesame seed just before serving. Serve with fruit salads. Makes 1¾ cups.

FRENCH THOUSAND ISLAND

½ cup salad oil
¼ cup white vinegar
¼ cup chili sauce *or* catsup
½ cup evaporated milk
2 hard-cooked eggs, chopped
¼ cup finely chopped green pepper
2 tablespoons finely chopped onion
1 small clove garlic
½ teaspoon salt
Dash pepper

Combine salad oil, vinegar, and chili sauce. Gradually beat oil mixture into evaporated milk with rotary beater or electric mixer. Stir in remaining ingredients. Chill. Remove garlic before serving. Serve with tossed green salads. Makes 2 cups.

CRANBERRY DRESSING

In small bowl, beat one 8-ounce can jellied cranberry sauce till smooth. Gradually beat in ¾ cup salad oil. Blend in 3 tablespoons lemon juice and ¼ teaspoon salt. Serve with fruit salads. Makes 1¾ cups.

ZIPPY EMERALD DRESSING

    1 cup salad oil
    ⅓ cup vinegar
    ¼ cup chopped onion
    ¼ cup snipped parsley
    2 tablespoons finely chopped green
       pepper
    2 teaspoons sugar
  1½ teaspoons dry mustard
    ½ teaspoon salt
    ⅛ teaspoon cayenne

Combine all ingredients in screw-top jar. Cover; let stand at room temperature 1 hour. Shake to blend thoroughly. Serve with seafood or tossed green salads. Makes 1½ cups.

USING HERBS AND SPICES

A sprinkling of various herbs and spices gives salads distinction. Add them in small amounts, about ¼ teaspoon for four servings. Taste before adding more. For best flavor results, blend the seasonings with a little oil, then stir into the chosen dressing.

Crush dried herbs or snip fresh ones before using. If substituting fresh for dried, use 3 times more fresh herbs. Below are basic types of salads with the herbs and spices that accent them best.

Bean: oregano, savory, tarragon
Beet: chervil, dill, thyme
Coleslaw: caraway seed, celery seed, dill, poppy seed, tarragon, thyme
Cucumber: basil, chervil, dill, tarragon
Egg: caraway seed, chili powder, curry powder, dill, tarragon
Fish and Seafood: basil, celery seed, curry powder, dill, oregano, tarragon
Fruit: allspice, cinnamon, clove, ginger, mint, nutmeg, rosemary, tarragon
Meat: basil, chervil, dill, rosemary, tarragon, thyme
Potato: caraway seed, chervil, curry powder, dill, oregano, savory
Poultry: basil, curry powder, marjoram, tarragon, thyme
Tomato: basil, chervil, dill, oregano, savory, thyme
Tossed Green: basil, chervil, dill, marjoram, tarragon
Vegetable: basil, chervil, dill, oregano, savory, tarragon

TWO-WAY DRESSING

    3 tablespoons sugar
    1 teaspoon salt
    1 teaspoon dry mustard
    ¼ teaspoon white pepper
    ½ teaspoon onion juice
    ¾ cup salad oil
    ¼ cup white vinegar

For clear dressing: Combine all ingredients in screw-top jar. Cover and shake. Chill. Shake again just before serving. Serve with vegetable salads. Makes 1 cup.

For creamy dressing: In small mixer bowl, combine first 4 ingredients; add onion juice. At medium speed on electric mixer, beat in oil, a little at a time, alternately with vinegar and ending with vinegar. Makes 1 cup.

ZESTY RUSSIAN DRESSING

    1 package creamy Russian salad
       dressing mix
    ⅔ cup tomato juice
    ¼ cup vinegar
    1 tablespoon salad oil

In screw-top jar, combine all ingredients; cover and shake well. Chill. Makes 1 cup.

TOMATO SOUP DRESSING

In screw-top jar, combine one 10¾-ounce can condensed tomato soup, 1 cup vinegar, ½ cup salad oil and 1½ teaspoons Worcestershire. Add 2 tablespoons sugar, 1 tablespoon grated onion, 2 teaspoons dry mustard, 1½ teaspoons salt, ½ teaspoon paprika, ¼ teaspoon garlic powder, and dash cayenne. Cover; shake. Chill. Makes 2¼ cups.

CHILI FRENCH DRESSING

In screw-top jar, combine ⅓ cup salad oil, 2 tablespoons vinegar, 2 tablespoons catsup, 2 teaspoons grated onion, 1 teaspoon prepared mustard, ¾ teaspoon chili powder, ½ teaspoon salt, ¼ teaspoon sugar, ⅛ teaspoon dry mustard, dash pepper, dash paprika and few drops bottled hot pepper sauce. Cover and shake well. Chill. Makes about ⅔ cup.

MAYONNAISE AND COOKED DRESSINGS

LEMONADE DRESSING

    1 6-ounce can frozen
        lemonade concentrate
    2 beaten eggs
    ⅓ cup sugar
    1 cup whipping cream, whipped

Thaw concentrate. In small saucepan, combine eggs, lemonade concentrate, and sugar. Cook and stir over low heat till thickened. Cool. Fold in whipped cream. Chill. Serve with fruit salads. Makes 3 cups.

COOKED DRESSING

Combine 2 tablespoons *each* all-purpose flour and sugar, 1 teaspoon *each* salt and dry mustard, and dash cayenne in top of double boiler. Add 2 slightly beaten egg yolks and ¾ cup milk; cook and stir over *hot, not boiling,* water till thick. Stir in ¼ cup vinegar and 1½ teaspoons butter. Cool. Makes 1 cup.

MAYONNAISE

    1 teaspoon salt
    ½ teaspoon dry mustard
    ¼ teaspoon paprika
        Dash cayenne
            • • •
    2 egg yolks
    2 tablespoons vinegar
    2 cups salad oil
    2 tablespoons lemon juice
    1 tablespoon hot water

Combine salt, dry mustard, paprika, and cayenne; blend in egg yolks. Stir in vinegar. Add oil, 1 teaspoon at a time, beating with rotary beater or electric mixer till ¼ cup has been added. Add remaining oil in increasing amounts, alternating the last ½ cup with lemon juice. Beat in water. Makes 2 cups.

RED CURRANT DRESSING

    ½ cup currant jelly
    ¼ cup mayonnaise
    ¼ cup whipping cream, whipped

With rotary beater, beat currant jelly till soft and smooth. Blend in mayonnaise. Fold in whipped cream. Makes about 1 cup.

BLUE CHEESE MAYONNAISE

Combine 2 tablespoons crumbled blue cheese, softened, and ½ cup mayonnaise. Beat till smooth. Stir in 4 teaspoons milk and few drops bottled hot pepper sauce. Serve with salad greens. If desired, crumble extra blue cheese over top. Makes ½ cup.

HONEY MAYONNAISE

Blend ½ cup mayonnaise, 2 tablespoons honey, 1 tablespoon lemon juice, ½ teaspoon celery seed, and ¼ teaspoon paprika. Serve with fruit salads. Makes ¾ cup.

DRESSING TIPS

French dressings—cling readily to greens and marinate vegetables. The tart-sweet ones add tang to fruit salads.

Mayonnaise and salad dressings—with their varied combinations, heighten the flavor of meat, seafood, egg, and handsome molded salads.

Cooked dressings—add luscious appeal to potato salads. Sweet cooked dressings are especially good as fruit toppings.

Cheese-flavored dressings—used with vegetables, make exciting companions.

Sour cream dressings—add zip to fruit and vegetable salads. They're delightful with main dish salad bowls.

This easy version of Thousand Island salad dressing continues as a great favorite. The creamy pink dressing is colorful with flecks of green pepper, chives, and pimiento to lend a note of cheer. Spoon it from a handsome server onto crisp lettuce wedges and garnish with sliced eggs.

THOUSAND ISLAND

> 1 cup mayonnaise
> 3 tablespoons chili sauce
> 1 tablespoon chopped green pepper
> 1 teaspoon chopped canned
>   pimiento
> 1 teaspoon chopped chives

Blend ingredients thoroughly. Chill. Serve with lettuce wedges. Makes 1¼ cups.

FRUIT DIP FLUFF

In small saucepan, combine ½ cup sugar, ⅓ cup light corn syrup, and ¼ cup hot water. Heat slowly, stirring till sugar dissolves. Then boil without stirring to soft-ball stage (236°). Gradually beat hot syrup into 1 stiffly-beaten egg white. Add dash salt and few drops vanilla. Cool.

Fold in ½ cup mayonnaise and 1½ teaspoons shredded orange peel; chill. Serve on fruit or as a strawberry dip. Makes 1⅔ cups.

APRICOT DRESSING

Blend together ⅓ cup mayonnaise or salad dressing and ⅓ cup apricot preserves. Whip ½ cup whipping cream just till soft peaks form; gently fold into apricot mixture. Serve with fruit salads. Makes 1⅓ cups.

PARMESAN DRESSING

Combine 1 cup mayonnaise and 1 tablespoon anchovy paste. Stir in *half* envelope (1 tablespoon) Parmesan salad dressing mix, ¼ cup water, and 2 tablespoons vinegar. Serve with vegetable salads. Makes 1½ cups.

CAPER MAYONNAISE

Combine 1 cup mayonnaise, ¼ cup coarsely chopped drained capers, 3 tablespoons chopped onion, and 2 tablespoons chopped toasted almonds. Heat through; or chill. Serve with seafood salads. Makes 1½ cups.

DAIRY DRESSINGS

SWEET-SOUR DRESSING

Combine 1 cup dairy sour cream and 2 tablespoons white vinegar. Stir in 2 tablespoons sugar and ½ teaspoon salt. Chill. Toss with shredded cabbage. Makes 1 cup.

TARRAGON DRESSING

Combine 1 cup dairy sour cream; ½ cup mayonnaise; 1 teaspoon vinegar; ½ teaspoon dried tarragon leaves, crushed; and ¼ teaspoon seasoned salt. Chill. Serve with seafood or vegetable salads. Makes 1½ cups.

MUSHROOM DRESSING

1 3-ounce can chopped mushrooms, drained (½ cup)
1 cup dairy sour cream
⅓ cup mayonnaise or salad dressing
2 tablespoons well-drained pickle relish
2 tablespoons milk
¾ teaspoon salt
½ teaspoon Worcestershire sauce

Chop any large pieces of mushrooms. Combine with remaining ingredients; chill thoroughly. Serve with lettuce wedges or vegetable salads. Makes 2 cups.

COTTAGE CHEESE FLUFF

1 cup cottage cheese, not creamed
Non-caloric liquid sweetener equal to 2 tablespoons sugar
4 teaspoons lemon juice
½ cup skim milk

In blender container, combine cottage cheese, sweetener, and lemon juice; blend till creamy. Add milk, a tablespoon at a time, till of desired consistency. Serve with shredded cabbage or lettuce. Makes 1 cup.

NIPPY NECTAR DRESSING

Beat together one 3-ounce package cream cheese, softened; 2 tablespoons honey; 1 teaspoon grated lemon peel; 1 tablespoon lemon juice; and ⅛ teaspoon salt. Gradually add ½ cup salad oil, beating till mixture is thickened. Chill. Serve with fruit. Makes 1 cup.

CUCUMBER DRESSING

Blend together ½ cup finely chopped unpared cucumber, 2 tablespoons mayonnaise, 1 tablespoon lemon juice, ⅛ teaspoon salt, and ⅛ teaspoon paprika. Whip ½ cup whipping cream just till soft peaks form. Fold into cucumber mixture. Chill. Serve with seafood salads. Makes 1¼ cups.

CREAM FRENCH DRESSING

With electric mixer, blend one 3-ounce package cream cheese, softened, with 1 tablespoon milk. Stir in ½ teaspoon sugar, ½ teaspoon paprika, and ¼ teaspoon salt. Gradually add 1 tablespoon vinegar, then 6 tablespoons salad oil, beating till fluffy. Chill. Makes ¾ cup.

WALNUT DRESSING

Blend together ⅓ cup mayonnaise; ¼ cup chopped walnuts; and 2 to 3 tablespoons frozen orange juice concentrate, thawed. Whip ½ cup whipping cream just till soft peaks form; fold into mayonnaise mixture. Chill. Serve with fruit. Makes 1½ cups.

CHEF'S CHEESE DRESSING

Thoroughly combine 3 ounces blue cheese, crumbled (¾ cup); ½ cup olive or salad oil; 2 tablespoons white vinegar; 1 tablespoon lemon juice; 1 teaspoon anchovy paste; and ½ clove garlic, minced. Season to taste. Chill. Stir before serving. Makes 1 cup.

LOW CALORIE • LOW CALORIE

Complement a pretty molded fruit salad with the mellow flavor of creamy Banana Cheese Dressing. It's a dressing good any season of the year and not limited to molded gelatin salads. Try it with a fresh fruit plate in summer, or spoon over canned or citrus fruits during winter.

BANANA-CHEESE DRESSING

Blend one 3-ounce package cream cheese, softened, with 2 tablespoons milk. Mash 1 fully-ripe banana (½ cup); add 1 tablespoon *each* sugar and lemon juice, and dash salt. Stir banana mixture into cheese mixture. Serve with fruit salads. Makes 1 cup.

BERRY SOUR CREAM SAUCE

    1 cup dairy sour cream
    ½ 10-ounce package frozen sliced
        strawberries, thawed (½ cup)

Blend cream and fruit. Chill. Serve with fruit salads. Makes about 1¼ cups.

DAIRY FRUIT DRESSING

Combine ½ cup dairy sour cream, 1 tablespoon honey, 1 teaspoon lemon juice, and ¼ teaspoon salt. Chill. Serve with sweetened or canned fruit. Makes about ½ cup.

AVOCADO DRESSING

Sieve 1 large ripe avocado, peeled (about ¾ cup); immediately add 2 to 3 tablespoons lemon juice. Stir in ½ cup light cream, ¾ teaspoon salt, ½ teaspoon prepared mustard, and ¼ teaspoon Worcestershire sauce. Chill. Serve with shredded cabbage or lettuce wedges. Sprinkle with ¼ cup crumbled blue cheese, if desired. Makes 1 cup.

Fresh vegetable texture from cucumber, radishes, green pepper, and green onion gives Crunchy Cream Dressing its name. This sour cream dressing tops off any green salad but is especially good on lettuce or cabbage. Additional green pepper rings or cucumber twists make notable garnishes.

CRUNCHY CREAM DRESSING

- ½ cup finely chopped unpared cucumber
- 2 tablespoons finely chopped green pepper
- 2 tablespoons finely chopped green onion
- 2 tablespoons thinly sliced radishes
- 1 cup dairy sour cream
- ½ teaspoon salt
  Dash pepper

Combine cucumber, green pepper, onion, and radishes. Stir in sour cream, salt, and pepper; mix well. Chill thoroughly. Serve over lettuce or cabbage salads. Makes 1½ cups.

SPICY FRUIT DRESSING

Combine 1 cup dairy sour cream, ½ cup apple cider *or* apple juice, ½ cup salad oil, ½ teaspoon ground cinnamon, ¼ teaspoon ground nutmeg, and dash salt; beat with rotary beater till smooth. Chill thoroughly. Serve with fruit salads. Makes 2 cups.

MARMALADE DRESSING

Blend together ½ cup dairy sour cream, 2 tablespoons orange marmalade, 2 teaspoons lemon juice, ¼ teaspoon paprika, and dash salt. Gently fold in ½ cup whipping cream, whipped. Chill thoroughly. Serve with fruit salads. Makes about 1½ cups.

YOGURT SALAD DRESSING

    1 cup plain yogurt
    2 teaspoons milk
    1 teaspoon lemon juice
    ¼ teaspoon garlic salt
    ¼ teaspoon onion salt
      Dash dried rosemary leaves,
        crushed

Combine all ingredients; chill. Serve with vegetable salads. Makes 1 cup.

CREAMY CHEESE DRESSING

In screw-top jar, combine ¾ cup dairy sour cream and 2 ounces blue cheese, crumbled (½ cup); stir in 2 tablespoons milk. Add 1 tablespoon salad oil, 2 teaspoons grated Parmesan cheese, and dash *each* onion salt, garlic salt, pepper, and Worcestershire sauce; mix well. Add 3 tablespoons white wine vinegar; cover jar and shake well. Chill. Serve with vegetable salads. Makes 1⅓ cups.

ROSY SALAD DRESSING

Swirling cranberry relish adds glamour—

Combine one 8-ounce package cream cheese, softened, and 1 cup dairy sour cream; beat till smooth. Stir in ¾ cup cranberry relish. Chill at least 2 hours. Serve with fruit salads. Makes about 3 cups.

AVOCADO CREAM DRESSING

Tastes as good as it sounds—

    1 medium avocado, peeled and
        mashed
    ½ cup dairy sour cream
    2 tablespoons milk
    2 teaspoons lemon juice
    ½ teaspoon salt
    ¼ teaspoon dried chervil leaves,
        crushed
      Dash onion powder
    3 drops bottled hot pepper sauce

Combine all ingredients; chill. Serve with tomato or lettuce wedges. Makes 1 cup.

BLUE CHEESE DRESSING

    ½ cup mayonnaise
    ½ cup light cream
    1½ teaspoons lemon juice
    4 ounces blue cheese

Combine mayonnaise, light cream, and lemon juice. Crumble cheese into mayonnaise mixture; mix well. Chill. Serve with lettuce or tomato wedges. Makes 1½ cups.

FRENCH CHEESE DRESSING

    1 3-ounce package cream cheese,
        softened
    2 ounces blue cheese,
        crumbled (½ cup)
    ½ cup French salad dressing

Beat cream cheese and the blue cheese together. Stir in French dressing. Chill. If dressing thickens during refrigeration, stir in additional French salad dressing to desired consistency. Makes 1 cup.

CITRUS PEANUT DRESSING

    ¼ cup peanut butter
    ¼ teaspoon grated orange peel
    ¼ teaspoon prepared mustard
    ½ cup dairy sour cream
    3 tablespoons orange juice

Combine peanut butter, orange peel, mustard, and dash salt. Gradually stir in sour cream and orange juice. Serve with fresh fruit salads. Makes about 1 cup dressing.

HORSERADISH DRESSING

    ½ cup dairy sour cream
    ¼ cup mayonnaise or salad
        dressing
    1 tablespoon prepared horseradish
    1 teaspoon sugar
    ¼ teaspoon salt
    2 drops bottled hot pepper sauce
    2 drops Worcestershire sauce

Combine all ingredients; chill. Serve with meat or seafood salads. Makes 2 cups.

ROBUST RELISHES

Thank the early American Colonists for many tasty relishes filled with a sweet-sour piquancy. In those days, pickles and relishes were standard fare that appeared at every meal.

The relish, often a mixture of chopped vegetables or fruits, herbs, spices, and seasonings, adds flavor and zest to the main portion of a meal. The recipes in this chapter are adaptations of this basic theme. Serve them as a side dish with the main course or in conjunction with a lavish buffet menu.

A good relish should have attractive color as well as appetizing appearance. Most, but not all, relishes are crisp and contain fairly uniform size pieces combined with a small amount of liquid. The mixture should be moist, but never watery.

This tiered relish server invites dinner guests to help themselves to a triple treat of chilled relishes—Pickled Mushrooms, Cheese-fruit Relish, and Carrot-olive Slaw.

SUMMER CORN RELISH

Wonderful way to preserve fresh corn—

   2 cups sugar
   2 cups vinegar
1½ teaspoons celery seed
 ½ teaspoon turmeric
   2 cups chopped onion
   2 cups chopped tomato
   2 cups chopped cucumber
   2 cups corn, cut from cob
   2 cups chopped cabbage

In Dutch oven, combine first 4 ingredients and 1½ teaspoons salt. Heat to boiling; add vegetables. Cook, uncovered, 25 minutes, stirring occasionally. Pack in hot, scalded jars and seal. Makes 3 pints.

A platter of Sunburst Artichoke brightens a menu. Garnish the center with sprigs of parsley.

SUNBURST ARTICHOKE

1 artichoke
1 cup mayonnaise or salad
   dressing
2 teaspoons dry mustard
1 teaspoon Worcestershire sauce
3 hard-cooked eggs

Cook artichoke in boiling salted water about 30 minutes; drain. Chill. Pull off leaves; trim off points. Mix mayonnaise, mustard, and Worcestershire sauce.

Halve hard-cooked eggs crosswise; cut each half into 8 wedges. Top leaves with dollop of dressing; place an egg wedge at base of leaf. Arrange sunburst-fashion on platter.

CALIFORNIA GUACAMOLE

Peel and chop 2 large avocados. Peel and chop one large tomato, removing seeds; drain. Put avocado and tomato in blender or mixer bowl; add 2 tablespoons finely chopped onion and 1 tablespoon wine vinegar. Blend or beat till smooth. Season with ½ teaspoon salt and dash pepper. Serve over tomatoes. Makes about 2 cups.

BANANA CUTS

¼ cup honey
2 teaspoons lemon *or* lime juice
3 ripe bananas
1 cup shredded coconut, toasted*

Combine honey and lemon juice. Peel bananas; cut diagonally in thirds. Brush honey mixture on bananas; roll in coconut.

*To toast coconut, spread thin layer of coconut in shallow baking pan. Toast in oven at 350° till lightly browned, about 6 to 7 minutes. (Stir coconut or shake pan often during baking to toast evenly.)

APPLE RELISH

Combine 2 unpared tart apples, chopped; ¼ cup chopped onion; and ¼ cup chopped dill pickle. Combine ¼ cup sugar and 2 tablespoons vinegar. Toss with apple mixture; chill. Makes about 3 cups.

CARROT–OLIVE SLAW

*Use with Cheese-fruit Relish and Pickled
Mushrooms to make a tasty relish trio—*

  ¼ cup salad oil
   2 tablespoons vinegar
   2 tablespoons sugar
  ½ teaspoon salt
   3 cups shredded carrots
  ¼ cup sliced pitted ripe olives

Combine salad oil, vinegar, sugar, salt, and
dash pepper; toss lightly with carrots and
olives. Chill. Makes 2½ cups.

CHEESE-FRUIT RELISH

   1 16-ounce carton (2 cups) large
     curd cream-style cottage
     cheese, drained
   1 cup halved seedless green
     grapes
   2 tablespoons coarsely chopped
     pistachio nuts
  ⅓ cup mayonnaise or salad
     dressing
  ¼ teaspoon salt

Combine all ingredients; mix together lightly. Chill. Serve in relish dish or spoon into
lettuce cup placed in the center of a fruit
platter. Makes about 2⅔ cups.

PICKLED MUSHROOMS

  ⅔ cup tarragon vinegar
  ½ cup salad oil
   1 medium clove garlic, crushed
   1 tablespoon sugar
   2 tablespoons water
    Dash bottled hot pepper sauce
   1 medium onion
   2 6-ounce cans mushroom crowns,
     drained

Combine vinegar, salad oil, garlic, sugar,
1½ teaspoons salt, dash pepper, water, and
hot pepper sauce. Slice onion and separate
into rings; add to marinade along with mushrooms. Cover; refrigerate 8 hours or overnight, stirring several times. Drain before
serving. Makes 2 cups.

DILLED CARROTS

  ¼ cup finely chopped onion
   1 tablespoon snipped parsley
  ½ cup low-calorie Italian salad
     dressing
  ½ teaspoon dillweed
  ¼ teaspoon salt
    Dash freshly ground black
     pepper
      • • •
   1 16-ounce can (2 cups) whole
     carrots, drained

LOW CALORIE • LOW CALORIE

Combine onion, parsley, Italian salad dressing, dillweed, salt, and pepper and pour over
carrots in shallow dish. Cover; refrigerate
several hours or overnight, stirring occasionally. Drain before serving. Makes 2 cups.

DEVILED GUACAMOLE

   2 avocados, halved and peeled
   1 2¼-ounce can deviled ham
   2 tablespoons chopped green
     chilies
   2 teaspoons lemon juice
   1 teaspoon grated onion

Mash avocados with fork. Stir in remaining ingredients and dash salt; chill. Serve as
relish or dip. Makes 1½ cups.

BEAN RELISH

   1 16-ounce can whole green beans
  ⅓ cup vinegar
   2 tablespoons sugar
   1 teaspoon salt
   1 teaspoon dillseed
   1 teaspoon mixed pickling spices
      • • •
   1 medium onion, sliced and
     separated in rings
   1 tablespoon salad oil

Drain beans, reserving liquid. In saucepan,
combine reserved liquid with vinegar, sugar,
salt, dillseed, and mixed pickling spices; simmer 5 minutes. Add beans; heat through.
Cool mixture, then drain off excess liquid.
Toss beans with onion rings and salad oil.
Chill before serving. Makes about 2 cups.

PEPPY BEET SALAD

Spicy and pickly—

 1 16-ounce can sliced *or* diced
　beets
 ⅓ cup vinegar
 1 tablespoon sugar
 ½ teaspoon ground cinnamon
 ¼ teaspoon ground allspice
　Dash ground cloves
　　• • •
 ¼ cup pickle relish
 2 tablespoons chopped onion

Drain beets, reserving liquid. Add enough water to liquid to make 1 cup; add vinegar, sugar, cinnamon, allspice, and cloves. Bring to boiling. Stir in beets; bring to boiling again. Remove from heat. Chill beets in liquid. Drain; stir in pickle relish and onion. Mix well. Makes 2 cups.

GARLIC OLIVES

 ⅔ cup salad oil
 ⅓ cup wine vinegar
 3 cloves garlic, minced
 1 9-ounce can ripe olives,
　　drained (about 1½ cups)

Combine salad oil, vinegar, and garlic. Pour over olives. Refrigerate several hours or overnight, stirring occasionally. Drain before serving. Makes 1½ cups.

FRESH CUCUMBER RELISH

Refreshing hint of dill—

 3 medium cucumbers
 ½ medium onion
　　• • •
 ⅓ cup vinegar
 1 tablespoon sugar
 ½ teaspoon salt
 ¼ teaspoon dried dillweed

Slice cucumbers in half lengthwise; scoop out seeds and discard. With food chopper using coarse blade, grind cucumbers and onion; drain. Stir in remaining ingredients. Chill thoroughly. Makes about 1¾ cups.

TOMATO-PEPPER RELISH

Combine 3 cups diced tomatoes, 2 cups chopped green pepper, and ¼ cup Italian salad dressing. Chill several hours, stirring occasionally. Just before serving, drain well. Makes 4 cups relish.

CONFETTI RELISH

 1 16-ounce can French-style green
　　beans, drained
 1 12-ounce can whole kernel corn,
　　drained
 1 8½-ounce can peas, drained
 1 6-ounce can sliced mushrooms,
　　drained
 ¼ cup chopped onion
 ¼ cup diced canned pimiento
 ⅓ cup white wine vinegar
 ¼ cup sugar
 1 teaspoon salt
 ½ cup salad oil

Combine first 6 ingredients in large bowl. In screw-top jar, combine vinegar, sugar, and salt; cover and shake till sugar is dissolved. Add oil and shake well. Pour oil mixture over vegetable mixture. Chill several hours, stirring occasionally. Drain well before serving. Makes about 5 cups.

DEVILED EGGS

 6 hard-cooked eggs, halved
　　lengthwise
 ¼ cup mayonnaise or salad
　　dressing
 1 tablespoon finely chopped onion
 1 tablespoon finely chopped
　　pimiento-stuffed green olives*
 1½ teaspoons prepared mustard
 ⅛ teaspoon salt
　　Dash pepper
　　Paprika

Remove egg yolks from whites. Mash yolks and combine with next 6 ingredients. Refill egg whites, using pastry tube, if desired. Chill. To serve, sprinkle tops with paprika.

*Or, substitute crisp-cooked and crumbled bacon, chopped canned pimiento, snipped chives, sweet pickle, or snipped parsley.

CHERRY RELISH

- 1 20-ounce can pitted tart red cherries
- ½ cup raisins
- ½ cup honey
- ½ cup vinegar
- ¼ cup brown sugar
- ½ teaspoon ground cinnamon
- ⅛ teaspoon ground cloves
- ½ cup chopped pecans
- 1 tablespoon cornstarch
- 1 tablespoon cold water

In 2-quart saucepan, combine cherries, raisins, honey, vinegar, brown sugar, cinnamon, and cloves. Cook slowly, uncovered, for 30 minutes. Stir in nuts. Combine cornstarch and water; gradually stir into cherry mixture. Cook, stirring constantly, till mixture thickens and bubbles. Chill. Makes 2½ cups.

CHEESE-ONION MARINADE

A choice barbecued meat partner—

- 3 ounces blue cheese, crumbled (¾ cup)
- ½ cup salad oil
- 2 tablespoons lemon juice
- 1 teaspoon salt
- ½ teaspoon sugar
  Dash pepper
  Dash paprika

. . . .

- 4 medium onions, thinly sliced and separated into rings (about 4 cups)

Mix all ingredients except onion rings. Pour mixture over onion rings and refrigerate at least 3 to 4 hours. Makes about 4 cups rings.

APPLESAUCE RELISH

- 1 16-ounce can applesauce
- ¼ cup red cinnamon candies
- 1 teaspoon prepared horseradish

In saucepan, combine applesauce, candies, and horseradish. Cook and stir over medium heat till candies are dissolved. Cool, refrigerate till ready to serve. Makes 2 cups.

COMBINATION RELISH

- 1 teaspoon salt
- 1 cup chopped cabbage
- ½ cup chopped carrots
- ¼ cup sugar
- 1 tablespoon dry mustard
- 1 teaspoon cornstarch
- ⅓ cup vinegar
- 1 8-ounce can whole kernel corn, drained
- ¼ teaspoon celery seed

Mix salt with cabbage; let stand 1 hour. Drain well. Cook carrots 3 to 5 minutes in small amount of boiling water; drain. In saucepan, combine sugar, mustard, and cornstarch. Blend in vinegar and ¼ cup cold water. Cook and stir over medium heat till mixture thickens and bubbles. Add cabbage, carrots, corn, and celery seed. Bring to boiling; cook 5 minutes. Chill. Makes 1⅔ cups.

CELERY CRAN-RELISH

Using coarse blade of food chopper, grind 1 pound fresh cranberries; 2 cups coarsely chopped celery; and 1 medium unpared apple, cut up. Stir in 1½ cups sugar and 2 tablespoons lemon juice; chill. Keeps in refrigerator several weeks. Makes about 4 cups.

PICKLED APRICOTS

- 1 cup dried apricots
- 1 cup brown sugar
- ¼ cup vinegar
- 2 inches stick cinnamon
- 6 whole cloves
- 24 to 30 walnut halves

Rinse apricots. In saucepan, cover apricots with 1-inch water. Cover and simmer gently for 15 minutes. Drain, reserving ¾ cup apricot liquid. In saucepan, combine reserved apricot liquid, brown sugar, vinegar, stick cinnamon, and whole cloves. Stir in apricots; return to boiling and simmer, covered, 10 minutes more, or till tender.

Cool apricots in syrup. Refrigerate till ready to serve. At serving time, remove apricots from syrup. Fill each apricot half with a walnut half. Makes 2 to 2½ dozen.

BUYING, STORING, AND PREPARING

Being a successful salad maker is not difficult, but it does necessitate adequate planning. Charts, buying and storing know-how, and preparation tips can ease this job.

This final chapter comes to the rescue with all the information a homemaker needs. Becoming familiar with the how-to's of making attractive garnishes for salads is not complicated. The ones pictured at left are described on page 154.

Citrus Garnishes are an easy way to vary and flatter salad servings.

The Orange Chrysanthemum makes a beautiful centerpiece on a fruit platter.

A bouquet of Vegetable Flowers is turned out in a jiffy by using cookie cutters.

Serve mayonnaise in a Cucumber Basket to pass with a vegetable salad.

HOW MUCH AND HOW MANY

Food	Amount
Cereals	
Macaroni	4 ounces uncooked (1 to 1¼ cups) = 2¼ cups cooked
Rice, long-grain	6½ to 7 ounces uncooked (1 cup) = 3 to 4 cups cooked
packaged precooked	1 cup uncooked = 2 cups cooked
Spaghetti	7 ounces uncooked (1½ to 2 cups) = 4 cups cooked
Dairy Products	
Blue cheese, crumbled	4 ounces = 1 cup
American or Cheddar cheese, shredded or cubed	1 pound = 4 cups
Sour cream or yogurt	8 ounces = 1 cup
Whipping cream	1 cup unwhipped = about 2 cups whipped
Fresh Fruit	
Apple, chopped	1 medium = about 1 cup
Banana, sliced	1 medium = ⅓ to ½ cup
Grapes, halved and seeded	1 pound = 2 cups
Lemon, juice	1 medium = 3 tablespoons
grated peel	1 medium = 1 teaspoon
Orange, juice	1 medium = about ⅓ cup
grated peel	1 medium = about 2 teaspoons
Peach or pear, sliced	1 medium = ½ cup
Strawberries, sliced	1 quart = 4 cups
Fresh Vegetables	
Cabbage, shredded	1 medium head = 8 cups
Carrots, shredded	1 pound (without tops) = 3 cups
Celery, diced or chopped	8 branches = 2¾ cups
Green onions, sliced with tops	7 onions (1 bunch) = about ½ cup
Green pepper, diced	1 large (6 ounces) = 1 cup
Iceberg lettuce, torn in bite-size pieces	1 small head = 4 cups
	1 medium head = 6 cups
	1 large head = 8 cups
Onion, chopped	1 medium = ½ cup
Potato, cooked and cubed	4 medium = 4 cups
Radishes, sliced	1 bunch = about 1 cup
Meat and Seafood	
Chicken, cooked and diced	
Broiler-fryer	about ¾ cup per pound
Stewing chicken	about 1 cup per pound
Two chicken breasts, 10 ounces each	1½ to 2 cups diced *or* 12 thin slices
Shrimp, cleaned and cooked	2 ounces raw in shell *or* 7 or 8 ounces frozen, shelled *or* one 4½- or 5-ounce can = 1 cup

Food	Amount
Nuts	
Almonds	1 pound unshelled = ¾ to 1 cup shelled
Pecans or walnuts, halved	
or chopped	1 pound unshelled = 1½ to 1¾ cups
Miscellaneous	
Cherries, whole candied	1 pound = 2¼ cups
Coconut, flaked	3½ ounces = 1⅓ cups
shredded	4 ounces = 1⅓ cups
Gelatin, unflavored	1 ounce = 4 tablespoons
	1 envelope = 1 tablespoon
flavored, packaged	3 ounces = 7 tablespoons

COMMON CAN AND JAR SIZES

Container	Approximate Net Weight or Fluid Measure	Approximate Cups
8 ounce	8 ounces	1
Picnic	10½ to 12 ounces	1¼
12 ounce (vacuum)	12 ounces	1½
No. 300	14 to 16 ounces	1¾
No. 303	16 to 17 ounces	2
No. 2	20 ounces (18 fluid ounces)	2½
No. 3 cylinder *or*		
46 fluid ounce	51 ounces (46 fluid ounces)	5¾
No. 10	6½ to 7¼ pounds	12 to 13

WEIGHTS AND MEASURES

1 dash = 1/16 teaspoon	1 gram = 0.035 ounces
3 teaspoons = 1 tablespoon	1 kilogram = 2.21 pounds
4 tablespoons = ¼ cup	1 cup = 8 fluid ounces
5⅓ tablespoons = ⅓ cup	2 cups = 1 pint
8 tablespoons = ½ cup	4 cups = 1 quart
10⅔ tablespoons = ⅔ cup	4 quarts = 1 gallon
16 tablespoons = 1 cup	8 quarts = 1 peck
1 ounce = 28.35 grams	1 quart = 946.4 milliliters
1 pound = 453.59 grams	1 liter = 1.06 quarts

GUIDE TO BUYING FRUIT

Apples: For best flavor choose those having good color for the specific variety. They should be firm to the touch. Avoid those which yield to slight pressure and are soft and mealy. Good salad apples include Delicious and Golden Delicious, sweet; Cortlands, mild; McIntosh and Winesaps, slightly tart; and Jonathans and Staymans, tart.

Apricots: Avoid apricots feeling soft or looking shriveled and wilted. Good ones appear golden-yellow, plump, and fairly firm.

Avocados: They vary in size, shape, and color from green to almost black. If ripe, they will yield to gentle pressure.

Berries: Look for berries that are firm, plump, and full-colored. They should be bright, clean, and fresh in appearance. Only strawberries should have a hull (stem cap) attached when mature.

Figs: Buy figs for immediate use since they are very perishable. Fully ripe fresh figs should be fairly soft to the touch. One with a sour odor indicates it is overripe.

Grapefruit: Pick those that are firm, well-shaped, heavy for their size, and smooth textured. The color of the skin is not always a good way to judge flavor and ripeness. Grapefruit, even though ripe, may have a green tinge. Russeted fruit often is tastier and juicier than the brightly colored fruit.

Grapes: Choose well-formed grape clusters. Color is an excellent guide to ripeness. Darker varieties should be free of green tinge, and green grapes should show a slight amber blush. When ripe, all grapes should be fairly soft and tender to the touch.

Kiwi: Kiwi fruits are imported from New Zealand. Sometimes called Chinese gooseberries, these brown fuzzy-skinned fruits will be soft to the touch, like an avocado, when ripe. To serve this fruit, peel and slice.

Lemons: Buy those that are moderately firm, fine textured, and heavy for size.

Limes: Green ones are more acid than the yellow-colored ones. Both should be heavy for their size, indicating high juice content.

Mangoes: They will vary in size from a plum to an apple and from yellow to red in coloring. The smooth skin is often speckled with black. Select those that are solid and not too soft to the touch.

Melons: Good melons show no evidence of a stem at the blossom end. Good, ripe cantaloupes have delicate aroma and a thick netting that stands out. The skin under the netting should have a yellow tinge. Ripe honeydews should have a pleasant aroma and creamy-yellow rinds. Watermelons should have dull surfaces and be symmetrical in shape. Color and aroma are the best guides to choosing melons.

Nectarines: Choose as for peaches.

Oranges: Look for oranges that are heavy for their size, firm, and with skins that are not too rough. Naval oranges are seedless, slightly thick-skinned, and are easy to peel and segment, making them good for salads. Temple oranges are very juicy, easy to peel, and have a rich flavor.

Papayas: Look for greenish-yellow to full-yellow color and flesh that will give slightly when fruit is pressed in palm of hand.

Peaches: They should be plump and fairly firm. Depending on variety, the skin color should be white or yellow with a red blush.

Pears: When ripe, they will yield to gentle pressure at the stem end. Colors range from creamy yellow to russet.

Persimmons: Choose ones that are firm and shapely, plump, and highly colored (orange-red). Handle gently because they are delicate. They resemble large ripe tomatoes in shape and firmness. Be sure stem cap is attached when buying.

Plums: Pick plums that are plump, full-colored, and soft enough to yield to slight pressure. Softening at the tip is usually a sign that the fruit is mature. Avoid those that are shriveled and hard.

Pomegranates: Those with thin skins of bright purply-red color and fresh appearance are the best ones to buy.

GUIDE TO BUYING VEGETABLES

Artichokes (globe): Choose artichokes that are heavy, compact, and have a plump globe with large, tightly-closed, fleshy leaf scales. Good green color is also important.

Asparagus: Select asparagus spears that have tightly closed buds at the top with straight, tender, and fresh-appearing stalks. There should be little tough base to trim off.

Beans: They should have crisp, long, straight, blemish-free pods that can easily be snapped between the fingers. Varieties include green and waxy yellow.

Cabbage: Well-trimmed, reasonably solid heads that are heavy for their size are the best quality. For green cabbage, the leaves should be medium green. Varieties include Savoy cabbage, with yellowish crimped leaves; Celery cabbage, often called Chinese cabbage; and red cabbage, identical to green cabbage except in color.

Carrots: Choose those that are firm, brightly-colored, smooth, clean, and well-shaped.

Cauliflower: Fresh cauliflower has bright green leaves surrounding the firm, closely-packed, creamy-white curd. Avoid heads that have yellowed or withered leaves attached. Leaves occasionally found growing through the curds do not affect quality.

Celery: Purchase celery having fresh branches brittle enough to snap easily. Avoid wilted looking stalks that feel rough or puffy. Pascal celery is the most common variety.

Cucumbers: Bright green cucumbers that are firm, well-shaped, and fresh-appearing are the best buy. Dull green ones are indicative of lower quality. Cucumbers are waxed before being sold to help retard evaporation and enhance the appearance.

Garlic: Consisting of many smaller sections, called cloves, garlic is usually purchased in bulbs. Pick those that are plump, firm, and have unbroken outer skins.

Mushrooms: Fresh mushrooms should look fresh and feel dry and firm. Small brown spots or opened caps indicate more mature mushrooms. These still have a delicate flavor.

Onions: Buy regular dry onions that are well-shaped, hard, and have dry skins. They should not be wet or feel soggy at the necks. Bermuda onions, perfect for salads or sandwiches, are flat and yellow or white. Green onions, sometimes called scallions, should have crisp green tops and white roots 2 to 3 inches long. Leeks look like large green onions and should also have bright green tops. Fresh chives are usually purchased as potted plants. Both roots and tops are used. Color should be bright green.

Parsley: Used mainly for garnish, parsley should be bright and fresh in appearance.

Peppers: The most common pepper is the green (bell) pepper. When fully mature, their color turns red. Choose those that have good shape, firm exterior, thick flesh, and bright, uniform glossy color.

Potatoes: "Baking" potatoes generally are too mealy in texture to be satisfactory for salads. The round, waxy types of potatoes are best for salads. They should have shallow eyes and be reasonably clean, smooth-skinned, and firm. Avoid those that are bruised, wilted, or sprouted. Some red potatoes are artificially colored with a non-toxic substance to help their appearance and preserve their freshness.

Radishes: Choose those that are smooth, crisp, firm, and well-formed. If the tops are still intact when purchased, they should be fresh and bright green.

Spinach: When buying spinach, look for fresh-appearing leaves with rich green color. Wilted or yellow leaves indicate spinach that is not fresh, therefore, undesirable.

Tomatoes: Handle these gently since ripe tomatoes are very delicate. Select those that are firm, well-formed, and free from blemishes. If not for immediate use, choose tomatoes having a greenish cast; ripen at room temperature. Avoid tomatoes that look yellow or wrinkled. The small cherry tomatoes are also good for salads. Their usual size is from 1 to $1\frac{1}{2}$ inches but some are 2 inches in diameter.

SHOPPING FOR
SALAD GREENS

Create tossed salads that boast flavor and appearance variety. Thanks to modern production and processing techniques, salad greens in assorted green shades and leaf shapes appear in grocery stores throughout the year. The salad green repertoire is not limited to the eight standards shown here. Leaf lettuce, for instance, comes in red-leafed or more ruffled salad-bowl versions.

Curly endive—narrow, fine, tight curls on heavy → rib. Dark green outer curls; heart is pale.
    Selection: Crisp, fresh leaves; tender stalks.
    Storage: Keeps in plastic bag in crisper of refrigerator 1 week or more.
    Flavor: Slightly bitter.

Romaine—cylindrical or elongated head with coarse, stiff leaves. Has a heavy midrib.
    Selection: Well-trimmed, full head. Rich green outer leaves with minimum blemishes.
    Storage: Keeps in plastic bag in crisper of refrigerator about 1 week.
    Flavor: Sharp, butter-nut.

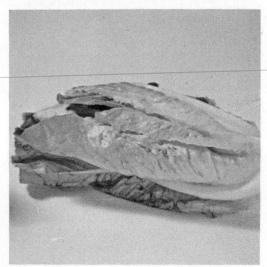

Escarole—rich green outer leaves; broad, slightly curly. Heart well-branched; appears bleached.
    Selection: Fresh, crisp, and tender.
    Storage: Keeps in plastic bag in crisper of refrigerator 1 week or more.
    Flavor: Slightly bitter.

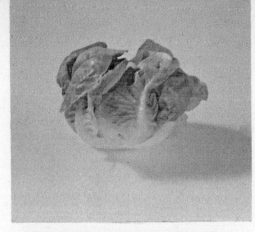

Bibb lettuce—small cup-shaped head.

Selection: Soft-texture green leaves.

Storage: Keeps in plastic bag in crisper of refrigerator a few days only.

Boston lettuce—soft head. Inner leaves feel oily.

Selection: Fairly firm head; fresh, soft-textured leaves. Big Boston leaves are brown on edges.

Storage: Keeps in plastic bag in crisper of refrigerator 1 or 2 days.

Flavor: Sweet, delicate.

Leaf lettuce—loose, non-head forming leaves.

Selection: Soft, tender leaves. Avoid wilted or decayed-looking bunches.

Storage: Keeps in plastic bag in crisper of refrigerator a few days only.

Flavor: Sweet, delicate (like Bibb).

Watercress—long stems; green round leaflets.

Selection: Bright green, crisp, and clean.

Storage: Put stems in jar of water; cover. Chill.

Flavor: Pungent, mustard-like.

Iceberg lettuce—most popular. Solid head.

Selection: Medium weight for size. Slight "give" when squeezed lightly. Leaves free from decay.

Storage: Keeps in plastic bag in crisper of refrigerator about 1 week.

Flavor: Sweet, mild.

FOOD STORAGE GUIDE

Apples: To keep crisp and tangy, store in refrigerator or some equally cool spot.

Apricots and *Peaches:* Ripen at room temperature. Refrigerate to prevent spoilage.

Avocados: Ripen at room temperature; refrigerate (up to 3 days) till needed.

Berries: Refrigerate, unwashed and dry, immediately. Use quickly. Wash for use.

Citrus Fruits: Refrigerate to keep grapefruit, oranges, and all citrus fruits juicy.

Figs: Use immediately; refrigerate briefly.

Grapes: Refrigerate. Use quickly.

Kiwi: Need no refrigeration.

Mangoes: Ripen at room temperature. Use immediately or refrigerate briefly.

Melons: If kept at room temperature (1 to 3 days) before use, meat will ripen.

Nectarines: Refrigerate briefly.

Papayas: Ripen fruit at room temperature. Refrigerate fully-ripe fruit for brief period.

Pears: Ripen at room temperature. Refrigeration of ripe fruit prevents spoilage.

Persimmons: Ripen best at room temperature. Refrigerate ripe fruit for short time.

Plums: Refrigerate ripe fruit immediately.

Pomegranates: Store briefly at room temperature away from light. Refrigeration keeps fruit moist. May be kept frozen.

Vegetables may require one of the following storage methods—

Moist cold: Refrigerate, covered, in crisper bin, plastic bag, or covered jar.

Dry cold: Place in *cool*, dry, dark area.

Artichokes: Store briefly in moist cold.

Beans, Green and Wax: Store in moist cold.

Cabbages: Store in moist cold.

Carrots: Store in moist cold. Keep well.

Cauliflower: Store in moist cold.

Celery: Store in moist cold for crispness.

Cucumbers: Store in moist cold.

Garlic: Store, covered, in dry cold.

Onions: Store in dry, not necessarily cold area. Never store with potatoes. Absorb moisture from potatoes, causing decay.

Green Onions: Store briefly in moist cold.

Mushrooms: Store briefly in moist cold.

Parsley: Store briefly in moist cold.

Peppers: Store briefly in moist cold for crispness and flavor retention.

Potatoes: Store in dry cold as greening takes place rapidly at room temperatures. Affected potatoes have bitter taste.

Radishes: Store briefly in moist cold.

Spinach: Store briefly in moist cold to retain crispness and fresh flavor.

Tomatoes: Store briefly in moist cold.

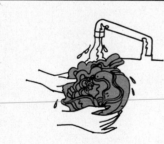

To prepare lettuce for use, discard discolored or wilted leaves. Rinse thoroughly and quickly under cold water. For lettuce cups, core head, then run water through core to loosen. Drain; gently remove cups.

For lettuce cups from compact head—wash, core, and drain head. Turn top down on cutting board. Press with palms of hands, and gently push from side to side to loosen. Remove cups as needed.

Toss or drain greens for full-flavored salads. Toss leafy greens in clean kitchen towel or paper towels. Use rack or paper towels to drain thoroughly. Water dilutes dressing and dressing coats dry leaves evenly.

PREPARATION TIPS

Kitchen shears are faster and easier than a paring knife for seeding grapes. First, cut grapes in half, then snip out seeds. Grapes are ready to use.

Tomato skins loosen by plunging them for a few seconds in boiling water. Another method is to twirl them over a flame for just a moment.

Score raw potatoes around center. Cook, covered, in boiling salted water. Spear spuds with fork in score mark and start peeling there.

Cut avocados in half lengthwise, cup in palms of hands and gently twist. Tap seed with sharp edge of knife. Twist and lift or gently pry seed out.

To snip parsley, rinse thoroughly. Drain. Remove stems and put parsley in measuring cup. With shears in downward position, snip leaves.

When salad calls for marshmallows, use miniatures or snip large ones. Dip shears in confectioners' sugar or water first to prevent sticking.

To remove crown from whole pineapple, grasp crown in one hand and pineapple in other. Twist crown one way, pineapple the other.

To section citrus fruit, peel fruit removing excess membrane. With knife, cut into center of fruit between one section and membrane. Slide knife down other side of section next to membrane.

To remove rind, cut wide strips from top to base, cutting just deep enough to remove eyes. Remove any remaining eyes with point of paring knife.

To serve pineapple in shell, quarter fruit and crown. Core. Using grapefruit knife, separate fruit from rind; slice and arrange in shell.

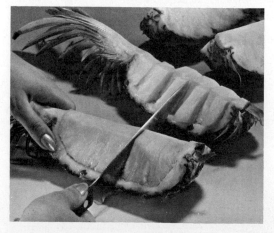

To cook artichoke, remove stem, 1 inch of top, and leaf tips. Remove outer leaves. Brush cut edges with lemon juice. Simmer, covered, in boiling salted water and a little salad oil 20 to 30 minutes.

GELATIN TERMS TO KNOW

Almost firm: Chilled gelatin mixture appears set, but is sticky to the touch.

Firm: Chilled gelatin mixture is completely set and ready to unmold.

Fluffy, light and fluffy: Air is whipped into gelatin till volume is about double.

Foamy, light and foamy: Air is beaten into gelatin till mixture appears frothy.

Fold: Ingredients are added gently to mixture. With spatula, cut down through mixture; go across bottom then up and over, close to surface. Turn bowl often.

Gelatin, unflavored: One envelope of this granulated protein equals 1 tablespoon. This amount sets 2 cups liquid (including liquid used for softening).

Gelatin, flavored: This packaged mixture contains gelatin, sugar, fruit acids, flavors, and coloring. The 3-ounce size sets 2 cups liquid and 2 cups drained fruit.

Mounds when spooned: Chilled gelatin mounds when dropped from a spoon.

Partially set: Chilled gelatin is the consistency of unbeaten egg whites.

Soft peaks: Mixture is beaten till peaks form and tips curl when beaters are lifted.

Stiff peaks: Egg whites are beaten till peaks stand up straight when beaters are lifted, but whites are still moist and glossy.

GELATIN TECHNIQUES

Adding fruits, vegetables, meat, etc.: Chill dissolved gelatin till partially set; fold in food so that it will be evenly distributed throughout. If during chilling gelatin becomes too stiff, set bowl of gelatin in pan of hot water. Stir till gelatin is liquid again; rechill till partially set.

Adding carbonated beverages: Cool dissolved gelatin to room temperature. Rest carbonated beverage bottle on rim of bowl; pour slowly down side of bowl. Gently stir up and down. Chill immediately till firm.

Whipping soufflé-type salads: Chill mixture of gelatin and mayonnaise or salad dressing till partially set, then whip till fluffy. Or, pour gelatin-mayonnaise mixture into freezer tray; chill in freezer till ice crystals form around edges. Whip till fluffy.

Unmolding gelatin salads: Loosen gelatin around edges of mold with spatula. Dip mold to rim in *warm* water for a *few seconds*. Tilt mold slightly easing gelatin away from one side to let air in. Tilt and rotate so air can loosen gelatin all the way around. Place serving platter upside down over mold. Hold platter and mold together; invert and shake gently to release. Carefully lift off mold. If gelatin does not release, tilt mold again or redip quickly in warm water.

Arranging fruit: Spoon thin layer of dissolved gelatin in bottom of mold. Arrange fruit. Chill till *almost* firm. Add remaining dissolved gelatin.

Preparing layered salads: Chill first gelatin layer till *almost* firm. Pour second layer over; chill till *almost* firm. Repeat layering as desired.

GARNISHING GLAMOUR

CUCUMBER BASKET

Hollow out a 3-inch length of unpared cucumber, leaving ¼-inch base and walls. Mark lengthwise strips around outside. Pare down every other strip of peel, *almost* to base. Crisp in ice water; drain. Pare strips of peel from remaining cucumber. Shape in circles; secure with wooden picks at base of basket. Fill with mayonnaise. Trim with parsley.

ORANGE CHRYSANTHEMUM

Score peel of 2 or more oranges into 8 sections, *cutting to, but not through,* base of peel. Gently remove peel from fruit, keeping shell in one piece. Pull fruit sections of 1 orange apart slightly; remove excess membrane. Use remaining fruit for salad.

With scissors, cut sectioned peels into small "petals," *cutting to, but not through,* bases. Replace prepared orange in 1 shell. Insert this shell into remaining petaled shells.

VEGETABLE FLOWERS

Slice pared large carrot and turnip crosswise, ⅛ inch thick. Cut flowers using cookie and tiny hors d'oeuvres cutters.

To prepare centerpiece pictured, thread green onion tops over wooden skewers. Attach desired flowers to ends of skewers. Use green onion and carrot pieces for centers.

CITRUS GARNISHES

Rose: Starting at stem end of lemon and/or lime, cut peel around fruit in continuous spiral. With stem end in center, curl into rose shape. Secure with wooden pick. For larger rose, curl several peels together.
Cartwheels: Slice fruit ⅛ inch thick. Notch peel around outside as desired.
Twists: Make 1 cut into fruit slice; twist.
Curls: Cut ⅛-inch citrus slice in half, *cutting to, but not through,* one edge of peel. Remove fruit from one half. Curl peel.

Tomato Roses: Turn tomato, stem end down. With sharp knife, cut 5 or 6 petals, cutting through skin but not into seed pocket. Gently separate petals slightly. Season with salt and pepper to taste. For added color, sprinkle center with sieved hard-cooked egg yolks. Use to garnish buffet platters or tossed salads. Tiny cherry tomato rosettes are particularly suitable to garnish individual salad servings.

Turnip Lilies: Here's an elegant-looking trim that's simple to make. For each lily, cut 2 *thin* crosswise pared turnip slices. Curve one slice into cone shape. Shape second slice around cone in opposite direction. Insert thin strip of carrot down center of cone. Secure lily with wooden picks. Crisp in ice water. Rutabaga slices are a good substitute if turnip is not available.

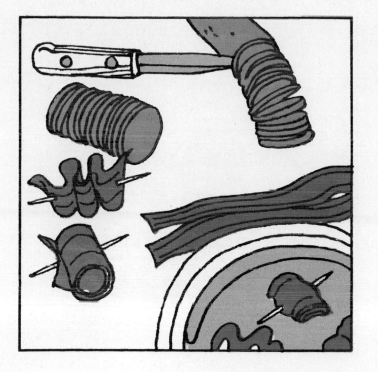

Carrot Corkscrews: Insert point of short-bladed paring knife into pared whole carrot, *cutting to*, *but not through*, center at slight angle; rotate carrot slowly, cutting a continuous spiral. Make deeper cut into carrot, if necessary, to make corkscrew flexible. Chill in ice water to open.

Carrot Curls: Rest pared carrot on cutting surface. Shave a thin and wide lengthwise strip of carrot with parer, pushing parer away from you. Roll up long slice; secure with wooden pick. Crisp in ice water; remove pick before serving.

Carrot Zigzags: Rest pared whole carrot on cutting surface. Make a thin, wide lengthwise strip of carrot with parer, cutting away from you. Thread on wooden pick accordion style. Crisp in ice water; remove pick before serving.

Fruit Baskets: Halve large grapefruit. With grapefruit or paring knife, cut around each section to loosen fruit; remove fruit from sections, leaving membrane intact. Snip out whole membrane.

Leaving 1 inch uncut in center of opposite sides, cut around each grapefruit half with paring knife ⅜ inch below rim to make basket handles. Carefully lift up the 2 resulting cut strips and tie together with ribbon of desired color.

Refill cavity of basket with a fruit salad combination containing the grapefruit sections. If desired, top fruit with miniature scoops of sherbet made with spoon or melon ball cutter. Serve immediately.

For smaller fruit salad serving, make basket from large orange, following directions above. Use orange sections in the fruit salad.

Radish Roses: Cut root tip off radish, then cut 4 or 5 thin petals around radish, leaving a little red between the petals. Use a grapefruit knife or point of paring knife. (If desired, leave on some green leaves at stem for trim.) Chill in ice water till petals spread open like a flower. Use radish roses as a relish or plate trim.

Petaled Daisies: Starting at root tip, score 6 petals on radish with point of knife. Following markings and beginning at tip, cut thin petals following shape of radish *almost* to base (stem end). Chill in ice water till petals open. Use as a relish or plate trim.

Radish Accordions: Cut long radishes crosswise, *cutting to, but not through*, in 8 narrow slices. Chill in ice water so slices will fan out, accordion style.

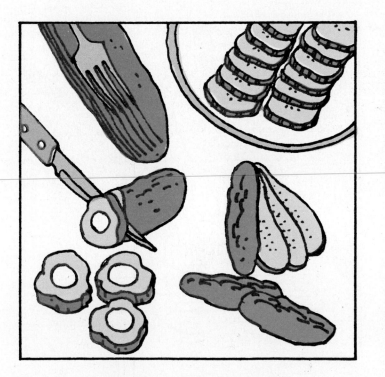

Scored Cucumbers: For fancy cucumber slices, run tines of fork lengthwise down unpared cucumber, pressing to break through peel. Repeat around entire cucumber. Slice straight across or on the bias. Use in tossed salads or as a relish.

Pickle Fans: Slice pickle lengthwise *almost* to stem end, making thin slices. Spread each fan and press uncut end of pickle so fan will hold its shape.

Stuffed Pickle Slices: Cut thin slice from stem end of large dill pickle. Hollow pickle with apple corer. Stuff with softened cream cheese or any spreading cheese. Chill well, then slice crosswise.

Pickle Accordions: (not shown) Cut off ends of pickles, then slice crosswise, *cutting to, but not through*, pickle. Bend pickle gently so slices separate at top.

Zigzag Melon Bowls: For attractive serving "bowls," cut small cantaloupe in half zigzag fashion by inserting knife into center of melon at an angle. Pull knife out and make next cut at reverse angle. Repeat around melon. Pull two halves apart; remove seeds. It might be easier to make heavy paper pattern and draw where cuts are to be made; carve along lines. Fill bowls with a salad mixture.

Scalloped Melon Bowl: Set watermelon on end. Cut thin slice off bottom to make it sit flat. Cut top third off melon. Using a cup as guide, trace scallops around edge of melon. Carve scalloped edge following pattern. Scoop out fruit. Using melon ball cutter, if desired, or large spoon, cut up pieces of fruit to be used in salad. Refill shell with fruit mixture.

Apple Rings: Pare or leave peel on apples. Cut out core using apple corer. Slice to desired thickness. Keep bright by brushing with ascorbic acid color keeper or lemon juice mixed with water.

Frosted Grapes: Combine slightly beaten egg white and a little water. Brush mixture over cluster of grapes using pastry brush. Sprinkle with granulated sugar; dry on rack. Use as a plate garnish.

Cheese Apples: Moisten shredded cheese with mayonnaise or salad dressing. Roll in balls. Make an indentation in each end. Insert whole clove in one end and half a green wooden pick in other end. Roll in paprika for rosy color.

Make balls from process cheese by cutting with melon ball cutter or forming with hands. Repeat with cloves, picks, and paprika.

INDEX

A-B

WINGS OF AN ARTIST

CHILDREN'S BOOK ILLUSTRATORS TALK ABOUT THEIR ART

Introduction by Julie Cummins
Activity Guide by Barbara Kiefer

HARRY N. ABRAMS, INC., PUBLISHERS

Editor: Howard W. Reeves
Designer: Edward Miller

Library of Congress Cataloging-in-Publication Data

Wings of an artist : children's book illustrators talk about their art.
p. cm.
Summary: More than twenty illustrators of children's books, including James Ransome, Robert Sabuda, Maira Kalman, and Maurice Sendak, talk about their work.
ISBN 0-8109-4552-5
1. Illustrators Juvenile literature. 2. Illustrated children's books Juvenile literature. 3. Illustration of books—20th century Juvenile literature. [1. Illustrators.]
NC965.W56 1999
741.6'42'0922—dc21
[B] 99-25906

Published in 1999 by Harry N. Abrams, Incorporated, New York

Printed and bound in Hong Kong

ABRAMS

Harry N. Abrams, Inc.
100 Fifth Avenue
New York, N.Y. 10011
www.abramsbooks.com

CONTENTS

INTRODUCTION

The expression "seeing the world through rose-colored glasses" implies pleasant, carefree surroundings with nothing unpleasant or negative to mar the view. In reality, a rose-colored point of view is monochromatic, unimaginative, and static in its sameness. In contrast, a kaleidoscope provides a multi-colored view with brilliant patterns and designs that are constantly changing. Which offers the most interesting and stimulating perspective?

The world of children's book illustration is such a kaleidoscope, offering imagination, creativity, and artistic ingenuity in a tangible, satisfying, and enduring form—a picture book. Parents who recognize the importance of art literacy in their children's formative years will find no better resource. Picture books offer an interesting and enjoyable experience that can build art appreciation, visual literacy, and self-esteem in a child.

In words and a visual image, most created specially for this book, these twenty-three illustrators express the meaning of art and the impact of artistic form on their childhood. Taken together, the words and pictures of these artists demonstrate the power of art in children's lives, the spirit of creativity, and the significance of visual images and how they speak to children.

From realism to impressionism; from traditional techniques such as woodcuts and scratchboard to textural images using collage; from humorous, cartoonish styles to sophisticated oil renderings: all representations of art are appropriate for children and all of them exist in picture books. Art literacy is as simple as opening the pages of a children's book.

Woodleigh Marx Hubbard comments that in her work she attempts to 'match the exuberance, delight, and vitality of children." The wonderful array of illustrations in this book provides a means for interpreting and expressing human experience as well as imparting cognitive information.

The last entry is by Jean and Mou-Sien Tseng who beautifully sum up the book's essence: "Imagination and creativity are the wings of the mind."

It is our hope that this volume will allow a child to stretch his or her own wings and begin to soar.

Julie Cummins

GRAEME BASE

I've never been able to see something beautiful, especially something of the natural world, and simply enjoy it for what it is—I have to try to capture it! Instead of turning into some weirdo collector, I have, over the years, channeled this urge into recreating on paper the things I see in real life and in my head. For me this is a basic need. If I am not creating something or planning what I'm going to do next, I get all restless and fidgety. I suspect I could get help for this, but instead I make picture books.

This illustration of Firny, Pearl, and Bert, characters from *The Sign of the Seahorse*, was done a few years ago as a commission. It hasn't been published before and I rather like it, so I thought I'd take this opportunity to show it off! The original book was inspired by my first experience scuba diving—I was totally blown away by the beauty of the world beneath the waves and knew immediately, while I was still underwater, that this was going to be my next book

9

DAVID CATROW

Today's Spelling words!
cat bat hat
rat vat that
fat spat sat
gnat pat chrysanthemum

One day in Mrs. Canary's first-grade art class the most amazing and wonderful creature was born.

"Mr. Catrow, all our birds will look the same!" Mrs. Canary squawked, her arms flapping in her massive flowered Tahitian muumuu. She looked like she would suddenly fly up and perch on the plaster bust of President James A. Garfield.

"I can't do it . . I won't do it," I thought—

maybe out loud—my hands getting too sweaty to hold my crayon.

"Then Mister, you're excused," she said with stiff red lips.

Though I spent the rest of class with my head on my desk, some good had come from this misfortune. I had confronted my first editor—and survived! I realized I was a true artist and no one was going to extinguish the creative fire within.

DAVID DIAZ

I spun around the room and realized that everything, everything, everything I saw had started as an idea that someone had drawn. The fork, the lamp, the clock, all the little parts in the clock and even the machine that made the little parts in the clock work had started as drawings. At some point someone had even drawn the pencil I now drew with. My head spilled! I knew right then that I would never run out of ideas for things to draw.

LEO AND DIANE DILLON

When faced with illustrating a subject that has been done many times before, our first thought is how we can show it in a new way.

Mother Goose conjures up images of a sweet old lady telling stories to a group of rapt children. Upon further thought, we wondered how she got her stories and rhymes. She has a great imagination, of course, but she might like some new adventures and inspiration. That is why we created a flying machine for her. Now she can soar amongst the clouds with her beloved geese to faraway lands with new tales to tell.

12

RICHARD EGIELSKI

When I was little, I drew pictures with a plain, No. 2 pencil on lined, loose-leaf paper. If I pressed too hard, I would make holes in the paper. The lines were always in my way, and when I erased, the paper would tear.

Then I saw "The Jon Gnagy Show." He drew pictures on T.V.! Starting with a circle or a square or a triangle, he would show you how to make a face or a building or a tree. That Christmas I got a Jon Gnagy art kit. It had black charcoal pencils and thick drawing paper and, best of all, a gummy, kneaded eraser.

I drew and drew until I wore down my pencils and used up my paper. So, for my birthday, I got art supplies. Colored pencils. Paper. Watercolors. Art supplies were like toys for me, and drawing and painting was just like playing with them.

One day our school went on a trip to an art museum. For the first time I saw paintings. Landscapes. Seascapes. Portraits. Self-portraits. Still lifes. Huge fantastic pictures. I imagined myself as an artist, in my studio, with my paints and canvases and easel, and I was happy.

14

DIANE GREENSEID

By the time I was a teenager, I knew I wanted to do something creative with my life. I just wasn't sure which way to go. I loved to dance, take photographs, and create things in general. I took all kinds of art classes, but it wasn't until I took a children's book illustration class that everything fell into place.

One of the things I value most about being a children's book illustrator is that I get to incorporate my playful side into my pictures. I have always been a tad silly! I used to laugh so hard in class that I couldn't stop; make funny faces; and play with made-up and real words like "mamaliga," "zombatutski," and "birky-in-the-bugner." In my artwork I continue to play, but now with visual elements like color, movement, and humorous characters that fit the stories I am to illustrate.

I feel very fortunate that as an adult I get to stay at home in my studio and paint pictures that include a people-eating chair, a girl that turns into a chicken, or beauty-queen cats that ride in floats!

WOODLEIGH MARX HUBBARD

My entire purpose in illustrating is to match the exuberance, delight, and vitality of children. This illustration depicts how I feel about being an illustrator—the utter joy of imagination gone wild.

My father is an arist. I grew up surrounded by his paintings, my mother's writings, and the boundless creativity of my brothers and sisters. In every art class I took, my instructor cried,

"You have no talent. Give it up!" I could not. I would not. I live to paint. Painting is my life. I love illustrating picture books. I receive deep satisfaction and pleasure from working with children. They continually inspire me and bring laughter into the bargain.

Remember, if you have a dream—never, never, never give it up.

Woodleigh

SUSAN JEFFERS

H ORSES MAKE ME HAPPY. Who knows why. Dreaming horses. Drawing horses. Riding horses. Whatever makes you happy or sad, you can draw it or write about it (no matter what anyone else says). What makes you happy?

17

We always look for art. We see it in the night sky, the glow of light on a child's face, the magic of a good story, the fantastic world of dreams, the fury of storms, the sound of a voice, the mystery of animals, and the security of a warm lap and loving arms. We find art everywhere.

STEVE JOHNSON AND LOU FANCHER

WILLIAM JOYCE

I was a weird kid. Most of the time I pretended I was from another planet and had super powers. This presented some problems at school. Math? Look out. Geography? Uh-oh. Spelling? Yikes. Why did Mississippi always have to be spelled with I's instead of O's? But art class, the library, and recess, that's where the action was for me. I was crazy for stories and pictures and made-up things.

A smart librarian led me to a book called *Where the Wild Things Are.* I guess she knew a wild thing when she saw one. That's when I decided I wanted

to be a writer. I acted up less and drew more. I learned to spell (sort of) so I could write stories.

I had a lot of help. My family and teachers encouraged me and exposed me to all kinds of art: movies, books, plays, T.V., paintings, music, photography.

I don't pretend to be from another planet anymore—but I get to make up characters who are. It's my job. And in some weird way it's like getting paid for recess.

When I was in seventh grade, the kindly, curly and somewhat cross-eyed Mrs. Walters told me that I was a GOOD writer and drawer. That was that!

Maira Kalman

MICHAEL McCURDY

Daddy's studio was a small room upstairs in our house on Grassy Sprain Heights in Yonkers, New York. He worked as a commercial artist, sometimes traveling to New York City and other times working at home. Sitting at his desk, Daddy created pictures for advertisements like women's hair coloring products and insurance companies. I was fascinated by his work area. His desk was filled with all kinds of compartments and—what seemed to me—secret drawers. There were cubbyholes for pencils and pens, T squares and line gauges, and special places to keep ink and illustration board. When I was very young, I began to draw pictures too. One day Daddy gave me a piece of black drawing board. He called it "scratchboard." He would scratch into it with a sharp point to reveal a white undercoating. In this way he created pictures. I also used a sharp point and scribbled white lines all over Daddy's gift to me. Maybe it was at this moment that I became what I still am today, an artist making pictures by bringing dark surfaces into the light. Maybe Daddy started something.

Susan Meddaugh

In elementary school, when I drew pictures, they always told a story. I knew I was an artist. I just didn't know what kind.

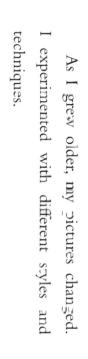

As I grew older, my pictures changed. I experimented with different styles and techniques.

Was it luck or fate that I took a job in a publishing house designing children's books? I worked on other people's stories, picking type and interviewing artists. After a while I thought: I will do my own books.

So I'm drawing stories again and I guess you could say I'm back where I started. But sometimes you have to try on a lot of hats before you find the one that fits. And sometimes the perfect fit turns out to be the one you tried on first.

Paul Meisel

For as long as I can remember, I have dreamed that I was flying high above the trees and rivers and houses and people. My imagination soars. The sky is limitless. As a child, every painting, sculpture, and piece of art I saw in a museum or book was a feather added to my wings. Every picture I drew, a feather. Every hug from my parents and grandmothers, another feather. Every laugh with my brothers and friends, more feathers. Every snuggle with my dog. Feathers. Every time I played ball. Feathers, feathers, feathers.

Now I am older and I have many feathers in my wings, a number of them from looking at and creating art. In my work, as in my life, the challenge is always there to soar ever higher, to never stop flying.

I am often asked how my interest in art began. "Did an artist were never discouraged, they were never your parents artists?" "Was there an artist gallery or exactly encouraged either. Despite these setbacks, I an elementary art teacher influence you?" "Were museum exhibit that sparked your interest?"

I was born in the small, rural town of Rich Square, North Carolina in 1961, six years after Mrs. Rosa Parks refused to give up her seat on a bus in Montgomery, Alabama, sparking the Montgomery bus boycott and fueling the Civil Rights Movement.

I was raised by my grandmother, away from my brothers and sister. I had a lot of time to draw. I copied the images around me—pictures from coloring books, characters from Disney and MAD magazine, Saturday morning cartoons, comic books, and the Bible. There were few children's books in my home other than those I checked out of my school library (there was no public library in town).

Although my drawing and dreams of becoming

enrolled at the Pratt Institute to study illustration. I wondered if a black man could make a living as an illustrator. All of that changed after meeting Jerry Pinkney. He lectured at Pratt and later taught a senior illustration class that I would occasionally attend as a junior. I reconnected with Jerry after graduating from Pratt, while working on my first children's book, *Do Like Kyla.*

I am so thankful for Jerry and other African-American artists and illustrators who worked so hard to open doors for my generation. Jerry is someone by whom standards can be measured, not only in his artwork but in his personal life as well. Today I still turn to Jerry for his continued support and unwavering enthusiasm. My portrait captures Jerry in the midst of abstraction—calm and smiling.

JAMES RANSOME

24

ROBERT SABUDA

Scissors: for cutting things out when I'm lazy

X-acto® knife: for cutting things out when I have to pay attention

Band-Aid®: for when I'm cutting things out and not paying attention

White tape: really strong

Double-sided tape: so strong it wouldn't even *consider* having only one sticky side

Banana: snack

Rubber cement: for making Booger Balls

Transparent tape: kind of strong

Protractor: I have no idea what this does—it just makes me look smart

White glue: "Mold and vermin proof"

Paint: for finger painting to make collage paper

Brushes: for mixing colors and slopping paint around

Triangle: for making sure things are straight when I need them straight

No. 2 Pencil: for making beautiful drawings

The other end of a No. 2 Pencil: for when the drawings aren't so beautiful

Ruler: because I'm bad at math

Knitting needle: to score heavy paper when I'm making pop-ups

The best part about being an artist is that you get to make messes and not have anyone yell at you to CLEAN THAT UP THIS *VERY MINUTE!*

MAURICE SENDAK

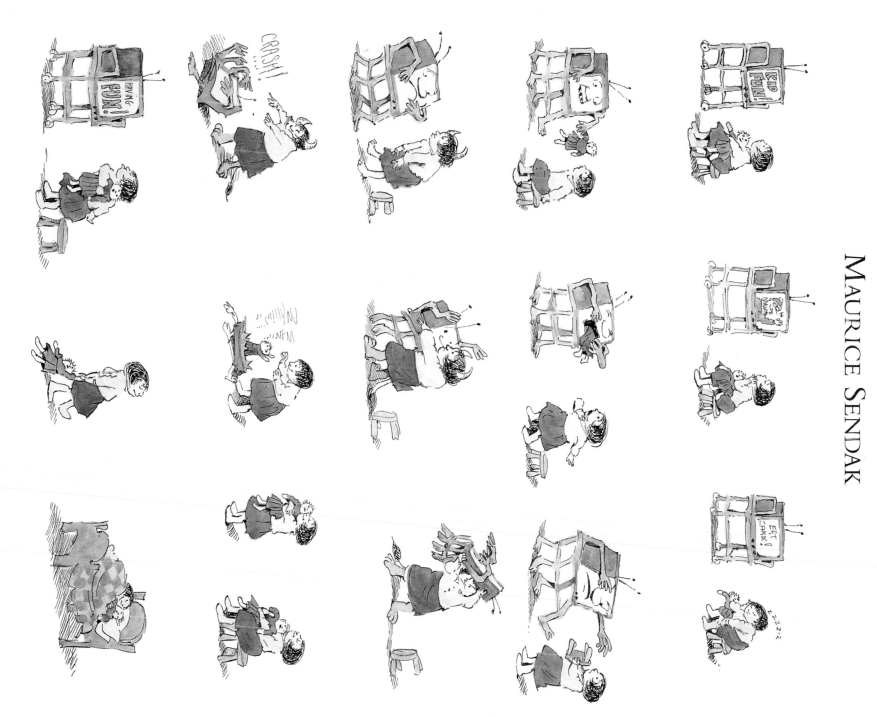

I have been doodling with ink and watercolor on paper all my life. It's my way of stirring up my imagination to see what I find hidden in my head. I call the results dream pictures, fantasy sketches, and even brain-sharpening exercises. They are the only homework I've ever energetically applied myself to, the only school that ever taught me anything.

The example shown here popped into my head without any preparation. Spontaneous sketching gives me great pleasure. I recommend doodling as an excellent exercise for stirring up the unconscious, just as you would stir up some mysterious soup all the while hoping it tastes good.

DAVID SMALL

When I was a boy I lived with my parents in Detroit. This was not where I would have lived had I been given the choice. Given my way I probably would have lived in Candy Land. But the fact is Detroit—then a harsh and aggressive city—made art and music all the more sweet in my life, more urgent, and more of a necessity. Seen in that light, it was the perfect place for me to grow up.

27

JEAN AND MOU-SIEN TSENG

A Journey to the West is perhaps the most exciting adventure in Chinese literature. In these tales, our hero, the Monkey King, is always getting himself into trouble, despite his ability to transform into seventy-two different creatures and travel one hundred thousand miles in one somersault. He creates havoc everywhere, from the Dragon Palace on the ocean floor to the Jade Emperor's Palace in the clouds. As punishment, the Monkey King is ordered to escort the T'ang Monk to the Buddhist Heaven of the West. It is a long, dangerous journey, full of demons wanting a bite of the Monk in order to become immortal. With wisdom and cunning,

the Monkey King outsmarts his enemies and accomplishes his task.

Every time we read *A Journey to the West* we are awed by its power and vitality. The Monkey King thrives through the imagination and creativity of the story's author, even five hundred years after its creation. It is our hope that our illustrations are as exciting and wonderful for others as the Monkey King tales are for us.

Imagination and creativity are the wings of one's mind. Or these two wings, you will fly high and far.

Illustration: Conquering the Goldfish Demon from *A Journey to the West*

Invitations to Fly: An Activity Guide

The rich images and imaginative narratives contained in this book are ideal for introducing children to many aspects of visual art. The activities suggested here are meant to lead children back into the book to think more deeply about their responses to the pictures and ideas they have encountered. In addition, these activities may also provide opportunities to take wing into more formal inquiry about art history, artistic production, and aesthetic evaluation. As children wonder about and consider the process of creating art, and as they consider their own objective and subjective responses to works of art, adults may support their questions with more formal instruction, with information, lessons, and techniques that could deepen their aesthetic understanding.

The following activities are addressed to children. Younger children will need adult supervision to help explain terms as well as carry out some of the exercises. Older children may need little if any guidance once begun, but should be reminded to consult a dictionary for any unfamiliar terms as well as available art appreciation books to round out their experiences. (Throughout "classmates" may be translated as family, friends, and library reading group partners.) References to particular artworks have been avoided so that these activities may be used with other pictures and books as well as artwork in museums and galleries.

1. This book has introduced you to twenty-three artists. As you read their words and look carefully at the pictures they chose to include, think of some ways in which these artists are alike and different. For example: When did the artists decide they wanted to draw and paint? What encouraged them to become artists? What difficulties did some of them overcome? What types of pictures do they like to draw? What details do they like to include? Interview members of your own class using similar questions. Make a comparison chart of the artists and then make one of your classmates.

2. Many of the artists included pictures of themselves (self-portraits) or people they know (portraits), in their illustration. Make a list of those artists who have drawn self-portraits. Make another list of those artists who drew portraits of other people. How have the artists shown more about the person than just what they look like? Draw a picture of yourself (or of a classmate). In addition to physical details like eye color and hair color, try to show something about your personality and your likes and dislikes.

3. Some artists create their pictures by looking at things in front of them. Others create imaginary worlds. In which pictures could the artists have been painting something from real life? In which pictures could the artist only have been imagining the scene? Make a drawing of something you can see. Then turn it into something that could exist only in your imagination.

4. Artists can choose to view a scene from far away or to look at something up close. How many different points of view, or perspectives, can you find in these pictures? How does the artist's point of view affect your feelings about the picture? Draw a scene that is close to you. Then imagine that you are a worm or a bird in the air looking at the same scene. How would the perspective in your drawing change?

5. When authors write stories they choose words to tell what is happening, to describe scenes, or to express how characters feel. Artists use things like lines, shapes, and colors to "tell" their stories. For example, thick vertical lines tend to seem steady and secure. Thin, sketchy lines might suggest nervousness or excitement. An artist might choose zigzag or diagonal lines to show action or curving lines to convey rest or quiet. Shapes can also imply meaning. Rounded, flowing shapes might seem natural and alive while sharp-edged or pointed shapes seem active or tense. Look at the illustrations in the book and choose those where you think the artist used lines and shapes to say something. Make a list of the things the artists were trying to tell you with lines and shapes. Draw a picture with pencils, paints, or crayons or create a collage—a picture using cut paper, fabric, or even wood—that conveys a feeling of happiness or excitement. Then create a picture of something frightening or gloomy.

6. You may be aware of how colors can affect your feelings. Name some color associations you know (red with anger, yellow with warmth). Look at the illustrations in the book and see how the artists have used color. Tell how an artist's choice of colors makes you feel. Create a color painting that expresses a feeling. See if your classmates can guess what emotion you are trying to express.

7. The ways the artists chose to combine different colors can also affect your feelings. Color complements (colors opposite each other on the color wheel) like red and green, blue and orange, or violet and yellow, look vivid and alive when used together. Colors from the same family, like gray-blue, pale blue, and blue-violet, may cause a more restful, tranquil feeling. Notice the types of color schemes chosen by each of the artists in this book. Which ones seem to jump off the page? Which are quiet? How do these colors match what the artists are trying to say? Draw two pictures of the same scene, one using color complements and another using shades of one color. Discuss the differences with your classmates.

8. All of these artists are such masters of visual storytelling that you can tell a story from their pictures without reading the words that accompany them. Choose one of the illustrations in the book and create your own story to go with it. Add more pictures to create a picture storybook.

9. Explore the techniques used by the different artists. On your canvas (your paper or board) paint an object like an apple, a seashell, or a vase with flowers, using transparent watercolor (color mixed with lots of water). Then use a thicker paint like tempera or acrylic. Now try scratchboard or crayon resist drawings. Experiment with cut-paper collage using different papers and textures to create a still-life design. A still life is a picture that shows a still-life design. A still life is a picture that shows mostly inanimate (nonliving) things. Once you have tried different techniques can you tell what original material each artist used?

10. The way the artist arranges or composes a picture can create a feeling of movement and rhythm. Choose one of the illustrations and create (or select) a musical accompaniment. Which picture might have a whole orchestra tell its story? Which might have a single instrument? Would the song be fast or slow, loud or soft?

11. Now that you have spent some time looking and thinking about the artists in this book, choose one or more of these artists to study in depth. At your library, find as many books by the artist as you can. Find out more about the artist's life by doing library research or visiting an artist's website. Present your findings about the artists to your reading group, classmates or the other classes in your school or library.

Big dreams with little space to grow

The decade's wave of immigrants had origins in Italy, Poland, Russia and Hungary. These disparate countries would often be represented in a single city block or one rundown tenement building—vacated by earlier immigrants from England, Ireland and Germany. Once again, newcomers changed the face, and faith, of American cities, bringing Catholic majorities to neighborhoods in Buffalo, Cleveland and Chicago, while Eastern European Jews crowded into New York's Lower East Side. Close quarters promoted the rapid spread of air- and waterborne diseases, as did the scarcity of both plumbing and ventilation. In 1901 the most sweeping in a series of tenement-regulation laws passed, requiring better sanitation arrangements and more windows giving access to light and air. But implementation, championed by reformers Robert DeForest and Jacob Riis and resisted by landlords, was slow to come.

New arrivals also faced harsher prejudices than earlier immigrants had. Well before he became President, Woodrow Wilson characterized them as "men of the lowest class from the South of Italy, and men of the meaner sort out of Hungary and Poland, men out of the ranks where there was neither skill nor energy, nor any initiative or quick intelligence." In spite of—or perhaps because of—sentiments like these, new Americans were eager to take part in one available advantage: free education. This was "the treasure that no thief could touch, not even misfortune or poverty," recalled Russian immigrant Mary Antin. "The doors stood open for every one of us."

In 1909 an alley between Boston tenement buildings doubled as a ballpark for children. By the end of the next decade, nearly 80 percent of the city's residents were either foreign-born themselves or the children of foreign-born parents.

Leslie Towns Hope, immigrant

Before there was Leno, Letterman, Carson or Paar, Americans had Hope. Few immigrant success stories are as inspiring as that of the star of some 70 films and 500 TV shows. Born in 1903 in Eltham, England, as Leslie Towns Hope, one of seven sons of a struggling stonemason, he immigrated with his family to Cleveland in 1908. Starting out in vaudeville, Bob Hope became famous in 1938 as the host of a weekly NBC radio broadcast. His monologues were a torrent of topical one-liners, delivered in a machine-gun cadence that suited the new medium. "You can make people laugh anytime if you're talking about things they are already thinking about," he once explained. By the time Hope made the film *The Road to Singapore* with chum Bing Crosby in 1940, he had cemented his comic persona as an inept lover and cowardly braggart. Offscreen he was anything but dumb: Savvy investments eventually made him among the country's richest entertainers.

Hope spent decades ceaselessly repaying his adopted country for his good fortune. During World War II he traveled more than a million miles to entertain war-weary GIs and sailors; his USO shows were as much a part of military life as K rations and reveille. After V-J Day, Hope refused to be demobilized; he went on to entertain U.S. troops in Korea, Vietnam and the gulf war. At home, he gave away millions of dollars through his foundation. His efforts earned him five honorary Oscars, 54 honorary university degrees and an estimated 2,000 awards and citations, including a 1963 congressional gold medal that called him "America's best Ambassador of Good Will." Hope responded to the honor in typical fashion: "I received this for going outside the country; I think they're trying to tell me something."

The natty young Bob (right, about eight years old) progressed to army boots and camouflage (top, entertaining troops off Bahrain in 1987).

"England occupies a warm spot in my affections. It was the scene of my greatest performance. I was born there."

From the Pilgrims in 1620 to Tibetan Buddhists in 1999, religious oppression has sparked immigration to America.

A NATION OF BELIEVERS

Ever since the Puritans landed at Plymouth Rock, preachers have warned that America is falling into godlessness. Yet this country has never strayed far from its religious roots. And though nativists have prophesied since the mid-19th century that the nation's essential character would be washed away by waves of immigrants, the newcomers—like the Pilgrim Fathers before them—have almost always carried faith in their baggage.

By 1900, fully a third of the nation's 75 million people were either foreign-born or the children of foreign-born parents. Of those new Americans, the largest number were Roman Catholic. As persecution mounted in Russia and Eastern Europe, America's Jewish population rose as well—from 250,000 in 1880 to over two million in 1915. Still, Protestants remained the majority in the U.S., their ranks replenished by a steady stream from Germany and Scandinavia.

At mid-century that majority still held. In 1960, Protestant church membership (all denominations) was approximately 64 million; Catholics numbered 42 million. There were some 5.5 million Jews and fewer than three million members of Eastern Orthodox churches.

In the 1990s, religion's grip is stronger than ever. In 1997, 67 percent of Americans identified themselves as church members, up from 43 percent in 1910. Thanks to a new wave of immigration, Hindus and Muslims (in 1990, 227,000 and 527,000 members, respectively) are growing in number. The New Age movement has spawned a panoply of sects. But such diversity is part of a long American tradition: As early as 1898, Asian immigrants on the West Coast had established a Young Men's Buddhist Association.

The high point of immigration to the U.S. in the first half of the century was in 1907, when 1.3 million sought welcome here. But that banner year was exceeded in 1991, when 1.8 million applied for residency. Many of those applicants had been living here illegally and seized upon the provisions of a special amnesty act to allow them and their families to stay.

NUMBER OF ALIENS DEPORTED OR REQUIRED TO DEPART	PERCENTAGE OF U.S. IMMIGRANTS ADMITTED FROM ASIA	COUNTRY SENDING THE MOST IMMIGRANTS TO THE U.S.
1907: 995	1907: 3.2	1907: Italy (22.2%)
1950: 579,105	1950: 1.8	1950: Germany (51.6%)
1996: 55,171	1997: 33.3	1997: Mexico (18.4%)

1910–1919

LIFE Two sounds defined the decade. First there was the clatter of machines—machines for transport and for manufacture, machines that changed America forever. Then came the thunder of guns, as war engulfed the world.

GRANGER COLLECTION; RIGHT: BROWN BROTHERS

D.W. Griffith (above) steered film away from melodrama and slapstick, but Ziegfeld relied on the tried-and-true formula of giving his audience an eyeful (right).

Preceding pages: In the fall of 1918, American soldiers charge across the battlefield of Meuse-Argonne. Among the U.S. troops was Capt. Harry S Truman.

On stage and screen, glorious excess

Irving Berlin wrote that a pretty girl is like a melody. But a lot of pretty girls? That, Florenz Ziegfeld calculated, is a spectacle people will pay to see. Ziegfeld, former manager of a sideshow strong man, put his insight to work—and thus was born Broadway's best-loved revue. "Out of the vulgar leg show, Ziegfeld has fashioned a thing of grace and beauty," cooed a reviewer in 1907. He also booked comedians like W.C. Fields, Will Rogers and Fanny Brice, who debuted with "Sadie Salome," a Berlin tune, in 1910. Much of the attraction was that Ziegfeld spared no expense—he once spent $300 apiece for onstage pillows—in realizing his vision.

Just as *Ziegfeld's Follies* peaked in New York, one Hollywood director, David Wark Griffith, gave us filmdom's first epic, a three-hour Civil War drama called *The Birth of a Nation*. Glorifying the Ku Klux Klan and depicting blacks as predators, the movie drew criticism from both white and black leaders. Despite its inflammatory content, *Birth of a Nation* established the modern cinematic vocabulary. Shifting camera angles, crosscutting, closeups, wide shots—we owe them all to Griffith's work.

A killer at sea, and one at home

When RMS *Titanic* scraped its hull on an iceberg and sank into the North Atlantic on April 14, 1912, the disaster grabbed headlines and the national consciousness like none before it. The passenger list on the world's largest and most luxurious ship (one sixth of a mile long, with a price tag of $7.5 million) mirrored the social order: Each person's station in life would decide his or her chance of escaping death. Hyped as unsinkable, the *Titanic* left England for New York with only enough lifeboats for half the ship's passengers. Whose lives were worth saving? It was this deadly calculation that gripped the public. All but one of the 50 children who died had been traveling in steerage. Three quarters of those in third class drowned, while nearly two thirds of those in first class were saved (among them the wife of industrialist John J. Astor).

Today the story of the 1,500 dead still tugs at our memory, but nearly forgotten is the far greater loss of life caused by a worldwide influenza epidemic that began in 1918. In less than a year, more Americans were killed by Spanish flu than died in both world wars.

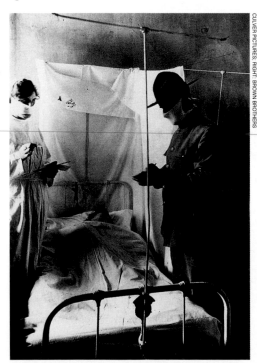

In New York (right), a hand-lettered precursor of the news ticker brings word of the *Titanic*. Around the world, flu victims (above) were hospitalized, but doctors could do little. The global death toll was 30 million.

1910–1919

The little car that could—and did

Tough enough to climb stairs, inexpensive enough ($850) to fit a prosperous farmer's budget—the Model T, introduced in 1908, proved so popular that its maker couldn't meet demand. So in 1913, in Highland Park, Mich., Henry Ford installed his industry's first assembly line. Each worker performed just a few simple movements. "The man who puts in a bolt does not put on the nut," Ford explained. Production septupled by 1916, to 585,388 cars a year; the price plummeted to $360. But employee turnover soared under the new system, thanks to the crushing monotony of assembly-line labor. So Ford doubled wages, offering those who qualified—partly by avoiding gambling or boozing—a princely $5 a day. Suddenly, even the man who put on the nut could afford a Tin Lizzie. By 1921 more than half the cars sold in the U.S. were Model Ts. Gasoline-fueled mobility became a national birthright. And as the assembly line spread to other industries, boosting productivity and incomes, American life was further transformed: A nation of toilers morphed into a nation of consumers.

"I will build a car for the great multitude," vowed Henry Ford. His assembly line was inspired, in part, by slaughterhouse conveyor belts that moved carcasses to cutters.

FPG INTL.; RIGHT: BROWN BROTHERS

A tragic fire shocks the nation

The 500 employees of the Triangle Shirtwaist Company were about to head home on March 25, 1911, when a fire broke out in the cutting room. Feeding on piled scraps of cloth, flames raced through the factory, which occupied the top three stories of a Manhattan loft building. Workmen on the eighth floor got out fast, as did executives on the 10th. But on the ninth floor, the bosses had locked the exit to keep the seamstresses—mostly Jewish and Italian immigrants, aged 15 to 23—at their machines. Dozens crowded onto the rickety fire escape, but it collapsed under their weight. Others plunged to their death trying to slide down the freight elevator cable. By the time fire trucks arrived, with ladders that reached only to the sixth floor, desperate women were leaping from the windows. "I learned a new sound," a reporter wrote, "a more horrible sound than description can picture. It was the thud of a speeding, living body on a stone sidewalk." The final toll: 146.

The Triangle conflagration galvanized the drive for better working conditions. But it also showed how little workers' lives were worth in an age of no-holds-barred capitalism. The factory owners were acquitted of manslaughter charges. And though the families of 23 victims won a lawsuit, the judge awarded them just $75 apiece.

Conditions like those that caused the Triangle disaster (right) dramatized the need for reform. One notable labor supporter was Socialist Eugene V. Debs (above), a five-time presidential candidate who received hundreds of thousands of votes.

PHOTOFEST; RIGHT: CULVER PICTURES

In the golden age of silents, two giants meet

Charlie Chaplin and Helen Keller were among the most celebrated people in America when they met in Hollywood in 1918. Keller, who was a renowned author and lecturer, had gone west that year to appear in a movie. Blind and deaf from the age of 19 months, she had learned to speak, read and write with the help of teacher Anne Sullivan, who became her constant companion. With Sullivan's assistance Keller had graduated from Radcliffe College. Now she was traveling the continent, drawing attention to the plight of the disabled. A movie, Keller felt, would spread her message and help support her household. "As the dungeon of sense in which I once lay was broken by love and faith, so I desire to open wide all the prison-doors of the world," she wrote of her hopes for the project.

While in California, she and Sullivan dined with Chaplin, who had made his signature picture, *The Tramp,* three years earlier and had just inked a million-dollar deal for his next eight films. And what did the movie star and the Hollywood newcomers talk about? Him, mostly, and his troubled marriage to young actress Mildred Harris. Also in attendance were muckraking author Upton Sinclair and his wife, Mary Craig Kimbrough. The following day, Chaplin screened two of his films for Keller and Sullivan, who interpreted. Though unable to see his flickering image, Keller took huge pleasure in the films, proving no more immune to Chaplin's charms than millions of others.

Keller would "listen" to a speaker by placing her fingers on that person's lips and voice box, as she does here with Chaplin.

The war to end all wars

In November 1916, Woodrow Wilson was reelected on the slogan "He kept us out of war." Four months later, after German U-boats sank three U.S. ships—and intelligence agents intercepted a German telegram proposing an alliance with Mexico—Wilson committed his nation to history's first global conflict, already three years old. "The world must be made safe for democracy," the President declared. The job, leaders in Congress said, would take six weeks.

In fact, it took until November 1918. Along the way, a peacetime army of 200,000 was transformed into a fighting force nearly five million strong. At Soissons, Saint-Mihiel, Meuse-Argonne, U.S. troops helped break the war's long stalemate. Their morale crumbling, Germans revolted. The guns soon fell silent.

U.S. combat losses were relatively light—53,000 dead, compared with Europe's millions. But the doughboys had seen horrors that changed them forever. There were changes at home, too. Wartime industry had given blacks and women new opportunities and new impatience with second-class citizenship. In fact, many Americans sought new freedoms and new kinds of fun. They would find both in the 1920s.

After months in muddy trenches, a shipload of Marines (left) reach port in Hoboken, N.J. Women welcomed soldiers home (above), then set about winning the right to vote.

Henry Beck,
factory worker

**Beck (above) worked at one of the largest
woolen worsted mills in the world.**

Born in 1898, Henry Beck was just 14 when he joined his father and a cousin at Wood Mill, in Lawrence, Mass. Although his family had been weavers in Germany, they had worked at home on handlooms. An American textile plant in 1912 was a very different kind of workplace. Its air was full of choking dust and the deafening roar of machinery; employees worked 10-hour days, six days a week, for an average of 14 cents an hour. That year, 25,000 of Lawrence's mill hands staged a three-month walkout, during which two workers were killed by state militia. But with the help of a radical union called the Industrial Workers of the World, the strikers won a raise—and frightened textile manufacturers in New England into hiking wages.

Beck, a skilled machine operator, went to school part-time but progressed slowly: Although he was born in the U.S., his first language was German, and he was still struggling to make it past second grade when he started work at the plant. Then, at 18, he got lucky—and got out. "Henry had a Sunday-school teacher who knew he and his cousin were bright lads," says great-nephew Fred Arold. She helped arrange for the boys to attend nearby Mt. Hermon prep school, where they did chores to help pay their way.

Beck was drafted during his first year and served in France with the Army medical corps in World War I. But he finished at Mt. Hermon after the Armistice and went on to study medicine at Harvard and two other schools. After earning his M.D., he married his sweetheart, Annie Mae, and moved to Gray, Maine, where patients sometimes paid him in farm animals or land. He practiced there until his death in 1957.

"My husband said it was pretty noisy [in the mill] with the shuttles going back and forth, but they got used to it."

BIG BOSS MEN

In the century's first decades, most of the richest men in America made their living by making things—or rather, hiring others to make them. To build their steel mills and railroads, industrialists felled forests and leveled mountains. Today's top tycoon (and the first to break the $100 billion net-worth barrier) is software-maker Bill Gates, whose primary product is not a tangible object but a set of computer codes. The Fortune 500 is full of moguls who produce services, not goods.

But one thing hasn't changed: Big earners tend to be big givers. An early model was Scottish-born Andrew Carnegie (1835-1919), who doled out $350 million, endowing colleges, medical research and 2,800 libraries. "A man who dies rich dies disgraced," wrote the bobbin boy turned steel baron.

Gates, who has so far parted with $6.5 billion, may not die poor—but even Carnegie may have had trouble giving away all of the Microsoft Midas's fortune.

By some calculations, John D. Rockefeller (above) was the richest American ever. His Standard Oil fell victim to trust-busting in 1911. Bill Gates (right), who cofounded Microsoft at 21, has also been attacked as a monopolist.

Sally Fields (above) as a union supporter in the 1979 movie *Norma Rae.*

The nation's first modern trade unions took shape in the 1880s. But it wasn't until 1935 that the National Labor Relations Act guaranteed workers' rights to organize and to bargain collectively.

PERCENTAGE OF U.S. NONFARM WORKERS IN MANUFACTURING INDUSTRIES
1919: 39.36
1950: 33.72
1998: 14.87

PERCENTAGE OF ALL U.S. WORKERS IN LABOR UNIONS
1900: 3.3
1930: 6.8
1940: 15.7
1953: 26.9 (the peak year)
1998. 13.9

"Now, MUSH!"

"**Now, MUSH!**" Thornton's command cracked out like a pistol-shot. Buck threw himself forward, tightening the traces with a jarring lunge ... His great chest was low to the ground, his head forward and down, while his feet were flying like mad, the claws scarring the hard-packed snow in parallel grooves. The sled swayed and trembled, half-started forward. One of his feet slipped, and one man groaned aloud. Then the sled lurched ahead in what appeared a rapid succession of jerks, though it never really came to a dead stop again ... half an inch ... an inch ... two inches ...The jerks perceptibly diminished; as the sled gained momentum, he caught them up, till it was moving steadily along.

—Jack London [8, with his wife, Charmian], *The Call of the Wild,* 1903

SO FAR AS I CAN NOW RECALL, the first knowledge that I got of the fact that we were slaves, and that freedom of the slaves was being discussed, was early one morning before day, when I was awakened by my mother kneeling over her children and fervently praying that Lincoln and his armies might be successful, and that one day she and her children might be free.
Booker T. Washington [3]
Up from Slavery, 1901

WHO WILL REMEMBER, passing through this gate, /The unheroic dead who fed the guns? Who shall absolve the foulness of their fate— Those doomed, conscripted, unvictorious ones?
Siegfried Sassoon [2]
On Passing the New Menin Gate (near a WWI battle site), 1918

NO ONE WHO, LIKE ME, conjures up the most evil of those half-tamed demons that inhabit the human breast, and seeks to wrestle with them, can expect to come through the struggle unscathed.
Sigmund Freud [4]
Complete Psychological Works, 1905

ANY FOOL CAN DESTROY TREES. They cannot run away; and if they could, they would still be destroyed—chased and hunted down as long as fun or a dollar could be got out of their bark hides, branching horns, or magnificent bole backbones ...Through all the wonderful, eventful centuries since Christ's time—and long before that—God has cared for these trees, saved them from drought, disease, avalanches, and a thousand straining, leveling tempests and floods; but He cannot save them from fools—only Uncle Sam can do that.
John Muir [1]
Our National Parks, 1901

SOMETHING THERE IS that doesn't love a wall, That sends the frozen-ground-swell under it, And spills the upper boulders in the sun, And makes gaps even two can pass abreast.
Robert Frost [7]
Mending Wall, 1914

MOTION PICTURES are just a passing fancy and aren't worth comment in this newspaper.
Arthur Brisbane
Chicago Record-Herald, 1913

[T]HE MEN UPON THE FLOOR were going about their work. Neither squeals of hogs nor tears of visitors made any difference to them; one by one they hooked up the hogs, and one by one with a swift stroke they slit their throats. There was a long line of hogs, with squeals and life-blood ebbing away ... until at last each ... vanished with a splash into a huge vat of boiling water.

It was all so very businesslike that one watched it fascinated. It was pork-making by machinery, pork-making by applied mathematics.
Upton Sinclair [6]
The Jungle, 1906

IT'S THE BEST BAND IN THE LAND, They can play a bugle call like you never heard before, So natural that you want to go to war; That's just the bestest band what am, honey lamb.
Irving Berlin [5]
"Alexander's Ragtime Band," 1911

1920–1929

LIFE Radical ideas challenged the nation. Many, like the teaching of evolution, were knocked down. But the wildest notion of all, that the country's female half might have a say in its political future, actually caught on. So did bobbed hair and short skirts.

UPI/CORBIS-BETTMANN; RIGHT: BROWN BROTHERS

The Lone Eagle soars, the Bambino scores

Americans rooted wildly for Charles Lindbergh as he took off from New York, flying into a sodden dawn. Even the 40,000 raucous boxing fans who crowded into Yankee Stadium for a prizefight on May 20, 1927, were moved to stand, still and hushed, while a prayer was said for the 25-year-old aviator. On May 21, 1927, some 33 hours after he began the first solo transatlantic flight, Lucky Lindy landed at Paris's Le Bourget airfield. Despite his nickname, the slender and handsome Lindbergh actually placed his faith in meticulous preparation: The *Spirit of St. Louis* packed 451 gallons of gasoline but only five sandwiches. "If I get to Paris, I won't need any more. And if I don't get to Paris, I won't need any more, either," he explained. His heroics won him a $25,000 prize—and the adulation of the world.

Huge, homely and cheerily profane, George Herman "Babe" Ruth was as profligate as the aviator was austere. The slugger hit 60 home runs that year, pushing the Yankees to their fourth World Series title in seven years. America's heroes didn't have to be perfect, just larger than life.

At 170 pounds, Lindbergh (right, mobbed by fans in England) was called Slim. The Babe (above), at 220, was anything but.

Preceding pages: Washington, D.C., members of the National Woman's Party celebrate their new voting rights in 1920.

HEMINGWAY COLLECTION/JOHN F. KENNEDY LIBRARY; RIGHT: THE GRANGER COLLECTION

How ya gonna keep 'em down on the farm . . .

Americans who came of age during World War I were a disillusioned lot, so alienated from their parents' Victorian values that Gertrude Stein called them a "lost generation." But an influential part of that generation found themselves in Paris in the '20s. The mass migration of artists, writers and wannabes owed much to a disdain for Prohibition and provincialism, and perhaps even more to the lure of cheap steamship fares and a terrific exchange rate. "The scum of Greenwich Village, New York, has been skimmed off and deposited in large ladlesful" on the French capital, wrote Ernest Hemingway. Yet Hemingway himself was among the voluntary exiles, along with a passel of other luminaries-in-

the-making: writer F. Scott Fitzgerald, poet e.e. cummings, photographer Man Ray, sculptor Alexander Calder. These young wanderers clustered for support around a few more established expatriates, most notably Stein and poet Ezra Pound; they mingled at cafés and salons with a crowd of displaced European geniuses that included James Joyce, Pablo Picasso, Joan Miró and Marc Chagall. For all these émigrés, Paris offered an intellectual electricity that gave new meaning to the nickname City of Light.

A mustached Hemingway (left) reveled in Europe. His party at a café in Pamplona, Spain, included Lady Duff Twysden (second from left; she was the model for Lady Brett Ashley in *The Sun Also Rises*) and his first wife, Hadley. Josephine Baker (opposite), a St. Louis–bred singer and dancer, came to Paris with a musical revue—and stayed. Some African Americans found the city a refuge from the indignities of segregation; Baker herself became one of France's biggest stars.

The men who made the '20s roar

Before 1920, urban gangs were plenty nasty, but their ambitions were relatively modest: prostitution, gambling, providing hired goons for political machines. Then came Prohibition. Suddenly, millions of Americans were thirsty for an illegal substance—and organized crime became big business. Gangsters bought out breweries and hired legions of alky cookers and rumrunners. They shipped the hooch in armored trucks and hijacked those of other dealers. With tommy guns blazing, they battled for control of local markets. Instead of working for pols, they bought them (along with countless Prohibition officials) wholesale.

Bred in city slums, these poor boys made spectacularly good by doing bad. Many became national celebrities. In New York alone, there were Dutch Schultz, Jack "Legs" Diamond, Charles "Lucky" Luciano. But the capital of gangland was Chicago, and Chicago's king was Al Capone. Of the city's 400 gang hits per annum, a hefty number were traceable to Scarface Al—including the most outrageous of all, on Valentine's Day, 1929, when killers disguised as cops iced seven associates of George "Bugs" Moran. Yet Capone, who wore canary-yellow suits and rode in a seven-ton armored Cadillac, portrayed himself as a simple tradesman: "When I sell liquor, it's bootlegging. When my patrons serve it on a silver tray . . . it's hospitality."

KEYSTONE LEFT—CORBIS/BETTMANN-UPI

Legs Diamond (second from left, with brother Ed, mob bodyguard Fatty Walsh and Lucky Luciano) survived three shootings. The fourth did him in. Gangbuster J. Edgar Hoover (above) transformed a corrupt Bureau of Investigation into the "untouchable" FBI.

HANOVER

A southern organization when it was crushed by federal officials in the 1870s, the Ku Klux Klan came back nationwide five decades later. In 1925, Klan membership across the U.S. exceeded the population of Indiana, one center of KKK activity.

LAN - No. 1.

1920–1929

Hatred with a hooded face

After decades of dormancy, the Ku Klux Klan returned to stalk the land in the 1920s. The racist organization had been revived in 1915 by a Georgia preacher named William Joseph Simmons. But it attracted only a few hundred followers until 1920, when Simmons hired public relations consultant Edward Clarke to market the Invisible Empire. Clarke set up a system in which local recruiters (known as Kleagles) sold memberships, literature and regalia for a portion of the take. By 1925 they had signed up more than four million dues-paying members nationwide.

The old Klan had fed on the hostility of southern whites toward southern blacks. Now there were other hatreds to exploit, and fresh anxieties. African Americans were heading north, alarming paler folk along the way. Many smalltown whites felt threatened by Eastern European immigrants; by supporters of the Russian Revolution; by the freewheeling spirit of the Jazz Age. The new Klan added Jews, Catholics, leftists and the sexually "impure" to its enemies list. At its peak it controlled statehouses from California to Ohio. Masked Klansmen spread terror with arson, beatings and lynchings.

But murder was too much for most Klan members—as were a spate of scandals and factional feuds. By 1930 membership had shrunk to 100,000, mostly in the South. And in 1944 the Klan went back into hibernation, where it remained until the civil rights movement of the '60s promised fresh blood.

BROWN BROTHERS; RIGHT: CORBIS/BETTMANN-UPI

Prohibition goes down the drain

The century's third decade began not with a bang but with one last, lingering gulp. In January 1920, the 18th Amendment became law, banning the sale of beer, wine and liquor. Hailed as a noble experiment, Prohibition proved just the opposite: Procuring illegal refreshment became a national obsession. Bootlegging was a growth industry, sparking vicious turf wars among avaricious mobsters. The speakeasy emerged as a neighborhood institution; in New York City, it was estimated there were more than 30,000 by decade's end. At least one Virginia still owner was always glad to see law officers, who were among her best customers. "Wets" everywhere toasted Prohibition's demise in 1933.

John T. Scopes stirred up a different sort of legal storm when he defied Tennessee law by teaching the theory of evolution. His 1925 trial pitted proponents of evolution against fundamentalist Christians. Two eminent lawyers, Clarence Darrow and William Jennings Bryan, squared off in a Dayton, Tenn., courtroom. Despite Darrow's forceful defense of Darwin's theory, Scopes was found guilty and fined $100. Making monkeys of the teetotalers was permissible, but making men out of apes was not.

Federal agents (right) pour barrels of illegal booze into a Los Angeles gutter in 1920. A year earlier, Scopes (above) stood for sentencing.

The country swings to the sound of New Orleans

After the horrors of the Great War, Americans were done with marching—and ready for a new beat. They found it in the bobbing rhythms of such groups as King Oliver's Creole Jazz Band. From the sporting houses of New Orleans, jazz had wafted northward with the wartime migration of African Americans. By 1922, the year young Louis Armstrong joined Oliver's ensemble, jazz was drawing mixed-race crowds to clubs in Harlem and on Chicago's South Side. Many white musicians responded as if they had never heard music before. "Why isn't everybody in the world here to hear that?" songwriter Hoagy Carmichael wondered when he first encountered Armstrong's playing.

Jazz was more than the sound track of the era. It symbolized a way of life. Adventurous young women transformed themselves into "flappers," so dubbed for the sound made by unbuckled galoshes. Their bobbed hair, bound breasts and open interest in sex scandalized polite society. One New York preacher blamed the raw new music for promoting "nervousness, lawlessness [and] primitive and savage animalism."

ARCHIVE PHOTOS; RIGHT: COURTESY OF PAUL EDWARD MILLER

In 1923, Oliver's band (right) strikes a playful pose. Armstrong is in front on slide trumpet. A flapper (above) steps out.

Michael J. Meehan, stockbroker

The stock market frenzy of the '20s generated some eye-popping numbers: Before World War I, an estimated two million Americans owned stocks; by 1929, up to 20 million did. Reported stock volume ballooned from 160 million shares in 1925 to more than a billion in 1929. The Dow-Jones industrial average zoomed from 88 in September 1920 to nearly 400 just before the crash. But if the figures were wild, the men behind them were calm and calculating—and M. J. Meehan was among the shrewdest.

Born in Liverpool in 1892 to Irish parents who had recently left America (and would soon return), Meehan inherited a restless spirit. As a boy peddling cigars door-to-door in New York City, he impressed a Broadway ticket agent with his energy; when the man offered him a job, Meehan asked that it be in the company's Wall Street office. "Mike Meehan already knew where he was pointed," says grandson Michael Nesbit. Meehan befriended his stockbroker customers, who helped him get started on a new career in 1918 at an outdoor exchange called the Curb Market. M.J. Meehan & Co. later became one of the top brokerage firms on the New York Stock Exchange—and the first to open branches on transatlantic steamers.

One of Meehan's specialties was a stock with all the futuristic glamour that Internet start-ups hold today: the Radio Corporation of America (RCA). In those days, big investors might contract a broker to rope in thousands of small-time buyers; when the price reached a predetermined level, the insiders would sell, leaving the little guys holding the bag. Such practices helped inflate the speculative bubble that burst in 1929, and they were eventually banned. Meehan learned in 1936 that he was being investigated by the SEC, and after an 18-month retreat in a mental hospital, he was forced to retire. He died in 1948, but his firm survives—now run by his descendants.

Meehan (right) started out at an outdoor exchange where brokers wore funny hats so clerks could find them easily. It evolved into the American Stock Exchange.

"During one bear market, my grandfather let his maids and cook go. But he still went to work in a chauffeur-driven limousine."

DANCE FEVER

America kicked up its heels as never before in the '20s. Giddy with stock market winnings, bathtub gin and hot jazz, young people took up the frantic Charleston, a step that owed as much to slave dances as to European ballrooms. (One English newspaper found it "reminiscent only of negro orgies.") Pioneered by black dockworkers in Charleston, S.C., the dance reached whites via the *Ziegfeld Follies of 1923*. Another crossover craze was tap dancing. Long a staple of minstrel shows and the "colored" vaudeville circuit, tap gained a wider audience in 1921, when it was featured in *Shuffle Along*, the first of the decade's string of all-black Broadway musicals.

Like its hip-shaking cousins the black bottom and the shimmy, the Charleston incorporated expressive solo movements; that trend was taken to acrobatic heights in the lindy hop of the '30s and '40s and to spacey extremes in the rock dances of the '60s. Tap reached new levels of virtuosity with such performers as Bill "Bojangles" Robinson, the Nicholas Brothers and Fred Astaire but was eventually relegated to school talent contests and *The Lawrence Welk Show*. Toward the end of the century, however, the form enjoyed a renaissance, culminating in the '90s with the edgy avant-tap of Savion Glover's *Bring in 'da Noise, Bring in 'da Funk*.

Robinson (top right) in the '20s and Glover (bottom right) in the '90s updated a form rooted in slave dances and Irish jigs.

In the '20s it seemed that every taxi driver had a stock tip to share. Newspapers ran breathless stories about the riches ordinary folks were reaping on Wall Street; in the early months of 1928, according to one article, there were 300 new millionaires. Dealers in luxury cars and antiques prospered, as did owners of nightclubs and theaters. Then it all collapsed. Some brokers, like Michael Meehan, got out with their shirts; others wound up selling apples. (Contrary to legend, however, few leaped from windows.) Although the Depression ended in 1941, it took until 1954 for the market to return to precrash levels.

HIGHEST PRICE OF A SEAT ON THE NEW YORK STOCK EXCHANGE
1900: $ 47,500
1929: $ 625,000
1950: $ 54,000
1999: $2,600,000

DAILY AVERAGE VOLUME OF SHARES TRADED ON THE NYSE
1900: 505,000
1929: 4,300,000
1950: 2,000,000
1998: 637,590,000

VALUE OF $40 INVESTMENT IN ONE SHARE OF COCA-COLA AT ORIGINAL ISSUE
1919: $ 40
1929: $ 472
1950: $ 4,822
1998: $6,674,302

1930–1939

LIFE Shock waves from Wall Street threw bankers and factory hands out of work, farmers off their land and families onto breadlines. For this desperate decade, the theme song was "Brother, Can You Spare a Dime?"

The height of modern elegance

It began with a bet. Two giants of the automobile industry, John Jakob Raskob of General Motors and Walter Chrysler, dared each other to dominate New York City's skyline with the bigger building. Chrysler's was finished first, in 1930, and for a few months was the tallest building on earth. It was also among the most elegant examples of art deco, which, with its clean lines and geometric representation of nature, epitomized modernism. In 1931, Chrysler was bested by Raskob's 1,250-foot, 102-floor Empire State Building—a milestone in vertical engineering and the pinnacle of the deco style. Although architect William Lamb had been instructed only to make a building that resembled a pencil, the Empire State embodied the machine age even as it recalled Aztec pyramids. All 10 million bricks were stacked up in just over a year. Until 1970 it remained the world's tallest structure, weathering a plane crash and the cinematic ravages of a giant ape. Then the World Trade Center's twin towers opened at 1,368 feet. In 1973 all were topped by Chicago's Sears Tower, still the biggest in America at 1,454 feet.

ROB ATMIN IS THE IMAGE BANK; LEFT: LEWIS HINE/AVERY LIBRARY/COLUMBIA UNIVERSITY

Undaunted by altitude, Empire State builders (left) averaged two stories per week. Fifteen blocks north, a mosaic (above) added to Rockefeller Center's art deco ambiance.

Preceding pages: A Wisconsin farm family prays for rain (1936). Across much of America, drought added to the Depression's woes.

On *Kristallnacht,* Nazis destroyed 7,500 shops (above) and 177 synagogues nationwide and killed 91 Jews. Blaming the victims for the damage, authorities sent 30,000 to concentration camps. Albert Einstein (right, with British Prime Minister Winston Churchill) fled Germany in 1933—first to England, then to Princeton, N.J.

Fleeing the Führer

It began in 1933, within weeks of Adolf Hitler's ascension to power. First came boycotts and vandalism of Jewish businesses. In 1935 the Nuremberg Laws stripped Jews of their citizenship, the right to marry gentiles, even the right to frequent public parks. After the 1938 pogrom known as *Kristallnacht* ("night of broken glass"), the concentration camps began to fill with "non-Aryans"—and the killing began in earnest. Then, in 1939, Hitler invaded Poland, sparking World War II and exporting genocide beyond his own borders.

Among the 104,000 Jewish refugees who were permitted to enter the U.S. between 1933 and 1941 were some of the brightest cultural and intellectual lights of the century. Composers Kurt Weill and Arnold Schoenberg enriched American music. Hollywood snagged directors Billy Wilder, Fritz Lang, Otto Preminger and Ernst Lubitsch. The social sciences got Hannah Arendt and Bruno Bettelheim. But it was in physics that the haul was richest. Albert Einstein, Leo Szilard, Edward Teller—without such geniuses, there would have been no U.S. atomic bomb. In one of history's great ironies, Hitler's hatred furnished his enemies with the key to ultimate victory.

America tunes in

Except for their setting (New Jersey), *The War of the Worlds* and the *Hindenburg* disaster had little in common. But the fictional Martian invasion of October 1938 and the actual dirigible explosion of May 1937 were seared into America's consciousness by the same medium—one that shaped the years before World War II as surely as TV did the years after.

Radio's grip on the popular imagination matched that of the movies: When *Amos 'n' Andy* came on, many theaters shut off their projectors and piped in the 15-minute show. Across the country, families gathered to laugh at Fred Allen or ventriloquist Edgar Bergen and his dummy, Charlie McCarthy. Radio linked the living room to the real world, too. Millions experienced the *Hindenburg* tragedy through Herbert Morrison's commentary, which climaxed with an anguished "Oh, the humanity!"

Radio's surpassing power was to create pictures in people's minds. When Orson Welles presented *The War of the Worlds*, many *saw* the slimy invaders—and took his simulated news bulletins for the real thing. Highways were clogged with refugees. Police stations were swamped with calls. Analyzing the panic, one social scientist surmised: "All the intelligent people were listening to Charlie McCarthy."

OPPENHEIM & SINGER SERVICE; LEFT: CORBIS

The hydrogen-filled *Hindenburg* (left) exploded over Lakehurst, N.J., killing 36. Welles (above) was only 23 when his *War of the Worlds* panicked thousands.

METROPOLITAN OPERA'S BALLET

DECEMBER 28, 1936 **10** CENTS

Miracles of the media age

Before the era of fertility drugs and septuplets, five baby girls were able to stun modern science simply by surviving. In five centuries of recorded medicine, the Dionne sisters, born May 28, 1934, were the only quintuplets to live longer than an hour. By age three, wrote *Time* magazine, they had moved from "biological sideshow freaks into a more normal human status." That is, if you call it normal to be put on public display by one's parents. Oliva and Elzire Dionne, farmers in Ontario, let half a million visitors a year gawk at their girls, and by doing so built them a trust fund of nearly a million dollars.

While the Dionnes' seven other children went unnoticed, the "Quins" were a media magnet. At age six they were featured in a magazine whose medium—photography— offered a new way to see the world, whether wars or everyday life or multiple births. LIFE, the weekly picture magazine that debuted on November 23, 1936, had 235,000 subscribers before the first issue even hit the stands. Its runaway success caused one harried executive to grouse that "having LIFE isn't like having a baby. It's like having quintuplets."

Thank heaven for little girls: LIFE could count on Cécile, Annette, Marie, Yvonne and Emilie to boost sales. But the magazine liked pretty girls of all ages (above).

FPG INTL.; OPPOSITE: CORBIS/BETTMANN-UPI

A master athlete takes on the master race

Adolf Hitler had boasted that the 1936 Berlin Olympics would prove the superiority of the Nordic "master race" and the inferiority of all others. The only hitch turned out to be the U.S. team, which included 10 African American athletes. Nazi propaganda minister Joseph Goebbels dismissed them as "black auxiliaries," but they won 13 medals, eight of them gold. And the winningest competitor of all was an Alabama sharecropper's son named Jesse Owens.

Owens made his debut at the Games by tying an Olympic record in the 100-meter dash; he set a new one in the 200. In the long jump he established another record; when German champion Luz Long matched it, Owens came back and leaped even farther—twice. The Ohio State student earned his fourth piece of gold as part of America's record-breaking 400-meter relay squad, and finished with one of the highest medal totals in Olympic track-and-field history.

To Owens's relief, he never had to shake Hitler's hand. (Although U.S. newspapers accused Hitler of snubbing Owens, the Führer had in fact stopped greeting any winners early on.) But Hitler had to watch as Long, a classic Aryan blond, strolled the field with his arm draped across Owens's shoulders. The irate dictator didn't stay to see the victor crowned with laurels. "That's a grand feeling, standing up there," Owens later told reporters. Ideology aside, many Germans felt grand watching him: He received a thunderous ovation.

Owens (above, right) got a hero's welcome when he returned home, but he still couldn't ride at the front of a bus in several states. Hitler (opposite) greets his fans at Berlin's Olympic Stadium.

CECIL BEATON/VOGUE, CONDÉ NAST PUBLICATIONS INC.; LEFT: MPTV

A plantation and an abdication

The stock market crash of 1929 pushed joblessness as high as 25 percent in the 1930s. But even on painfully pinched budgets, more and more people—90 million per week in 1930— went to the movies. (An average week in 1990? Only 22 million.) Grim reality vanished when Fred and Ginger twirled or Shirley Temple sparkled. The decade closed with a Civil War epic based on the best-selling 1936 novel *Gone with the Wind.* In it, heroine Scarlett O'Hara marries three times, but never for love.

As Margaret Mitchell's book climbed the charts, a real-life romance grabbed headlines. Britain's new king, Edward VIII, had fallen crowned head over heels for married American Wallis Simpson. After the Baltimore socialite filed for divorce, her new beau revealed their plans to wed. But he did not have the support of Parliament, the Church of England or even his own family. On December 11, 1936, Edward abdicated, finding it "impossible to . . . discharge my duties as king as I would wish to do without the help and support of the woman I love." Sometimes reality beats fantasy.

Gone with the Wind **producer David O. Selznick (far left) shocked fans of the book by casting a British actress, Vivian Leigh, as Scarlett. Edward (above, with Simpson at their 1937 wedding) encountered more serious resistance when he tried to cast a divorced American as his queen.**

Charles Woodruff, farmer

It was the era of the Dust Bowl, when drought and soil mismanagement turned 150,000 square miles of America's breadbasket into a wasteland, and refugees fled west in rusty flivvers. But Woodruff, profiled in LIFE in 1937, farmed in Iowa, where the fields were (in the magazine's words) "as fat and fertile as the firm-kerneled corn and great-bellied hogs they nourish." He was lucky in other ways, too. Although the phrase "tenant farmer" conjures images of sharecroppers' shacks, Woodruff rented his 271 acres from an uncommonly generous landowner.

Howard Roach, scion of the big farm-management company J. Roach & Sons, shared operating costs and profits with Woodruff, 50-50. What's more, Roach gave his tenant a leg up. Woodruff had been struggling to support his wife, two children and a hired man when Roach bought him one of the area's first combines. "Charlie said, 'My God, Howard, I can't pay for that,'" recalls Roach's son Richard. Roach told Woodruff to use the machine to do jobs for other farmers; Woodruff could reimburse him with the fees. "Charlie raised enough that first fall to pay for the combine," says Richard, "and from then on things started to go better for him."

By the late '30s, Woodruff was on the cutting edge of agriculture. His farm, LIFE reported, "is very nearly as mechanized as a factory." To tend his cows and crops, Woodruff used a milking machine, a tractor and a dozen specialized gadgets. Still, he lived a traditional rural life. "He worked from daylight to dark," says Woodruff's son, Lowell. The family grew its own food; for fun there was fishing and, for the women, quilting bees. In 1941 (again with Roach's help), Woodruff bought his own spread. But he gave up farming in 1957 and—closing the circle—rented out his land. After five years as a handyman for Roach, Woodruff retired; he died in 1980.

At midday dinner, Woodruff (above, center) and his threshing crew enjoy roast beef from one of the farm's cows, served with homegrown vegetables. His wife, Blanche, and daughter, Mildred (standing), did the cooking and baking.

"My dad milked a lot of cows, raised a lot of hogs. Of course, it was seven days a week. But he loved being a farmer."

GROWING THE WEED

To Native Americans, tobacco was a sacrament. When European explorers brought it home, enthusiasts touted it as a cure-all. (Nicotine was named in honor of Jean Nicot, who used tobacco extract to treat the ailing stomach of France's Catherine de Médicis.) But for U.S. farmers, tobacco has long been something else: a major source of cash. The golden age began at the turn of the century, when machine-rolled cigarettes debuted. Annual consumption rose from 54 cigarettes per person in 1900 to 4,354 in 1963. The next year, the Surgeon General linked smoking to cancer, and the industry entered a decline. Today tobacco's best hope may lie, once again, in medicine: Scientists believe the plant can be genetically engineered to produce pharmaceuticals—including, ironically, anticancer drugs.

According to a recent Nationwide survey:

MORE DOCTORS SMOKE CAMELS THAN ANY OTHER CIGARETTE

● Like the rest of us, doctors smoke for pleasure. Their taste recognizes and appreciates full flavor and cool mildness just as yours does.

And when 113,597 doctors were asked to name the cigarette they smoked, more doctors named Camels than any other brand.

Three nationally known independent research organizations conducted the survey. They queried doctors in every branch of medicine.

R. J. Reynolds Tobacco Co., Winston-Salem, North Carolina

Your "T-Zone" will tell you

T for Taste...
T for Throat...

● Taste and Throat...your "T-Zone" ...that's your proving ground for any cigarette.

See how your own critical taste responds to the rich, full flavor of Camel's choice tobaccos. Tobaccos of uncompromising quality...tobaccos blended in the fine, traditional Camel way.

See how your throat reacts to the cool mildness of Camels.

See if Camels don't suit your "T-Zone" to a "T."

In 1915, less than 1 percent of U.S. farms used tractors. Then, in 1918, Ford began mass-producing the Fordson, and a revolution was launched. At first it seemed entirely benign: Farmers no longer had to reserve land for draft-animal feed; productivity soared. But crop surpluses brought low crop prices. To pay off equipment loans, farmers had to grow still more, which lowered prices further. Chemical fertilizers and pesticides helped some stay ahead of the game, but family farms increasingly gave way to giant agribusinesses.

PERCENTAGE OF AMERICAN POPULATION LIVING IN RURAL AREAS
1900: 60
1950: 36
1990: 25

PERCENTAGE OF AMERICAN LABOR FORCE WORKING ON FARMS
1910: 32
1950: 12.2
1998: 2.6

PER CAPITA ADULT CONSUMPTION OF CIGARETTES (IN POUNDS)
1900: less than .5
1950: 9.5
1997: 4.1

This great nation will endure as it has endured, will revive and will prosper. So, first of all, let me assert my firm belief that the only thing we have to fear is fear itself—nameless, unreasoning, unjustified terror which paralyzes needed efforts to convert retreat into advance.—Franklin D. Roosevelt [6], first inaugural address, 1933

GRACIE: ON MY WAY IN, a man stopped me at the stage door and said, "Hiya, cutie, how about a bite tonight after the show?"
George: And you said?
Gracie: I said, "I'll be busy after the show but I'm not doing anything now," so I bit him.
George: Gracie, let me ask you something. Did the nurse ever happen to drop you on your head when you were a baby?
Gracie: Oh, no, we couldn't afford a nurse, my mother had to do it.
George Burns and Gracie Allen [5]
Vaudeville routine

KANSAS FARMS ARE BLOWING through Nebraska at an accelerating rate. In the spring of 1934, the farms of the Dust Bowl . . . blew clear out to the Atlantic Ocean, 2,000 miles away. On a single day 300 million tons of rich top soil was lifted from the Great Plains, never to return, and planted in places where it would spread the maximum of damage and discomfort.
Stuart Chase
Rich Land, Poor Land, 1936

PROHIBITION IS AN awful flop.
We like it.
It can't stop what it's meant to stop.
We like it.
It's left a trail of graft and slime,
It's filled our land with vice and crime,
It don't prohibit worth a dime,
Nevertheless, we're for it.
Franklin P. Adams [3, with his wife, Esther]
New York World, 1931, satirizing a commission report that said both that Prohibition was unworkable and that it should continue

GATSBY'S BUTLER WAS suddenly standing beside us.
"Miss Baker?" he inquired. "I beg your pardon, but Mr. Gatsby would like to speak to you alone."
"With me?" she exclaimed in surprise.
"Yes, madame."
She got up slowly, raising her eyebrows at me in astonishment, and followed the butler toward the house. I noticed that she wore her evening-dress, all her dresses, like sports clothes—there was a jauntiness about her movements as if she had first learned to walk upon golf courses on clean, crisp mornings.
F. Scott Fitzgerald [1, with his wife, Zelda]
The Great Gatsby, 1925

ON THE EVENING of the first of March, 1932, an event took place which instantly thrust everything else, even the grim processes of Depression, into the background of American thought—and which seemed to many observers to epitomize cruelly the demoralization into which the country had fallen. The baby son of Colonel and Mrs. Charles A. Lindbergh was kidnapped—taken out of his bed in a second-story room of the new house at Hopewell, New Jersey, never to be seen again alive.
Frederick Lewis Allen
Since Yesterday, 1939

FANS, FOR THE PAST TWO WEEKS, you have been reading about a bad break I got. Yet, today I consider myself the luckiest man on the face of the earth. I have been in ballparks for 17 years, and I have never received anything but kindness and encouragement from you fans.
Lou Gehrig [4]
Bidding farewell to New York Yankee fans after illness forced his retirement, 1939

ART. II. THE OFFICERS . . . shall consist of a Grand Wizard of the Empire and his ten Genii; a Grand Dragon of the Realm and his eight Hydras; a Grand Titan of the Dominion and his six Furies; a Grand Giant of the Province and his four Goblins; a Grand Cyclops of the Den and his two Night Hawks; a Grand Magi, a Grand Monk, a Grand Exchequer, a Grand Turk, a Grand Scribe, a Grand Sentinel, and a Grand Ensign.
Ku Klux Klan Constitution

WITH THE SPIRIT of her people who would not know defeat, even when it stared them in the face, she raised her chin. She could get Rhett back. She knew she could. There had never been a man she couldn't get, once she set her mind upon him.
"I'll think of it all tomorrow, at Tara. I can stand it then. Tomorrow, I'll think of some way to get him back. After all, tomorrow is another day."
Margaret Mitchell [2]
Gone with the Wind, 1936

EDNA'S CASE WAS REALLY a pathetic one. Like every woman, her primary ambition was to marry. Most of the girls of her set were married—or about to be. Yet not one possessed more grace or charm or loveliness than she.
And as her birthdays crept gradually toward that tragic thirty mark, marriage seemed farther from her life than ever.
She was often a bridesmaid but never a bride.
Listerine Mouthwash advertisement, 1925

ONCE I BUILT a railroad, I made it run,
Made it race against time.
Once I built a railroad, now it's done—
Brother, can you spare a dime?
E.Y. Harburg and Jay Gorney
"Brother, Can You Spare a Dime?" 1932

1940–1949

LIFE The first half of the decade was soaked in blood.
Then, in a blinding flash, mankind's deadliest weapon
put an end to history's most terrible conflict. America
emerged a superpower, and the cold war began.

"This is no drill"

By 1941, war with Japan was considered inevitable. Even so, when Japanese bombers raided U.S. bases at Pearl Harbor in Hawaii, the December 7 attack was so unexpected that it was at first believed to be a drill. "I didn't even know they were sore at us," cried one sailor aboard the USS *Monaghan*. The toll was staggering: 21 ships damaged or sunk, 2,388 people killed. Nearly half the dead remain entombed inside the *Arizona* to this day.

News of the assault came via radio report, interrupting football games and concerts, and moving people to declare themselves ready to fight. "I want to beat them Japs with my own bare hands," said the first man to line up at a recruiting station in Norfolk, Va. On December 8, President Roosevelt asked Congress to vote on a declaration of war and received almost unanimous support. (The lone dissenter was Montana Rep. Jeannette Rankin, who had also voted against entering World War I.) Roosevelt labeled December 7 "a date which will live in infamy." But, he vowed, "we will gain the inevitable triumph—so help us God." Said Montana Sen. Burton Wheeler: "The only thing now is to do our best to lick hell out of them."

The USS *Arizona* (right) explodes after a bomb strikes its magazine. The advent of war precipitated many goodbyes (above).

BROWN BROTHERS; OPPOSITE: U.S. COAST GUARD

Delivered by a Coast Guard landing craft (above), GIs head for the beach—and withering German fire. A similar vessel (opposite) bears away the wounded.

Turning the tide on Normandy's beaches

As the troops crossed the Channel to Normandy, their officers recited the Order of the Day from Gen. Dwight D. Eisenhower. "You are about to embark on a great crusade," the statement read. "You will bring about the destruction of the German war machine, the elimination of Nazi tyranny over the oppressed peoples of Europe, and security for ourselves in a free world." Operation Overlord began before dawn on June 6, 1944. By the time D-Day was over, 132,000 Allied soldiers—American, British and Canadian—were standing on French soil.

The largest seaborne invasion in history, the Normandy landing marshaled 1,200 ships, 4,000 landing craft and 11,600 airplanes. Paratroopers hit first. Warships and bombers pummeled enemy positions. Then the infantry swarmed onto beaches code-named Gold, Juno, Omaha, Sword and Utah. Thanks partly to ingenious diversionary tactics (squadrons of phony tanks; sound effects faking a battle elsewhere), the Germans were caught off guard. Only at Omaha did they put up strong resistance, raining fire on U.S. soldiers from cliff-top bunkers. Ten thousand died—some drowned by their heavy backpacks as they waded toward shore—but Hitler's "fortress Europe" had been breached. With Soviet forces closing in from the east, the Nazis were on the defensive. Still, it would take another year for the great crusade to triumph.

"Swoonatra" sets young hearts aflutter

"Baffling," declared *Newsweek* in 1943. "He is undersized and looks underfed—but the slightest suggestion of his smile brings squeals of agonized rapture from his adolescent adorers." One psychiatrist theorized that it was the wartime absence of young men that made this stateside singer (4-F because of a punctured eardrum) the object of so much affection.

But girls know what they like. They didn't see the jug-eared, 138-pound beanpole that male journalists picked on. They saw Frank Sinatra's blue eyes and the way he delivered a song—making each one of them believe he sang to her alone. And when the kid from Hoboken debuted as a solo artist in 1942 (he had previously sung with the Tommy Dorsey Orchestra), his core fans, 12-to-16-year-olds dubbed "the bobby socks brigade," responded in kind. They lined up overnight on sidewalks, defying city curfews to ensure a seat at his shows. They wore blue polka-dot bow ties just like Frankie's. They saved his cigarette butts as holy relics. "Not since the days of Rudolph Valentino has American womanhood made such unabashed public love to an entertainer," noted *Time*.

It wouldn't be the last time, though. By the 1960s, Sinatra—perhaps wistful for the hysteria that once surrounded him—complained that too few deejays were "brave enough to give me equal time in Beatleland."

A pack of bobby-soxers swarm Sinatra (left) at a 1943 radio show in New York. Bobby socks (above) were a fashion must for teens during the '40s.

MARGARET BOURKE-WHITE; OPPOSITE: ARCHIVE PHOTOS

At home, new opportunities and new restraints

"We are a kindly, sentimental people about what women should or should not do," claimed *Fortune* magazine in 1943. "Many thoughtful citizens are seriously disturbed over the wisdom of bringing married women into the factories." But with a workforce drained of men, America desperately needed able hands and minds. Wisdom prevailed, encouraged by government propaganda assuring women that operating a drill press could be feminine. By 1945, when women made up 36 percent of civilian workers, the female labor force had grown by half in just five years.

While wartime America suspended its stereotypes about what work suited women, prejudice against Americans of Japanese descent intensified. In 1942, President Roosevelt ordered ethnic Japanese into 10 "relocation" camps in the western states. Many internees were U.S. citizens—some were veterans of World War I. Now they were prisoners, though no charges were ever brought against any of the 110,000 people who were rounded up. Property, farms, jobs and, most of all, a sense of belonging were lost during the three years that families spent in the camps. At war's end, the interned Japanese were released to begin rebuilding their lives. The women who had proved themselves in the workforce were also sent home, in order to create jobs for men returning from battle.

Japanese Americans were tagged (opposite, in Hayward, Calif.) and shipped to internment camps. In a Gary, Ind., factory (above), women welded steel plates for use on tanks.

DEFENSE DEPT.; LEFT: CULVER PICTURES

Islands of agony

For months after Pearl Harbor, Allied forces in the Pacific suffered disaster upon disaster. The Japanese conquered Hong Kong, Singapore and a string of islands stretching nearly to Hawaii. On Bataan and Corregidor, MacArthur's starving troops surrendered, only to die by the thousands on a forced march to prison camps. But in June 1942, U.S. planes and ships won the Battle of Midway, sinking four of Japan's biggest aircraft carriers. With that victory began the long campaign to roll back the Empire of the Rising Sun.

It was a grueling, inch-by-inch struggle. So many ships went down off Guadalcanal that one stretch of water was nicknamed Iron Bottom Bay. In New Guinea's jungles, soldiers were plagued by leeches, malaria and skin ulcers. From Saipan to Guam to Tarawa, corpses littered tropical beaches. When cornered, the Japanese launched terrifying banzai charges—suicide attacks with bayonets and clubs. At sea, kamikaze pilots used their planes as bombs. Under such conditions, one Marine recalled, "the veneer of civilization wore pretty thin." If the enemy would rather die than be captured, many GIs were happy to oblige.

By late 1944, MacArthur had retaken the Philippines; by spring 1945, Iwo Jima and Okinawa were in American hands. But the Japanese held on to their will to fight— until it was shattered by the power of the unleashed atom.

U.S. Marines (left) recharge aboard a transport ship after the battle of Eniwetok Atoll in 1945. The fight for Betio Island (above) in 1943 was among the fiercest of the Pacific war.

FPG INTL; RIGHT: WILLIAM VANDIVERT

A concentration camp prisoner stares blankly at his liberators. U.S. troops (right) stand amid the smoking embers of a barn in Gardelegen where 1,016 prisoners were burned alive by the German SS.

Face-to-face with the unthinkable

Adolf Hitler had long proclaimed his intention of making Europe "Jew free." But it was only as the advancing Allied armies liberated the concentration camps scattered across Germany and Eastern Europe in 1945 that the world learned the full extent—and confronted the horror—of the Nazis' systematic genocide. At Dachau, Auschwitz and dozens of other man-made hells, the smell came first, then the sight of emaciated corpses stacked like cordwood. Among the dead were living skeletons, many too weak to greet their rescuers. Gen. George S. Patton vomited. Battle-toughened GIs wept. Some took quick revenge on captured SS guards; others handed their pistols to freed prisoners. Sgt. Fred Friendly, later a pioneering TV news producer, wrote his mother, "Your son saw this with his own eyes and . . . aged 10 years."

More than six million Jews and millions of non-Jewish "undesirables"—leftists, Gypsies, homosexuals, Jehovah's Witnesses and others—perished in the camps' gas chambers, starved or were worked to death. A half century later, their shadow still haunts the world. "I never could dance about my liberation," said one former prisoner. "Not then and not now. I was numb. I just couldn't put all that suffering aside."

FDR's last journey

It seemed as if he had been President forever. Elected to an unprecedented four terms, Franklin Delano Roosevelt led his nation through the abyss of the Depression and the inferno of World War II. With fireside chats and an alphabet soup of social-welfare programs, he made millions of struggling Americans feel they had a friend in the White House. He carried his burdens ebulliently, despite the polio that had crippled him. Now he was poised to defeat Hitler. But on April 12, 1945, as Roosevelt signed documents at his retreat in Warm Springs, Ga., his strength gave out at last. "I have a terrific headache," he muttered, then slumped in his seat. Two hours later, FDR was dead.

His remains were loaded into a railroad car, on a platform that allowed the casket to be seen through the window. Crowds lined the tracks, weeping and singing hymns, as the train crept northward. The first stop was Washington, where an Episcopalian bishop, leading a memorial service at the executive mansion, quoted Roosevelt's first inaugural: "The only thing we have to fear is fear itself." Then the journey resumed. FDR's escorts included his wife, Eleanor, and two of his children (three sons were in uniform overseas); his dog, Fala; old friends, cabinet members, Supreme Court justices, 18 reporters and the new President, Harry S Truman. The train passed through Philadelphia and Manhattan, and reached Hyde Park, N.Y., on April 15. There Roosevelt was laid to rest in the rose garden of his boyhood home.

EDWARD CLARK; LEFT: UPI/CORBIS-BETTMANN

FDR's casket (left) is lifted onto the train in Washington, D.C. Chief Petty Officer Graham Jackson (above), who had often entertained the President in Georgia, plays "Going Home."

When the guns stopped

In the early weeks of 1945, as German forces were retreating, the Allies pressed them on two fronts. Nazi Propaganda Minister Goebbels rejoiced over the death of President Roosevelt, saying: "It is written in the stars that the second half of April will be the turning point for us." But the next day, Soviet troops seized Vienna. Soon American soldiers caught sight of the Russians along the Elbe River. The two armies approached each other warily—then broke out the beer and vodka and began waltzing. By month's end, Adolf Hitler had committed suicide. America's new Commander in Chief, Harry Truman, had the pleasure of declaring the war in Europe over on May 8—his 61st birthday.

Meanwhile, scientists had offered the President a new weapon: the atomic bomb. Advised that Japan appeared willing to fight indefinitely, he ordered the bomb dropped on Hiroshima. The August 6 blast killed 80,000 instantly; more than 100,000 would die from radiation. A second bomb at Nagasaki three days later killed 40,000. Truman promised "a rain of ruin" if Japan did not surrender. On August 14 the U.S. celebrated the long-sought peace. But the national mood shifted once again. As the U.S. watched Soviet-held territories fall to communism, the former dancing partners were on a path toward cold war.

U.S. and Soviet troops, anticipating victory, cut a rug at Cobblesdorf (right). At Pearl Harbor (above), sailors cheered Japan's defeat.

A woman of the world

When her husband was stricken with polio in 1921, she encouraged his political aspirations. As First Lady, she was his second set of legs and eyes, traveling the country to view New Deal projects and overseas on morale-boosting visits to U.S. troops. Eleanor Roosevelt garnered the admiration of a generation of women for revamping the role of White House wife: She held her own press conferences, attended by an all-female press corps. After Franklin D. Roosevelt died in April 1945, she might have left public life. Instead she became known as the First Lady of the World.

She earned the title at the United Nations, whose charter had been signed by 50 countries just months after the President's death. Mrs. Roosevelt seemed a natural choice for President Truman to send to the first General Assembly in December 1946. The future delegate—whose grace was grounded in strength, decency and modesty—did not agree; she needed to be persuaded by her children.

When FDR was President, "I was after all a private citizen," she said in 1947, "and for that reason I was freer than I am now." Though she may have compromised her own personal freedom, she passionately championed it for others, as when she challenged the Soviet Union's contention that there should be limits on liberty. It was the job of the U.N., she countered, to "consider first the rights of man . . . consider what makes man more free: not governments but man." In 1948 she helped draft the U.N.'s Declaration of Human Rights. Throughout her six-year tenure, Roosevelt remained as popular as ever, causing occasional speculation that the former First Lady might run for office. She did not but is still a role model for others who may.

In 1947, Roosevelt attended the second U.N. session with "a sincere desire to understand the problems of the rest of the world and . . . a real goodwill for all the peoples."

Go, Jackie, go!

Even if he hadn't opened modern big league baseball to African Americans, Jackie Robinson, the grandson of a slave, would still be remembered. He was too athletically gifted, too electrifying on the field and too poised off it to ever fade into anonymity. And in 1947, after he had been tapped by Brooklyn Dodgers general manager Branch Rickey to break baseball's color barrier, nearly every eye in the country was on him.

The pressures on the 28-year-old rookie were intense: Bigoted white players screamed skin-peeling racial epithets; opposing pitchers gunned for him; on road trips, some hotels barred him. Yet Robinson kept his cool and his brash onfield style (he batted .297, topped the league in stolen bases, was second in runs scored) while propelling the Dodgers to a pennant. Although his team lost the World Series to the Yankees, the Rookie of the Year had won something far more enduring. Said Rev. Jesse Jackson at Robinson's funeral in 1972: "Jackie as a figure in history was a rock in the water, creating concentric circles and ripples of new possibility."

By 1949, Robinson (here attempting to steal third base against St. Louis) was no longer the only black player in the majors but was still as fierce a competitor as ever.

Every house in Levittown (above, in 1949) sat on a 60-by-100-foot lot. As the suburbs swelled, so did the car culture; drive-in theaters (like the one opposite, in Los Angeles) multiplied from 743 in 1948 to 6,000 in 1961, their high point.

Crabgrass, station wagons and backyard barbecues

After years of privation, it was time for a boom—or maybe two. Returning vets kicked off both the greatest economic expansion and the biggest population explosion in the nation's history. In 1946 there were 3.4 million babies born in the U.S., a 13 percent jump over 1945; the number peaked at 4.3 million in 1957 and hovered in the ozone for seven more years. Where to put all those growing families? William Levitt came up with the answer: the two-bedroom equivalent of a Model T. His vision took root in 1947 in a Long Island potato field, and so began the suburbanization of America.

Levittown was a marvel of mass production. Each unit was assembled with prefabricated parts by specialized crews—one for white paint, one for red. The average contractor built four houses a year; Levitt churned out 36 a day, in five basic models. Prices started at $7,990. With the help of GI Bill loans, hordes of would-be Ozzies and Harriets could afford a home of their own.

As such developments spread across the country, critics assailed them as hotbeds of conformity, where the people were as soulless as the "ticky tacky" houses. But to residents, those dwellings were a piece of the American dream—even if they were a bit cramped. Levitt touted his creation as a cold war secret weapon: "No man who owns his own house and lot can be a communist. He has too much to do."

Art, in angles and drips

Before the war, Jackson Pollock was struggling for attention. But by 1949 his work was in five museums and selling well to collectors, though some critics still found his paintings as "unpalatable as yesterday's macaroni." Love him or hate him, Pollock and the abstract expressionism movement—which included Willem de Kooning and Robert Motherwell—wrested art away from representationalism. In Pollock's hands this meant dripping and spattering paint to imbue a canvas with tangible energy and rhythm.

Like Pollock, Martha Graham devised "an original way of communication," noted fellow dancer-choreographer Agnes de Mille. Years earlier, Graham had freed movement from the constraints of classical ballet and, in doing so, coined a new dance vocabulary. Hitting her stride in the '40s and '50s, she used her body as an emotional lightning rod to tell the stories of Medea, Joan of Arc, Clytemnestra and Emily Dickinson. Her school, founded to pass on her unorthodox ideas, today gives students a foundation in what is now mainstream modern dance. It remains true to Graham's philosophy: "Out of emotion, comes form."

MARTHA HOLMES; LEFT: GJON MILI

Martha Graham (left) said she wanted to "dance like that" after seeing a canvas by Wassily Kandinsky, a forebear of the abstract expressionists. For Pollock (above), paint was as much about movement as dance was.

LIFE For some, postwar America was the happiest place on earth: Suburbia expanded like a La-Z-Boy in front of a new TV. Still, there was trouble in paradise. Red hunts and fallout shelters betrayed the era's anxieties.

1950–1959

A no-win war

The cold war turned piping hot in June 1950 when communist North Korea invaded South Korea. President Truman sent in U.S. troops, and the U.N. backed him with a multinational force. Led by Gen. Douglas MacArthur, the "police action" wilted at first before the North Korean onslaught. But in September U.N. forces counterattacked at Inchon and pushed the Reds back across the 38th parallel.

Then things got crazy. Truman authorized MacArthur to invade North Korea. His troops made it almost to the Chinese border before they were routed by Mao Zedong's army. MacArthur publicly blasted Truman for refusing to bomb China—and when Truman fired him, Republicans howled for impeachment. (Senator Nixon accused the President of pandering to "the communists and their stooges.") The GOP swept the next election, putting a general named Eisenhower in the White House. By the time the war ended in 1953, some 54,000 Americans had died. And neither side had gained an inch of land.

In North Korea, Marines (right) fought Chinese troops and subzero temperatures. Two years after the war ended, U.S. troops still in South Korea (above) got a visit from Marilyn Monroe.

Preceding pages: On opening day, in 1955, Disneyland had 20,000 paying customers.

GEORGE ZENO COLLECTION; RIGHT: DAVID DOUGLAS DUNCAN

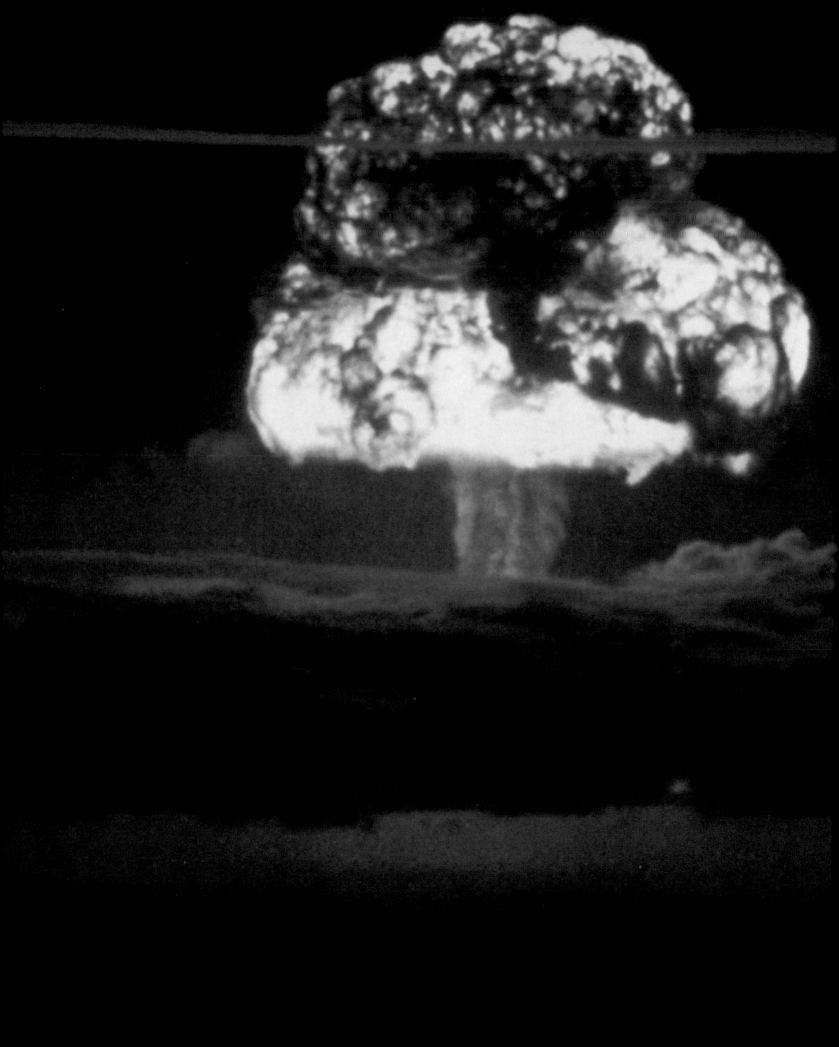

WALTER SANDERS; LEFT: U.S. NAVY

Life under the mushroom cloud

"I cannot tell you when or where the attack will come—or that it will come at all. I can only remind you that we must be ready when it does come." With that statement, President Truman ushered in the age of paranoia as defense policy. Four years after Hiroshima and Nagasaki, the Soviets also had atomic weapons. Truman raised the stakes in 1952 by testing hydrogen bombs with the force of 10 million tons of TNT. (The Hiroshima bomb had the equivalent of 15,000 tons.) Within 10 months, the U.S.S.R. added the H-bomb to its arsenal as well. Albert Einstein, whose research had led to the A-bomb, warned that "annihilation of all life on earth" was now possible. Paranoia thrived in domestic policy too, fueled by such skilled practitioners as Wisconsin's junior senator, Joseph McCarthy.

The public was bombarded with conflicting messages: first, that a person could survive a bombing by covering his head and ducking under a desk; then, that radioactive fallout might mutate the genes of every living thing for hundreds of miles. Even as the government claimed that the horror of nuclear weapons ensured they would never be needed, it made plans to evacuate the President and rescue works of art in the event of an attack. The Post Office optimistically offered to waive postage on letters sent to areas devastated by nuclear holocaust.

As the U.S. tested ever more powerful weaponry (left, an H-bomb explodes over Eniwetok Atoll in the Pacific), Americans learned to stop worrying and love their bomb shelters (above, in Long Island, New York).

Are you lonesome tonight?

Although there had been teenagers before the 1950s, the fact had attracted little public notice. But as postwar prosperity gave adolescents unprecedented buying power and leisure time, a new subculture seized the spotlight. Suddenly there were teen movies (*I Was a Teenage Zombie*), teen fashion (poodle skirts, ducktails) and, above all, teen music—a.k.a. rock 'n' roll. "Heartbreak Hotel" became Elvis Presley's first million-selling record in 1956; by 1958 he had 14 more. Listening to Presley was just part of the fun: To fully dig his electrifying blend of raunch and innocence, you had to *see* him. "Without my left leg, I'd be dead," said the King, whose lower-body language prompted screams from fans and groans from parents.

To witness Elvis in action (from the waist up, anyway), you didn't have to go to a concert hall or to a movie theater: You simply turned on *The Ed Sullivan Show.* Television ownership ballooned from 9 percent of U.S. homes in 1950 to 86 percent in 1959, changing the way Americans relaxed, related to one another and learned about the world. Across the country, living rooms were flooded with hypnotic images—news shows and game shows, soap operas and horse operas, *I Love Lucy* and *Dragnet*, *Howdy Doody* and *Queen for a Day.* The poet T.S. Eliot fretted over a medium "which permits millions . . . to listen to the same joke at the same time, and yet remain lonesome."

Most people, untroubled, just sat and stared.

In 1954 (above), 74 percent of those polled felt TV violence might turn kids to crime. Elvis (right) plays his hometown, Memphis, in 1956.

Hot rods and burgers to go

"What does that thing do?" asked Nikita Khrushchev, pointing to a Cadillac tail fin. The visiting Soviet premier was being rhetorical; he knew it served no mechanical function. But *did* it do something? Indeed it did: It made teenage boys and grown men swoon. It helped make cars as big as small ships — the 1959 Lincoln stretched more than 19 feet. And, as the Big Three in Detroit knew, it made car styles as transitory as hemlines. The glamour of fins, originally modeled after P-38 fighter planes, also blinded automobile aesthetes to basic safety requirements. "A square foot of chrome sells 10 times more cars than the best safety door latch," observed one industry executive.

Style and speed were the selling points for another roaring success of the era. As suburbia sprawled and car sales soared, America was increasingly a nation on the move. Why slow down for a meal? Inspiration struck a milk shake–mixer salesman named Ray Kroc while he was on a routine call to a California hamburger stand. Two brothers, Richard and Maurice McDonald, had worked out a way to make burgers and fries quickly and uniformly. "Each step was stripped down to its essence," noted Kroc, who acquired rights to the McDonald's company in 1954. He franchised their assembly-line approach to fried food and taught it at Hamburger University. By 1959, Kroc was moving 50 million burgers a year from 100 restaurants. Today there are franchises in more than 100 countries. The Golden Arches have marched across the globe.

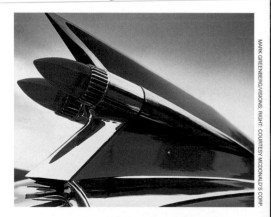

The first of Kroc's McDonald's (right, in Illinois) exemplifies space age style, as do the jet fighter fins of the '59 Cadillac Eldorado (above).

MARK GREENBERG/VISIONS; RIGHT: COURTESY MCDONALD'S CORP.

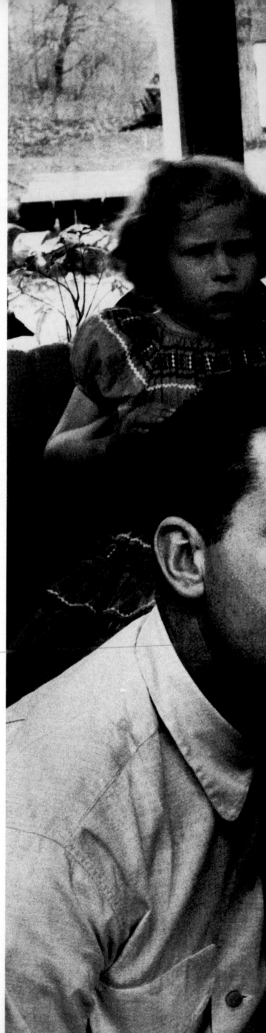

CORBIS/BETTMANN–UPI; RIGHT: ALBERT FENN

Among the plethora of products aimed at '50s kids were 3-D comic books (above). Illinois homemaker Jean Ryan (right), disabled by polio in 1952, watches as her son is vaccinated in 1955.

The luckiest generation?

Few children in history had it so good as those who grew up in the '50s. After relying for decades on childrearing experts who prescribed coldness and rigidity (no hugs or kisses; feedings on a strict schedule), parents were getting loose with Dr. Spock. "Every baby needs to be smiled at, talked to, played with," advised the kindly pediatrician, whose *Baby and Child Care* sold a million copies a year. Marketers, too, were eager to fulfill the needs of the biggest generation of Americans ever born. Hula Hoops, Barbie dolls, Davy Crockett caps—a cornucopia of *stuff* rained down on postwar kids. The baby boomers, wrote LIFE in 1958, "represent a backlog of business orders that will take decades to fill."

Even illness seemed powerless against those golden boys and girls, thanks to a new array of miracle drugs. But one virus imperiled the boomers: polio. The crippling disease reached epidemic proportions; playgrounds and pools closed to stem contagion. Then, in 1954, Dr. Jonas Salk introduced his vaccine. By decade's end, the threat had largely been vanquished.

Betty Friedan, housewife

"The problem lay buried, unspoken, for many years . . . Each suburban housewife struggled with it alone. As she made the beds, shopped for groceries, matched slipcover material, ate peanut butter sandwiches with her children, chauffeured Cub Scouts and Brownies, lay beside her husband at night—she was afraid to ask even of herself the silent question—'Is this all?'"

The author of those lines had intended more for herself. As a student at Smith College, Betty Goldstein excelled. But when she was offered a prestigious fellowship to continue graduate studies at Berkeley, she turned it down in order to keep a boyfriend: The cultural imperative to get a man and settle down was powerful in postwar America. Eventually she moved to New York and wrote for labor papers. She would marry and have three children with Carl Friedan, an ad executive. While pregnant with the second, Friedan says, she was forced to quit her job. But peanut butter and slipcovers were no substitute for the workplace.

In 1957, before her 15-year Smith reunion, Friedan prepared a questionnaire. In her classmates' responses she saw evidence of "the problem that has no name"—knowing there was

In 1960, Friedan spent time with (from left) Emily, Jonathan and Daniel in suburban New York. Six years after her book came out, she was divorced and a single mother.

life beyond housewifery but feeling guilty for desiring it. Working while her kids were in school (at times hiring a taxi to carpool for her), Friedan published *The Feminine Mystique* in 1963, naming the problem and prescribing a solution: treating women as human beings with purposes beyond serving their families. One child of the time remembers his own mother devouring the book "as if she were starving."

"There were twenty-eight wives ... Eighteen were taking tranquilizers; several had tried suicide."

TV FAMILIES

In the late '40s, Americans welcomed a new member to their households: television. Through the years it would become a surrogate parent to a generation of kids. However unrealistic the shows were (vacuuming in pearls, Mrs. Cleaver?), TV families married easily into our own. Their milestones became ours. In 1951 more people tuned in for the birth of Little Ricky on *I Love Lucy* than for Dwight Eisenhower's inauguration the following day. (Lucy's pregnancy also daringly implied that the Ricardos had overcome the sitcom standard of separate beds.)

Slowly, as advertisers no longer determined program content, TV families evolved. *The Brady Bunch* depicted life with step–siblings and perfect lawns. *All in the Family* tackled bigotry with humor. *Maude* grappled with legal abortion in 1972. The mom on *Roseanne* in the '80s would be a shock to her 1950s counterpart: If Roseanne Conner ever vacuumed (unlikely), it sure wasn't in pearls. More likely topics were teen sex and bankruptcy. TV had gotten closer to real life, but with a laugh track. On one popular family show of the '90s, *Party of Five*, there were no parents at all: Now the kids are running the fun house.

Though animated, Marge Simpson (below) was a more fully drawn character than Donna Reed's Donna Stone (left). But for both TV moms, a good coif was key.

Americans watch about 28 hours of TV each week. Is it coincidence that between 1980 and 1994 the number of obese children in this country almost doubled? Two important inventions, the remote control and the cordless telephone, eliminated the small but not insignificant calorie-burners of getting up to change the channel or answer the phone.

PERCENTAGE OF U.S. HOUSEHOLDS WITH TELEVISION	AVERAGE WEEKLY TV VIEWING HOURS, 1997–98 SEASON	PERCENTAGE OF U.S. WORKFORCE THAT IS FEMALE
1950: 9		1900: 18.1
1998: 98.3	Women: 31.45	1950: 28.8
	Men: 27.43	1997: 46.4
	Teens: 21.30	
	Children: 21.00	

You eat it, usually sitting in a booth in a bare, plain restaurant, with a mural of Vesuvio on the wall, a jukebox, and a crowded bar. The customers are Italian families, Bohemians, lovers, and—if a college is nearby—students and faculty members.—*The Atlantic Monthly,* Acquainting its readers with a new dish, pizza, 1949

MR. ARBUCK STARED WITH disbelief as the door shut firmly. "Hey, baby, let me in, baby. You like me, baby. I'm a liked guy. Didn't I pick up the check, five people, *your* friends, I never seen them before? Don't that give me the right you should like me? You like me, baby."

He tapped on the door gently, then louder; finally . . . he plunged down the stairs, slamming a fist against the wall. Just as he reached the bottom, the door of the girl's apartment opened and she poked out her head.

"Oh, Mr. Arbuck . . ."

He turned back, a smile of relief oiling his face: she'd only been teasing.

"The next time a girl wants a little powder-room change," she called, not teasing at all, "take my advice, darling: *don't* give her twenty-cents!"
Truman Capote [5]
Breakfast at Tiffany's, 1958

IT IS HARD TO UNDERSTAND why our town must be destroyed to make a bomb that will destroy someone else's town that they love as much as we love ours.
Sign outside Ellenton, S.C. (evacuated so an H-bomb plant could be built), 1952

IT'S NICE TO BE included in people's fantasies, but you also like to be accepted for your own sake
Marilyn Monroe [4]
1955

I HOPE I SHALL BE able to confide in you completely, as I have never been able to do in anyone before.
Anne Frank
The Diary of a Young Girl, 1952

I HAVEN'T WRITTEN anything about the "Big Picture," because I don't know anything about it. I only know what we see from our worm's-eye view, and our segment of the picture consists only of tired and dirty soldiers who are alive and don't want to die; of long darkened convoys in the middle of the night; of shocked silent men wandering back down the hill from battle; . . . of jeeps and petrol dumps and smelly bedding rolls and C rations and cactus patches and blown bridges and dead mules and hospital tents and shirt collars greasy-black from months of wearing; and of laughter too, and anger and wine and lovely flowers and constant cussing.
Ernie Pyle [2]
Here Is Your War, 1943

AT THE BEGINNING of the World Series of 1947, I experienced a completely new emotion, when the National Anthem was played. This time, I thought, it is being played for me, as much as for anyone else. This is organized major league baseball, and I am standing here with all the others; and everything that takes place includes me.
Jackie Robinson [1, with his wife, Rachel, and son Jackie Jr.]
Interview, 1948

LOU: WELL, ALL I'M TRYIN' to find out is what's the guy's name on first base.
Bud: Oh, no, no What is on *second* base
Lou: I'm not askin' you who's on second.
Bud: Who's on first.
Lou: That's what I'm trying to find out.
Bud Abbott and Lou Costello [3]
From the comedy routine "Who's on First?"
1945

I HAVE SENT THE FOLLOWING telegram to General Eisenhower at the Commodore Hotel in New York: "The people have made their choice and I congratulate you. That you may be the servant and guardian of peace and make the vale of trouble a door of hope is my earnest prayer. Best wishes. Adlai E. Stevenson."

Someone asked me, as I came in, down on the street, how I felt, and I was reminded of a story that a fellow townsman of ours used to tell—Abraham Lincoln. They asked him how he felt once after an unsuccessful election. He said he felt like a little boy who had stubbed his toe in the dark. He said that he was too old to cry, but it hurt too much to laugh.
Adlai E. Stevenson
Conceding the presidential election, 1952

THE TELEVISION ALSO served as a baby-sitter. You could just put your children in front of the TV and while they watched *Davy Crockett* and *Ding Dong School,* you could make supper. TV taught our children things that we couldn't teach them. It taught them right from wrong. TV was our information box and our link to the outside world, and, of course, it entertained us.
Harriet Osborn
Levittown resident

IN CASE OF A forced retreat of Red Army units, all rolling stock must be evacuated; to the enemy must not be left a single engine, a single railway car, not a single pound of grain or a gallon of fuel.
Joseph Stalin [6]
In a radio speech, 1941

LIFE It's a youthquake. The youngest President ever reigns over Camelot. Motown is the "Sound of Young America." But slain leaders and an unpopular war give youth a cynical outlook: Never trust anyone over 30.

1960–1969

**Previous pages:
The First Family
returns from a
vacation in
Florida, 1961.**

The day before his third birthday, John F. Kennedy Jr. (opposite) watched the procession bearing his father's casket. In 1966, Sen. Robert Kennedy (above) campaigned for a local candidate in Iowa.

The violent edge of the New Frontier

Never had so charismatic a family taken up residence in the White House. The handsome President had a penchant for sailing and touch football. The elegant, cultured First Lady invited Shakespearean actors and ballet companies to entertain at state dinners. The two children seemed picture-perfect, even as their mom insisted on a private, normal life. The dashing younger brother (with his own brood of eight) was attorney general and his brother's confidant. Behind the dazzle was the promise of a future as John F. Kennedy saw it: space travel, progress in arms negotiations, racial equality and a Peace Corps to aid underdeveloped countries. Though he blundered at the Bay of Pigs and was

criticized for acting slowly on civil rights, Kennedy made strides toward many of his goals. His vision for the country ended abruptly on November 22, 1963. On a visit to Dallas, the President was murdered as he rode in a convertible with his wife, Jacqueline, at his side. His assassin, Lee Harvey Oswald, was himself killed two days later.

Bobby Kennedy resigned as attorney general and in 1964 was elected senator from New York. Two months after the April 1968 assassination of Dr. Martin Luther King Jr., Kennedy was killed in Los Angeles. Dazed by the loss of its leaders, the country could barely recall a time when politics glowed with optimism and glamour.

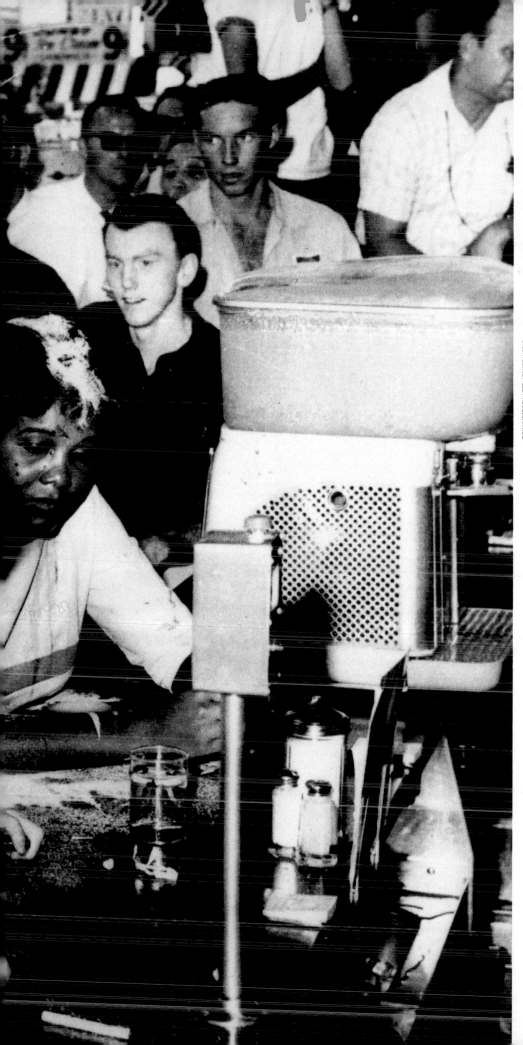

All God's children

In February 1962, John Glenn orbited smoothly overhead, but African American families could not travel freely about the South, barred, as they were, from hotels and rest rooms. The modern civil rights movement had been launched by the Supreme Court's 1954 *Brown* v. *Board of Education* decision, ruling segregated schools unconstitutional. But it took another decade of struggle before Congress passed the sweeping Civil Rights Act of 1964.

Inspired by Jesus and Gandhi, the crusaders—from Rosa Parks in her Montgomery bus to Freedom Riders in their Greyhounds; from teens who braved jeering mobs outside Central High in Little Rock to schoolkids who defied police dogs in the streets of Birmingham—countered violence with force of spirit. The climax came in 1963 when 250,000 marched on Washington, and Dr. Martin Luther King Jr. dreamed aloud that his children would someday be judged not "by the color of their skin, but by the content of their character." Legislation was passed the next year; fulfilling the dream would take a while longer.

King (above) is handcuffed in Atlanta in 1960. A mob pours scorn on a 1963 sit-in (left) at a Woolworth's lunch counter in Jackson, Miss.

WALTER IOOSS JR.; RIGHT: NEIL LEIFER

Sometimes, winning isn't the only thing

Sports and politics collided in 1967 when the heavyweight champ was barred from the boxing ring for opposing the Vietnam war. But sports also provided a relief from the era's tensions: Though victory was out of reach in Southeast Asia, it was available on the gridiron at home. January 15 saw the first Super Bowl, football's championship. Led by Vince Lombardi, the Green Bay Packers beat the Kansas City Chiefs 35–10, inaugurating an event that continues to grip the nation one Sunday a year.

The war revealed that our best fighter was a pacifist. Because he refused on religious grounds (he is a Muslim) to be inducted into the Army, Muhammad Ali was banned from boxing until vindicated by the Supreme Court in 1970. Ali's titles confirm his athletic prowess, but his years out of the ring show his strength of character.

Muhammad Ali, born Cassius Clay (right, in a 1966 bout), declared himself "The Greatest." And he was: stunning to look at, quick with a sound bite and unmatched in the ring. Another ace, quarterback Bart Starr (above), was MVP of the first Super Bowl.

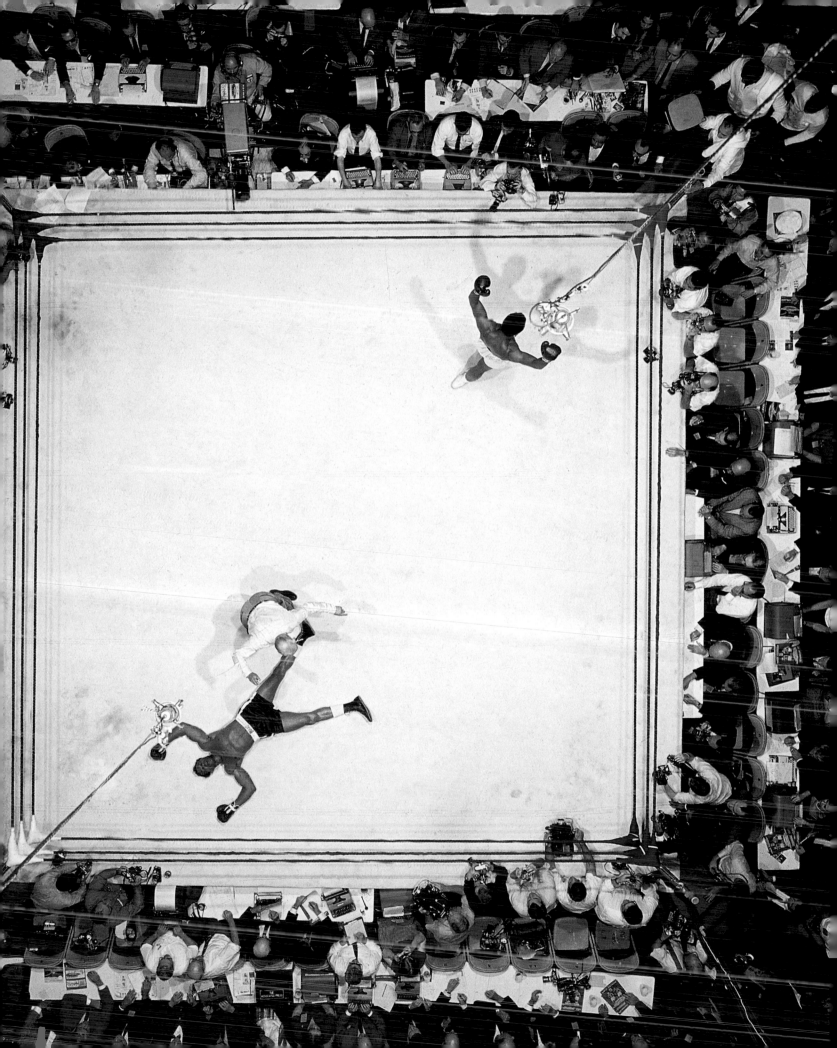

1960–1969

The long and winding road

1961: Four Liverpool lads. Pete out, Ringo in. Matching suits, mop-top cuts. *Meet the Beatles:* The smart one, the cute one, the quiet one, the drummer. "Love Me Do." (Instantly, fans oblige.) JFK airport: The Beatles have landed. John: "More popular than Jesus." Out with the suits, in with the beads, the beards. "All You Need Is Love." Paul loves Linda. John loves Yoko. John to Paul: "I want a divorce." 1970: "Let It Be."

John, Ringo, Paul and George gave the '60s its soundtrack, from innocence to protest.

ROGER MALLOCH/MAGNUM PHOTOS; LEFT: LARRY BURROWS

Into the quagmire

It began by fateful degrees. Eisenhower sent a few hundred military advisers; JFK sent a few thousand more. After a skirmish in the Gulf of Tonkin, President Johnson sent in combat troops. By 1967 there were almost 500,000 U.S. soldiers in Vietnam. Why were they there? The domino theory: If South Vietnam fell to communism, all of Southeast Asia would follow. Each week, hundreds of American boys died in the jungles. Still, the Vietcong and North Vietnamese body count was far higher, and U.S. officials insisted they saw light at the end of the tunnel. Then came the Tet offensive of '68, which revealed the tunnel to be a bottomless pit.

By then, America was tearing itself apart. No other war had poured through TV sets into the nation's living rooms, and this war was ugly indeed. Millions of young people turned against their parents; millions of all ages came to mistrust their government. Protest marches erupted into riots. Angry doves chanted, "Hey, hey, LBJ, how many kids did you kill today?" Johnson decided not to seek reelection, and voters turned to conservative Richard Nixon, who hinted at having a secret plan for peace. But the war dragged on.

Marines (left) recover a buddy's corpse during a firefight in 1966. Outside the 1968 Democratic Convention in Chicago (above), the scene of bloody riots, a protester and a soldier share a moment of peace.

1960–1969

The fire this time

When rioters rampaged through L.A.'s mostly black Watts district in August 1965, their battle cry was "Burn, baby, burn"—a phrase borrowed from a local deejay who had used it to introduce hot records. It took 1,000 police joined by 13,500 National Guardsmen to quell the weeklong insurrection; 34 people were killed (all but six of them African American) and 3,500 arrested. Frustration fueled the riot: Left behind by postwar prosperity, urban blacks suffered ills the civil rights movement, with its focus on southern segregation, had yet to address. Soon cities across America were burning, and young militants were shouting a new slogan: Black power.

Sparked by the arrest of a black motorist, the Watts riot left 150 blocks in ruins.

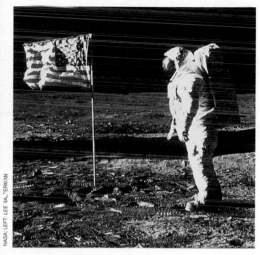

NASA; LEFT: LEE BALTERMAN

Fantastic voyage

The close of the 1960s was anything but serene: War dragged on in Vietnam, the counterculture raged against the establishment, and the U.S. and Soviet governments elbowed each other for the top spot in the arms race. Then, for a few hours on July 20, 1969, all divisions were forgotten as people around the world watched a miracle unfold in the Sea of Tranquillity.

NASA's third lunar mission (the previous two had orbited without landing), *Apollo 11* met John F. Kennedy's 1961 challenge to put an American on the moon. Some were cynical about spending $41 million on yet another outer-space joyride. "While we can send men to the moon, we can't get foodstuffs across town to starving folks in the teeming ghettos," scolded Rev. Jesse Jackson. But when the grainy black-and-white image of Neil Armstrong setting foot on the moon was broadcast—to 600 million viewers—cynicism turned to childlike wonder. Some people alternated viewing the closeup TV picture of the moon's surface with a naked-eye gaze at the real thing. It was baffling: One of us, from earth, was up *there*.

Buzz Aldrin celebrated a private communion before following Armstrong (Michael Collins stayed on the command module). The two frolicked in the moon's faint gravity, and for a moment the world's problems seemed a little less weighty to the spectators 240,000 miles below.

At home in Houston, Joan Aldrin (left, with son Andrew) is moonstruck at the sight of her husband, Buzz (above), on television.

Field of dreams

Gazing out over the crowd, singer Richie Havens uttered the definitive comment on the Woodstock festival: "I mean, like, wow!" For three days in August 1969, on a farm near Bethel, New York, close to half a million young people created an impromptu utopia. It could have been a bummer. Organizers of the rock fest—which featured such A-list artists as Jimi Hendrix, Janis Joplin and Jefferson Airplane— had expected only 50,000 attendees; along

with rain, mud and 20-mile traffic jams, there were shortages of food and shelter. Yet peace prevailed as concertgoers shared everything from hash pipes to nude backrubs. The crowning moment of the '60s counterculture, Woodstock seemed to prove that all you really did need was love (and a tab of acid). Then, in December, at a concert in Altamont, near San Francisco, Hell's Angels killed a spectator—and the hippie dream of heaven crashed to earth.

A local paper called the festival (below) "the biggest drug and sex orgy since the Roman Empire." But to the citizens of Woodstock Nation, the event was a celebration of youth and freedom, an outpouring of communal joy.

Eleanor Bralver, teacher

"I think I was born to be a teacher," says Eleanor Bralver, now 86 and the oldest faculty member in the Los Angeles Unified School District—possibly in the nation. Born to Polish and Russian immigrants who worked in sweatshops, Bralver earned two master's degrees and became a gym teacher at an inner-city school in Detroit in 1935. Six years later she married. Though she still loved her work, somehow her first maternity leave turned into an extended absence. "I stayed away from teaching for 22 years, until my son wanted to go to college, which was in 1968. I was 52 years old when they hired me back."

With race riots going on in Detroit at that time, and an environment where the faculty were often threatened by the students in their charge, the school system was pleased to see Bralver

return. Later her family would move to California, where Bralver has been teaching health at Sylmar High School ever since. There, she says, she has dealt with kids on drugs as well as runaways.

"Those of us who cover health are concentrating on critical social issues that are the heart of a functioning society," she says. "Drug abuse, teenage pregnancy, nutrition, eating disorders, gangs and violence, child and domestic abuse—we cover practically every ill that visits the human body, from warts to AIDS. We cover the poisoning of the environment, adolescent suicide." In 1999 she helped her students cope with their anger after the school shootings in Littleton, Colo.

Some of her current pupils are the children of former ones. But the issues they face are similar. When she began her career, "I had a large number of children coming from Italy—I had a

Bralver (at Sylmar in 1969) says, "I'll teach forever. I have no plans to do anything else."

set of twins called Primo and Secundo. When I taught in the '60s, Mexicans were the minority. Now a lot of them come from Mexico and South America. My curriculum really isn't that much different than it was back then. I always talked about premarital sex. But in those days kids were getting abortions. Today, people are keeping their babies.

"I'm known as a very open teacher," she says. "When I teach sex education, there are no holds barred. I figure I'll be the last person telling these kids [about sex], and I'm not afraid to tell them they're not old enough." Bralver's students appreciate her candor. One class presented her with a certificate commending her teaching and addressed to THE SEXIEST BROAD IN SYLMAR HIGH SCHOOL. It still hangs over her blackboard.

"In the '60s I had kids who OD'd in my class. People think the drug problem is worse today, but I don't think so."

CHILD LABOR

The national consensus that every child should be in school is of relatively recent vintage. Some two million children, aged 10 to 15, were hard at work in the U.S. in the first decade of the century. Little boys did 12-hour shifts in coal mines, factories, canneries; they hawked newspapers late into the night. In southern cotton mills, 25 percent of the workforce was under the age of 15, earning pennies a day. Finally, the Fair Labor Standards Act of 1938 placed limitations on child labor, partly to protect scarce jobs for adults.

Today, owing to compulsory education and better enforcement of child labor laws, the number of underage workers in the United States has dropped. (In some countries, particularly in the Middle East, Asia and Latin America, young workers may make up as much as 10 percent of the workforce.) But the problem has not been eradicated in America: A study by a Rutgers University labor economist estimated that 59,600 children under age 14 were illegally employed in 1996. Some 13,000 toiled in garment industry sweatshops. Hiring the young, and paying them less than legal workers, had saved employers as much as $155 million.

On farms, according to a 1997 news story, children younger than 14 who accompanied their parents to work could earn about $3.50 for picking a tray of blueberries, the equivalent of 12 pints. At work in New Jersey berry fields, the children said that picking fruit was the easiest way they'd found to earn money for designer jeans. But, said one 11-year-old child, "I'm not so good as older kids because I get only one or two trays."

Photographers spurred crucial reforms by showing children, like this little newsboy (c. 1910) at work.

A recent survey found that about 74 percent of public school teachers were female; their median age was 44; some 90 percent were white, and three quarters were married. Happily, only about 4 percent of those who were asked if they would again choose to go into teaching said they would not. Some 62 percent said they probably or surely would.

PERCENTAGE OF AMERICAN 5-TO-17-YEAR-OLDS ENROLLED IN SCHOOL
1909–10: 74.2
1949–50: 83.1
1994–95: 91.6

PERCENTAGE OF AMERICAN 17-YEAR-OLDS WITH A HIGH SCHOOL DEGREE
1909–10: 8.8
1949–50: 59.0
1994–95: 70.9

AVERAGE ANNUAL SALARY FOR TEACHERS
1909–10: $ 485
1949–50: $ 3,010
1994–95: $36,605

LIFE Shaken by Vietnam, Watergate, fuel shortages and recession, America was in an uncertain mood. While President Carter bemoaned the "crisis of confidence," the Me Generation flocked to discos for relief.

1970–1979

National Guardsmen killed four students (right) at Kent State University in 1970, rocking the antiwar movement. But the women's movement (above, in New York) was gathering steam.

Previous pages: As Saigon falls in April 1975, evacuees board a helicopter atop the U.S. embassy.

1970–1979

Sisterhood is powerful; so is pounding the pavement

Dormant since the fight for suffrage, feminism returned to boisterous life in the '70s. Inspired by the civil rights movement, the campaign for women's liberation was partly a product of the era's weakened economy, which forced large numbers of females into the workplace. Barred from many positions, denied freedoms that men took for granted, women revolted. Thousands hit the streets demanding that pay be equal and

childbearing be a choice. The decade would see the Supreme Court legalize abortion and the Congress promote equal opportunity in education. The Equal Rights Amendment, introduced in 1923, would finally pass Congress—only to fall three votes short of ratification by the states.

Changing the lawbooks was difficult enough; changing attitudes—and day-to-day relationships

with men—was sometimes even tougher. Sure, you could march against the male chauvinist pigs who ran the country; but what about the one who thought he ran your household? "By the time my husband walked in the door," said one frustrated homemaker, "all hell would break loose. He was responsible for all the evils of the world, and especially responsible for keeping me trapped."

1970–1979

Terror and triumph

If not for Mark Spitz, the 1972 Olympics might have been remembered only as a bloodbath. Ten days into the Munich Games, members of the Black September faction of the Palestine Liberation Organization invaded the Israeli team's dormitory, killed two coaches and seized nine hostages. The next day, five of the terrorists died in a shootout, but so did all their captives. Although the Games continued, competition was subdued.

Spitz, however, had already made an indelible impression. The 22-year-old swimmer won an unprecedented seven gold medals in four individual and three team events; each victory set a world record. "I am in a bit of a trance," Spitz said afterward, but he was alert enough to quit dental school and hit the endorsement circuit. Posters of the comely Californian were the best-selling souvenir in Olympic history.

Spitz's mustache and bangs were signs of his confidence: Most swimmers eschew excess hair, fearing that it will slow them down.

Nixon: ". . . and then you destroy yourself."

Maybe it seemed like a good idea at the time, secretly tape-recording every Oval Office conversation of his own presidency. Perhaps Richard Nixon just didn't want to miss one detail for his memoirs. And maybe it seemed smart to hire a team of operatives to fix news leaks and foil enemies.

It all started in 1971, when confidential documents on Vietnam showed up in *The New York Times*—and Nixon set up a "plumbers" unit to discredit the leaker, Daniel Ellsberg. That mission failed, despite a break-in at Ellsberg's psychiatrist's office. In June 1972, five of the agents were caught plumbing at Democratic National Committee headquarters in the Watergate complex. Press secretary Ron Ziegler denied any White House involvement in the "third-rate burglary attempt," and Nixon was reelected. But two young reporters from *The Washington Post* kept the story alive, and eventually the Senate held hearings. Nixon's underlings testified that he had helped orchestrate or cover up a slew of dirty tricks— and that it was all on tape. As the scandal unfolded, 25 people went to jail, including U.S. Attorney General John Mitchell. And on August 8, 1974, with his impeachment looming, Nixon became the first Chief Executive to resign in disgrace. Perversely, his wish was granted: His presidency may be the best documented ever.

White House counsel **John Dean** (left) confers with his wife, **Maureen**, during a break in his Senate testimony. **Nixon** (above) leaves Washington on August 9, the day after announcing his resignation.

MARK GODFREY/IMAGE WORKS; LEFT: BURT GLINN/MAGNUM PHOTOS

Two hundred candles

It was more than a birthday party, said one organizer—in the wake of Watergate, it was "a way of clearing the American soul." On July 4, 1976, the nation celebrated its bicentennial with a shindig that stretched from Mars Hill, Maine (where National Guardsmen greeted the dawn's earliest light with a 50-gun salute), to Pago Pago (where 15,000 American Samoans marked the day with pole-climbing contests and boat races).

New York City boasted the grandest pageantry: more than 200 sailing ships from 30 nations. But extravagance was everywhere. In Philadelphia, a million people watched a reenactment of the signing of the Declaration of Independence. In Chicago, 1,776 new citizens were sworn in. Starshine from Epsilon Lyrae, some 150 light-years away, was turned into electrical current in Hawaii and sent on to Boston to power replicas of Paul Revere's lanterns. Townsfolk in George, Wash., baked a 60-square-foot cherry pie. And in Seward, Nebr., a '70s time capsule was buried, to be dug up in 2076. Among its contents: a Teflon frying pan and a man's aquamarine leisure suit.

New York's Operation Sail (left) drew six million spectators; President Ford watched from an aircraft carrier. In Philadelphia (above), Uncle Sam himself joined the fun.

PHOTOFEST; LEFT: ENRICO FERORELL

Saturday-night tribal rites in a galaxy not so far away

If the '60s were set to anthems of peace and love, the '70s grooved to a different ethos altogether. Forget "smile on your brother." Try "get down, boogie oogie oogie."

Words without meaning were the core of disco, so called for the discotheques that spun records instead of featuring live acts. In this postwar, sexual revolution era, the most famous of nightspots was New York's Studio 54, where celebrities and nobodies boogied side by spandexed side. Observed Truman Capote from behind the velvet ropes: "Boys with boys, girls with girls, girls with boys, blacks and whites, capitalists and Marxists . . . one big mix." Mind-expanding psychedelic drugs were passé. Now, as one Studio 54 regular put it, "Let them eat coke."

Baby boomers, now in their twenties, flocked to other disco palaces across the country. One of them, deep in working-class Brooklyn, inspired the film *Saturday Night Fever,* which immortalized polyester suits, platform shoes and the words of the Bee Gees: "You should be dancing."

In 1977, dancers had Studio 54 (left) and moviegoers had C-3PO and R2-D2 (above), thanks to George Lucas's *Star Wars.*

A nuclear nightmare

For years, environmentalists had warned that nuclear power—enjoying a boom during the fuel-starved '70s—was a time bomb in America's backyard. In March 1979, a movie called *The China Syndrome* dramatized the dangers. Just days later the disaster almost happened: Pennsylvania's Three-Mile Island plant suffered a partial core meltdown. Children and pregnant women were evacuated; thousands more fled. Workers struggled to contain a huge bubble of radioactive gas. The crisis lasted a week. The nuclear industry never recovered.

A meltdown at Three-Mile Island (above) could have killed thousands.

Sherry Nicholson, secretary

Growing up in Luray, Va., Nicholson dreamed of getting a degree and running a business. But her mother, who worked as a secretary, suggested she take a typing course—just in case. It turned out to be sound advice. In 1965, during her senior year in high school, Nicholson got married; a baby boy arrived soon afterward. "That sort of knocked the heck out of going to college," she says. Two years later she had a daughter. And when the younger child entered kindergarten, Nicholson went to work. Her job: secretary to the guidance counselor at her children's school.

Her husband didn't like it. "Most middle-class women didn't work in the early '70s," says Nicholson. "It sort of undermined his masculinity, I suppose." But the family needed a house of its own, and that required a second income. Besides, work had always been a source

of pride for Nicholson, ever since she was a girl selling tickets to tourists at the Luray Caverns. After a year at the school, she left to become a bank teller but quickly grew frustrated. "My boss had been hit on the head too many times when he played football," Nicholson jokes. "The other teller and I pretty much ran the place, but we got paid teller salary and he got paid management." So back to the guidance counselor's office she went, and there she stayed until 1983, when her son departed for college.

Her marriage ended not long afterward. Nicholson was living with her daughter in a suburb of Washington, D.C., and working as a secretary to a magazine editor. "I had spent my entire life saying If I could just. If I just didn't have these children, If I had just gone to college." Now it was time for a change. Nicholson had begun taking college courses in whatever caught her interest: art, psychology, writing. She thought

Nicholson (above) found in secretarial work a path to independence. Today her daughter, an aspiring actress, makes a living the same way.

she might try to become a proofreader. But one day, as she was looking through the P's in the want ads, she came across an opening in property management—and saw a way forward.

Nicholson's clerical talents got her an entry-level job. She took real estate courses, picked experts' brains. Soon she was managing several buildings and overseeing a staff that included her own secretary. "I hope I treat her differently from the way I was treated," Nicholson says. "I don't ask her to make coffee." When Nicholson turns 55, she plans to retire and begin her next career: writing murder mysteries. Once again, those typing skills will come in handy.

"My husband didn't want me to work. The mind-set was, it shouldn't take two salaries to support a family. But I was adamant."

Typewriters went portable in 1909, electric in 1920. But by 1999 they had been replaced by computers in many offices.

FROM REMINGTON TO MACINTOSH

Offices used to be quiet places where the pervasive sound was the scratching of employees' pens. Then in 1874 the gun manufacturer E. Remington and Sons, of Ilion, N.Y., began marketing the first practical typewriter—and the peace was shattered. Inventors had been tinkering with writing machines since the 1700s, but those devices were slower than longhand, and many were as big as pianos. The speedy, compact (and noisy) Remington, principally designed by Milwaukee inventor Christopher Latham Sholes, unleashed a tide of paperwork that is still rising. But in 1977 a new machine appeared that would end the typewriter's reign. Invented by twentysomethings Steve Jobs and Steve Wozniak, the personal computer has made offices quiet again. Whether it makes them more efficient is debatable: According to one study, workers waste five billion hours a year "futzing" with balky computers.

Secretaries have existed since the beginning of civilization. In olden times, however, they were called scribes, and they were always men. They took dictation for merchants in ancient Rome and did bookkeeping for 17th century nobles. Then came the Industrial Revolution, and the need for secretaries exploded. Women proved adaptable to such new technologies as typewriters and telephones, and they could be paid less than men. By the 1930s, they had come to dominate the field.

NUMBER OF AMERICANS WORKING AS SECRETARIES

1900:   112,000
1950: 1,580,000
1997: 3,300,000

PERCENTAGE OF SECRETARIES WHO WERE WOMEN

1900: unknown
1950:   94
1997:   98

AVERAGE ANNUAL SALARY OF A SECRETARY

1951: $ 3,060
1975: $ 9,000 to 15,000
1997: $28,420

There was a strange stillness. The birds, for example—where had they gone? Many people spoke of them, puzzled and disturbed. The feeding stations in the backyards were deserted. The few birds seen anywhere were moribund; they trembled violently and could not fly. It was a spring without voices.—**Rachel Carson [6],** *Silent Spring,* 1962

JACK WOLTZ ALWAYS SLEPT ALONE. He had a bed big enough for ten people and a bedroom large enough for a movie ballroom scene, but he had slept alone since the death of his first wife ten years before …

On this Thursday morning, for some reason, he awoke early. The light of dawn made his huge bedroom as misty as a foggy meadowland. Far down at the foot of his bed was a familiar shape and Woltz struggled up on his elbows to get a clearer look. It had the shape of a horse's head. Still groggy, Woltz reached and flicked on the night table lamp.

Mario Puzo
The Godfather, 1969

I'VE GOT A GIRL NAMED Rama Lama, Rama Lama
    Lama Ding Dong.
She's everything to me
Rama Lama, Rama Lama Ding Dong.

The Edsels
"Rama Lama Ding Dong," 1961

NONVIOLENCE IS THE ANSWER to the crucial political and moral questions of our time; the need for man to overcome oppression and violence without resorting to oppression and violence.

Man must evolve for all human conflict a method which rejects revenge, aggression and retaliation.

Dr. Martin Luther King Jr.
Nobel Prize acceptance speech, 1964

THEY ARE VIOLENT when their interests are at stake. But for all that violence they display at the international level, when you and I want just a little bit of freedom, we're supposed to be nonviolent. They're violent in Korea, they're violent in Germany, they're violent in the South Pacific, they're violent in Cuba, they're violent wherever they go. But when it comes time for you and me to protect ourselves against lynchings, they tell us to be nonviolent.

Malcolm X [4]
Speaking in Detroit, 1965

LIKE A FEATHER CAUGHT in a vortex, [Ted] Williams ran around the square of bases … hurriedly, unsmiling, head down, as if out of praise were a storm of rain to get out of. He didn't tip his cap. Though we thumped, wept, and chanted "We want Ted" for minutes after he hid in the dugout, he did not come back …The papers said that the other players, and even the umpires on the field, begged him to come out and acknowledge us in some way, but he never had and did not now. Gods do not answer letters.

John Updike [1]
"Hub Fans Bid Kid Adieu," *The New Yorker,* 1960

IT WAS QUITE A DAY. I don't know what you can say about a day when you see four beautiful sunsets.

John Glenn [5]
First orbital flight, Mercury program, 1962

YOU'RE GONNA NEED a bigger boat.
Roy Scheider [3]
Portraying a police chief, to a shark expert (played by Robert Shaw) in *Jaws,* 1975

KENNEDY HAD BEEN CAMPAIGNING in an open convertible in California. He looked great … Nixon looked like death warmed over. We offered to put some makeup on him, but he said no because he didn't want people to say he used makeup and Kennedy didn't …When the first debate was over, I said, "My God, we don't have to wait for election night." I said, "I just produced a television show that elected a President of the United States." That was a travesty.

Don Hewitt
TV director of the Nixon–Kennedy debates, 1960

HOW MANY ROADS must a man walk down
Before you call him a man? …
The answer, my friend, is blowin' in the wind,
The answer is blowin' in the wind.

Bob Dylan [2]
"Blowin' in the Wind," 1962

I AM WRITING it in a hurry. I see death coming up the hill.

GI in Vietnam
Last letter, 1969

LIFE Forget "Less is more." Now more is more. More money. More BMWs. More Jacksons. More sequins. More TV channels. But also, more homelessness. More AIDS patients. And after the crash, more used BMWs for sale.

1980–1989

A time for healing

After a decade of self-doubt, America reclaimed its confidence in the 1980s. The atmosphere began to brighten on January 20, 1981, when Iran freed 52 hostages who had been seized at the U.S. embassy in Tehran 444 days before. Although their release had been negotiated under Jimmy Carter, it was Ronald Reagan who welcomed them home, getting his presidency off to a Technicolor-sunrise start.

For a new era to truly begin, however, old wounds had to be healed. Long after the last U.S. troops left Vietnam in 1973, the war continued to chafe at the body politic. Liberals saw it as an imperial adventure that should never have been undertaken; conservatives insisted that it was a just war, doomed by liberal opposition. In 1982, Maya Ying Lin made a place for the two to come together—a 493-foot wall in Washington, D.C. Lin, 21, an undergraduate architecture student at Yale, was the winner (out of 1,421 entrants) of a veteran-sponsored contest to design a memorial to Americans lost in Vietnam. Her stark design was almost as controversial as the war itself. But standing before the wall, visitors saw past their opinions to a deeper truth: the sacrifice of more than 58,000 Americans whose names were chiseled in black granite.

DANIEL SIMON/GAMMA LIAISON; RIGHT: CHRISTOPHER MORRIS/BLACK STAR

The freed hostages travel home (above). Said one vet at the wall (right), "It's the first time in 12 years that I haven't felt like an alien."

Preceding pages: Michael Jackson gets a jump on his brothers in 1984.

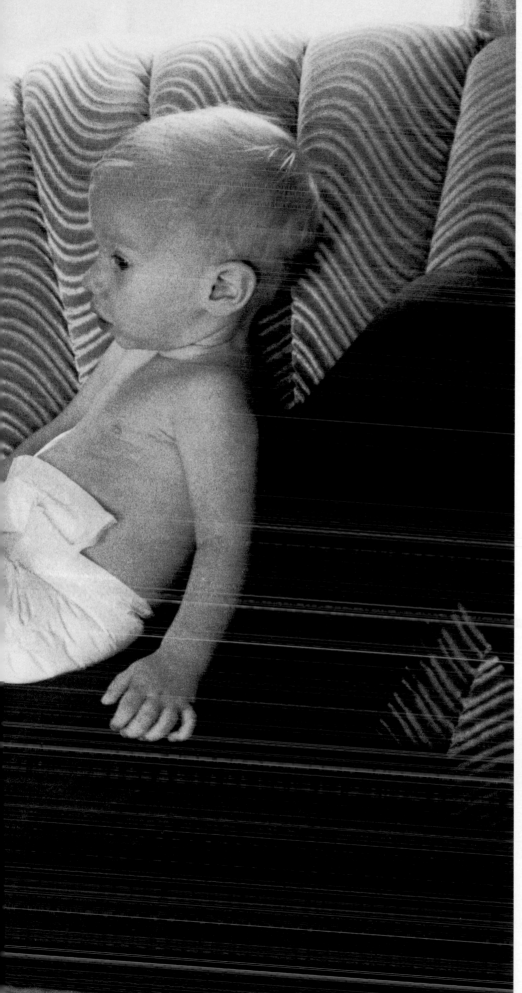

Could it happen to you?

Two epidemics swept the country in the 1980s. AIDS was one; fear, the other. By mid-decade, acquired immunodeficiency syndrome was America's top health concern, even though heart disease remained the No. 1 killer.

Because most early AIDS victims in America turned out to be male homosexuals or intravenous drug users, the religious right claimed that the illness was punishment for sinful lifestyles; many who lived with AIDS became outcasts. President Reagan, who took office the same year the first cases were identified, did not publicly utter the name of the disease until 1987.

Sex seemed to be the most common way to be infected, but misinformation was rampant. Could you also get it in restaurants? At the dentist? In a playground scuffle? The one certain thing was that there was no cure, as we were reminded when Rock Hudson, Doris Day's costar in *Pillow Talk* (1959) and other romantic comedies, died of AIDS in 1985. "Please God," said his friend Elizabeth Taylor, "he has not died in vain."

Hudson (above) died at 59. A Pennsylvania man (left), infected by blood transfusions, unwittingly passed the death sentence to his wife, who transmitted it to their son.

Disaster at 46,000 feet

By January 1986, the space shuttle program was five years old and the excitement was beginning to wane. But the 25th mission was going to be different. Riding with the *Challenger*'s crew of commander, pilot and specialists was the first ordinary American to be sent into orbit: a high school social-studies teacher from Concord, N.H., named Christa McAuliffe. In classrooms across the country, kids watched this 37-year-old mother of two embark on what she called "the ultimate field trip." (Her family watched from Cape Canaveral.) Seventy-three seconds later, the trip was ended by a blast so powerful that the sky rained debris for an hour.

The culprit was a leaky gasket. Engineers had known that O-rings sealing the shuttle's booster rockets grew brittle in chilly weather, and the mercury on the morning of the launch read 36°F. But the flight was already six days late, and impatience trumped caution. A presidential panel later charged NASA's managers and the O-rings' manufacturer with playing "Russian roulette" with the astronauts' safety. Seven lives were lost in the gamble, and the manned space program was grounded for more than two years.

The *Challenger* was nearly nine miles above the Atlantic, traveling at 1,977 mph, when its liquid-fuel tank exploded (right). The disaster was the worst in space-program history.

Living in a material world

Ronald Reagan vowed to make people feel better about the country, in part by fixing its ailing economy. He cut taxes and axed social programs; Wall Street responded by booming. But the trickle-down theory of Reaganomics—that spending by the rich would help the poor—failed to pan out. While the wealthiest Americans (including the new class of young urban professionals, known as yuppies) spent billions on foreign cars, imported water and tiny portions of nouvelle cuisine, homelessness was rampant. By August 1987, when the Dow-Jones average reached a dizzying 2,600, some 11 percent of Americans lived below the poverty line.

The boom went bust two months later, on October 19, as the Dow tumbled 22.6 percent—a free fall akin to that of the 1929 crash, which triggered the Great Depression. Fortunes were lost in seconds. Outside the New York exchange an investor shouted from a car roof, "Down with Reagan! Down with M.B.A.'s! Down with yuppies!" The bulls waited until 1990 to roar back stronger than ever: By the end of the '90s the Dow had left the 10,000 mark in its wake.

MICHAEL EVANS/SYGMA; LEFT: AP/WIDE WORLD

After the '87 crash (left, the floor of the N.Y. Stock Exchange), *The New York Times* said of Reagan (above), "With . . . the country anxious for leadership, it gets an astonishing rerun of Herbert Hoover."

Let freedom ring

For four decades, a pair of superpowers had wrestled for supremacy, and virtually every other nation had been swept up in the fray. Then, in 1985, Mikhail Gorbachev assumed the leadership of an exhausted Soviet Union. Besides decreeing *glasnost* (openness) and *perestroika* (restructuring) at home, he shocked the world by renouncing empire abroad.

In October 1989, Hungary became the first of Moscow's satellites to jettison communism, and the momentum quickly spread to East Germany. Guards who would once have shot anyone trying to jump the Berlin Wall watched champagne-swigging revelers take sledgehammers to the concrete. "I don't feel like I'm in prison anymore," exulted one man, speaking for millions. Over the next year, communist regimes were ousted across Eastern Europe. (China, having massacred prodemocracy demonstrators in Tienanmen Square, continued to resist the trend.) By the end of 1991, the Soviet Union had ceased to exist. The cold war was over, but a new world order had yet to take shape.

Built in 1961, the wall (left) dividing East and West Berlin was a 28-mile symbol of the cold war. It began to crumble in November 1989.

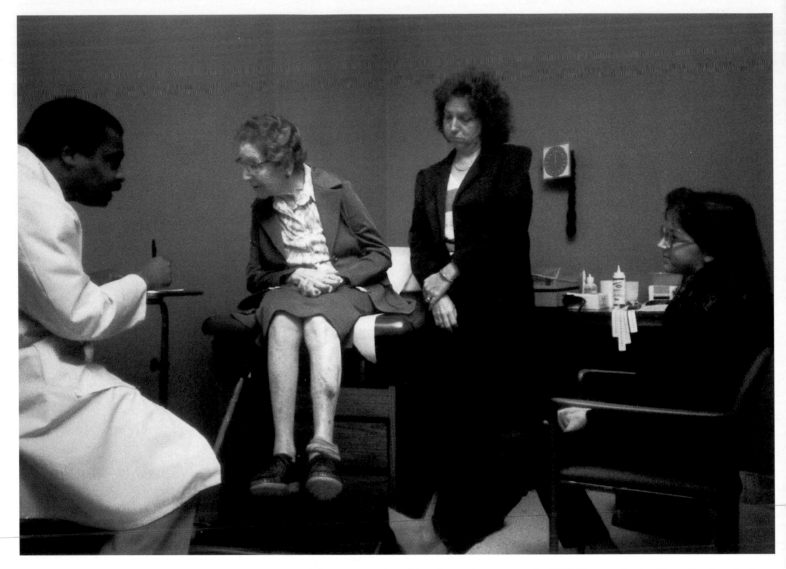

Fred Thomas, M.D.

"The only black teacher who ever thought I could be more than a plumber or a postman was Dr. Wendell Davis, my track coach. He grabbed me by the collar one day and said, 'Fred, you're a darned good student, and if you don't want to end up in jail for robbing someone to pay for a hamburger, you'd better get the heck out of Bryan.'" Fred Thomas was 14 and living in Bryan, Tex., with his mom, a launderer. He took the advice and, after college, enrolled in Meharry, a black medical school in Tennessee.

To repay his tuition, partly financed by the U.S. Public Health Service, Thomas was required to work in a community with a doctor shortage. In 1981, at age 28, he hung out a shingle in Lafayette, Tenn., a white, blue-collar factory town. "Older physicians, in retiring mode, left the door open for me," says Thomas. Despite wariness from some patients who had never had a black doctor, Thomas built a thriving practice. (A Ku Klux Klan member in full regalia once greeted him in town by lifting his sheet to say "Mornin', Doc!" Thomas had treated the man's sore throat.) Eventually, Thomas—who even made house calls—became one of the wealthiest people working in Macon County. He married, had three daughters, built a home outside town, bought a Mercedes and flew small

In 1988, Thomas treated Grandma Roark at the county hospital. "I knew everybody, and everybody knew me," he says.

planes. "Over 70 percent of my patients had private insurance," he explains.

Thomas saw that change by decade's end, when more people were covered by health maintenance organizations. "I don't really have anything good to say about HMOs," he says. Thomas, now 45 and back in Texas, complains that such companies focus too narrowly on the bottom line: "I like to make money too, don't get me wrong. But my personal satisfaction comes in knowing that I provided a service."

"My practice was word of mouth. The first day I saw three people, the second day I saw five. In six weeks, I was up to 25 a day."

Today 10 million Americans take *Ginkgo biloba* to enhance memory. From the leaves of a tree (left), it may help Alzheimer's-related dementia.

ALTERNATIVE MEDICINE

In late 20th century medicine, everything old was new again. Ancient herbal remedies gained legitimacy in Western eyes. Massage, which we always knew felt good, was found to *do* good, helping premature babies gain weight. The once exotic became commonplace as people popped echinacea (from a daisylike flower) at the onset of a cold, took valerian root as a natural sleep aid and used ordinary foods like garlic to ward off infection. By 1993, Americans were spending an estimated $14 billion a year on alternative treatments. And by 1996, more than a quarter of the nation's medical schools offered courses in alternative medicine, so called for the wider range of choices it offered patients. One of the leaders of the movement was Andrew Weil, a Harvard-trained M.D. who wrote for lay people about integrating alternative therapies, and trained doctors to use those therapies in their practices. Some physicians, however, were having none of it—pointing out that scientific evidence of the efficacy of many herbs was inconclusive. Because the FDA does not regulate dietary supplements, manufacturers are not required to meet any industry standard or warn buyers about side effects. To navigate this uncharted territory, said Weil, "we need a new generation of physicians who are trained to think differently."

Medical developments in this century have meant longer, healthier lives for most Americans. Among the advances in the past 100 years: chemotherapy (1910), insulin to treat diabetes (1921), penicillin (1928), kidney dialysis (1943), the birth control pill (1954) and Prozac (1987).

AVERAGE LIFE EXPECTANCY OF AN AMERICAN BORN IN
1900: 47 years
1950: 68
1991: 76

COST OF EACH DAY OF HOSPITAL STAY (AVERAGE)
1900: unknown
1950: $7.98
1990: $687

PERCENTAGE OF AMERICANS OVER 85
1900: 0.2
1950: 0.4
1990: 1.2
2000: 1.6 (projected)

1990–1999

LIFE The personal is public and tabloids reign supreme. Princesses confess to eating disorders and Presidents to sexual indiscretions. Trials are soap operas, lawyers are TV hosts, TV hosts are therapists. This is the information age?

For peace, justice and oil

By 1990, millions of Americans had grown up never knowing war. To Generation X, just entering their twenties, Vietnam was as much a history lesson as the Civil War. Then on August 2, Iraq's Saddam Hussein renewed a centuries-old land dispute and invaded Kuwait. In part, he wanted to use his neighbor's oil fields and harbor to ease the massive debt his nation had incurred during its war with Iran. After months of U.N. sanctions and threats, a U.S.-led coalition of 39 nations began bombing Iraq in January 1991.

"Our cause could not be more noble," said President Bush in one of several speeches he made to justify using military force to "liberate Kuwait." Some Americans believed that the need for cheap oil fueled U.S. involvement in the war, but others were wholehearted supporters of the effort and tied yellow ribbons on local trees.

The Persian Gulf war was different from earlier conflicts. Women flew combat missions. And the fighting played round the clock on CNN, as night-vision cameras transmitted green streaks of light—bombs over Baghdad—to viewers, some of whom noted that this war bore an unmistakable resemblance to a video game. That perception changed on February 24 when ground troops invaded; 100 hours later the fighting ended and negotiations began. Kuwait was freed of the Iraqi presence, but by 1999 Hussein had yet to comply fully with the cease-fire agreements. Most troubling was his refusal to allow inspection of chemical weapons plants. As long as Hussein remained in power, war in the region remained a constant threat.

U.S. Marines (right) patrol the Burgan oil fields. Iraqis set fire to hundreds of Kuwaiti oil wells and dumped 465 million gallons of crude into the Persian Gulf.

Preceding pages: In 1996, Britain's Princess Diana drew crowds at home. A year later, fleeing Paris paparazzi, she died in a crash.

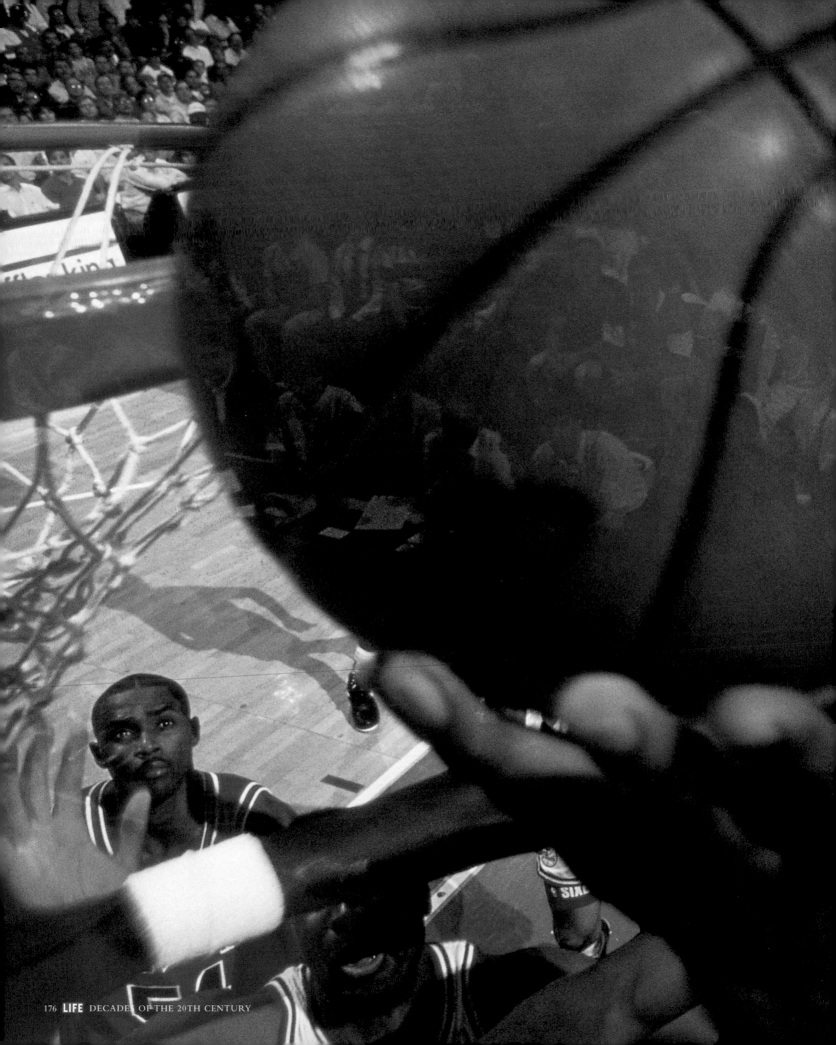

Extraordin-Air

Would it be going too far to call Albert Einstein the Michael Jordan of physics? Possibly. When the man who changed the meaning of the word "air" hung up his jersey in January 1999, basketball lost its greatest player ever. Jordan's average (31.5 points per game over 13 seasons) is the highest in NBA history; he led the league in scoring 10 times and herded the Chicago Bulls to six titles. But those stats were only part of what made him an international icon. Few athletes have matched his soaring grace, his competitive drive, his intense charisma—or his salesmanship. Hawking everything from shoes to underwear to batteries, Jordan transformed the endorsement business into an industry worth billions. His friend and rival Magic Johnson said it best: "There's Michael, then there's all the rest of us."

Kids worldwide wanted to be like Mike, as did his competitors (here, the Philadelphia '76ers).

Terror hits home

For those who dreamed that the end of the cold war would bring peace on earth, the '90s brought a rude awakening. From Rwanda to the former Yugoslavia, ethnic hatred proved as powerful a motive for bloodletting as ideology had. Meanwhile, America discovered that homegrown terrorists could be as ruthless as the foreign kind. The strangest of the lot was the Unabomber, a math professor turned hermit named Theodore Kaczynski, whose 17-year campaign of mail bombing killed three and injured 29 before he was arrested in 1996. But the deadliest U.S. terrorist of this decade (or any other) was the one who turned Oklahoma City's Alfred P. Murrah Federal Building into a slaughterhouse on April 19, 1995.

The blast, powered by a truckload of fertilizer and fuel oil, hit at 9:02 a.m. "It was just like an atomic bomb went off," said a survivor. The front of the nine-story building disintegrated, trapping scores of occupants beneath the rubble. Doctors had to free one woman by amputating her leg on the spot. An agonizing 43-day search turned up 168 bodies; among the dead were more than a dozen children in a daycare center. The horror was tempered by an outpouring of aid from around the country—and by the capture of the perpetrator. Timothy McVeigh, a Desert Storm vet with a penchant for antigovernment conspiracy theories, was sentenced to death in 1997; Army buddy Terry Nichols, who supplied him with bomb materials (but claimed not to know what they were for), drew life in prison.

The remains of the Federal Building (above) were torn down a month after the bombing. But the survivors (left) would be scarred forever.

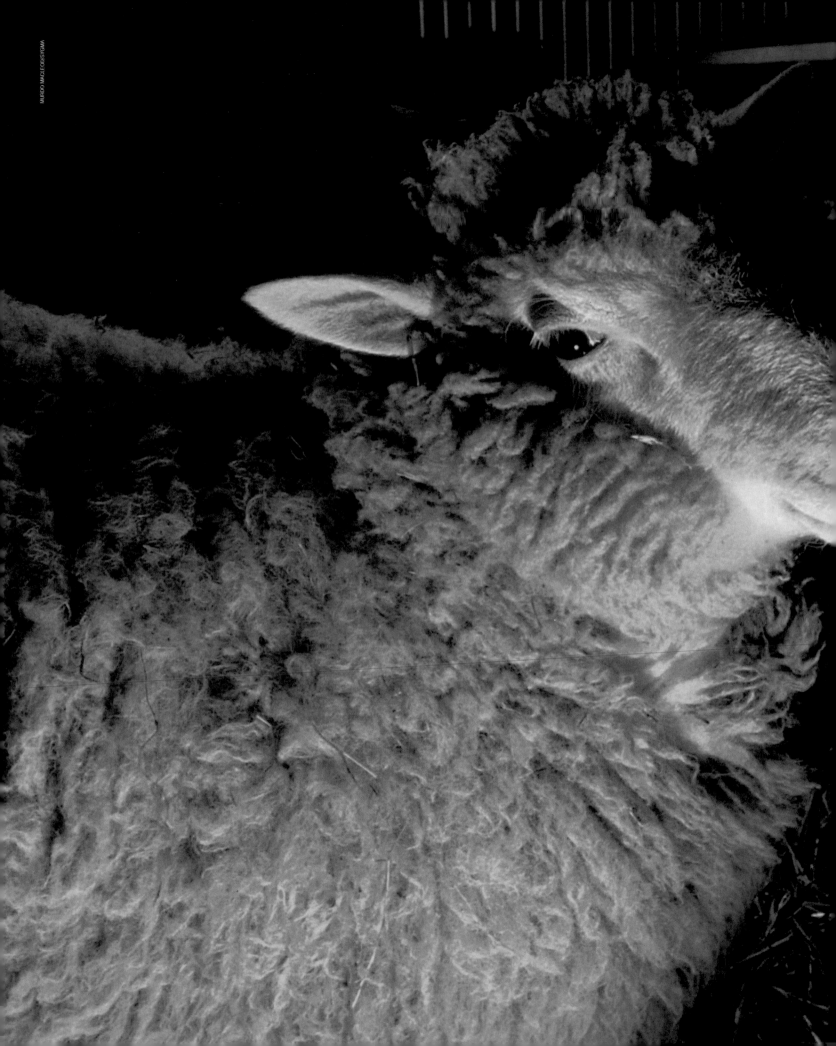

Send in the clones

In 1990, U.S. researchers set about mapping the 100,000 genes of the human body. Deciphering our DNA raised the hope of wiping out genetic illnesses—as well as the specter of baby Frankensteins created from a list of desirable physical and personality traits. By 1992 doctors could test embryos for genetic abnormalities like hemophilia. But the further implications of genetic engineering still lay in the realm of science fiction. Then in 1997 fantasy became reality as the world greeted its first clone of an adult mammal, a Scottish sheep copied from the mammary cells of another. Dolly's arrival inevitably gave rise to ethical conundrums about replicating people; legislators in several countries responded with bans on cloning humans. Said James Watson, who with Francis Crick discovered DNA's structure in 1953: "Moving forward will not be for the faint of heart."

Dolly (left), the creation of embryologist Ian Wilmut, meets with other cloned ewes in Edinburgh.

Trying times, televised

There have been many contenders for Trial of the Century, but two of the strongest took place at century's end. Each was a media event, a real-life soap opera whose titillating plot and riveting performances belied the seriousness of the charges. The first drama went on the air in January 1995, when O.J. Simpson was tried for the stabbing deaths of ex-wife Nicole Brown and her friend Ron Goldman. The former football hero's blood was allegedly at the crime scene; a glove with the victims' blood turned up at his home. But Simpson claimed he had been framed. The glove, said lawyers, was planted by Det. Mark Fuhrman, whose racial slurs had been caught on tape. Polls showed most white Americans thought Simpson guilty; most blacks believed him innocent. A mixed jury acquitted him.

"I did not have sexual relations with that woman—Miss Lewinsky," Bill Clinton declared in 1998. Or maybe he did. But had the President committed any impeachable offenses? Yes, said independent counsel Ken Starr, perjury and obstruction of justice. Starr had been appointed in 1994 to investigate a land deal Clinton made in Arkansas. Then Starr discovered Monica Lewinsky, a witness in a sexual harassment suit filed against Clinton by Arkansas clerk Paula Jones. Lured by tales of thong underwear, cigars and secretly taped girl talk, the nation tuned in to the second impeachment trial in U.S. history. On February 12, 1999, the Senate voted to acquit— and left America more confused than ever about the border between personal and political.

At a 1994 pretrial hearing, Simpson (above) heard a graphic account of his ex-wife's slaying. In 1998, the House voted to impeach President Clinton (right), seen on monitor.

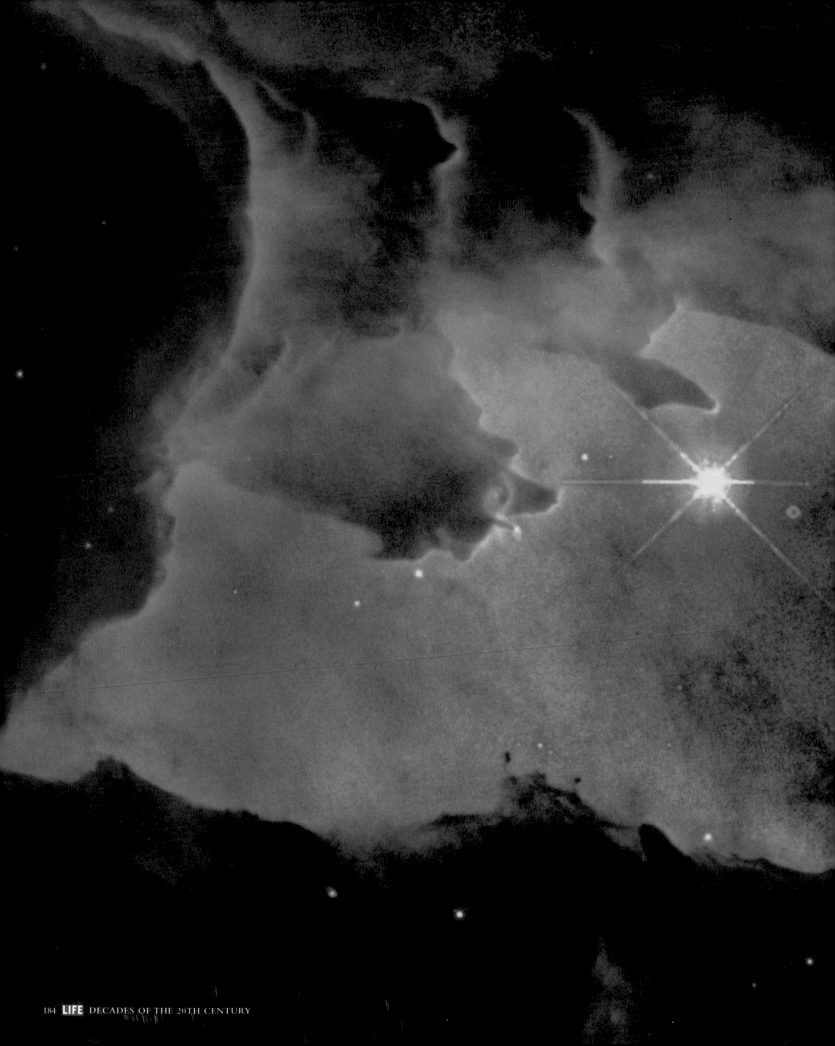

1990–1999

Starlight express

Launched in April 1990, the Hubble Space
Telescope began life as a $2 billion lemon.
But after shuttle astronauts repaired its mirror
in '93, the Hubble revolutionized astronomy.
Orbiting 380 miles above the earth, the
caboose-size scope lets us see nearly to the
edge of the cosmos, 13 billion light-years
distant. It has shown us stars aborning,
galaxies colliding, evidence of black holes.
The Hubble won't answer our most urgent
questions (Why are there school shootings?),
but it may help with some of the deepest
ones (How did the universe begin?). Its
images remind us how small our world is,
and how short our century has been.

**In the Eagle Nebula, 7,000 light-years away,
stars are born from gas clouds.**

Rand Miller, computer game designer

As a boy in New Mexico, Rand Miller loved two things: stories—particularly adventure tales like C.S. Lewis's *Chronicles of Narnia*—and computers. He would hang out at a local college and hack into its system. "At first," he recalls, "it was just playing games. One called Lunar Lander was just a table. It printed out how fast you were going, how much fuel you had left. It wasn't visual, it was all in your head." At age 16 he wrote

his first game, Swarms, which won third place in a national contest.

By 1979, Miller was in college and hating it. He dropped out, took a job at a bank, married and had the first of three daughters, Kinslee. "I was looking for software for her and realized how lame it was." Using early '80s graphics technology, Miller and his brother Robyn, an artist, designed a simple kids' game called The Manhole that allowed young users to navigate through a simulated urban landscape. After the success of a second game, Rand and Robyn quit their jobs to create a grown-up game, Myst.

Miller (at work in Spokane) personalized the company's offices with architectural details right out of its computer games.

Partly inspired by a Jules Verne novel, its lush graphics beckon the player to explore a deserted island and figure out what happened there. No guns, no exploding asteroids. Its beauty and brains made Myst a best-seller, bringing in well over $140 million. In 1999, Kinslee finished high school. "It's hard to believe," says Miller, who bought his daughter an iMac for graduation. "And here I am doing games for a living."

" There wasn't a command for 'the computer thinks now.' Just getting a computer to play ticktacktoe was a huge thing. **"**

FITNESS REVOLUTION

Logging long hours online may expand your mind—but your waistline will widen too. By 1998, 55 percent of Americans were overweight or obese, a remarkable fact considering all the money—$2.85 billion— shelled out on home fitness equipment alone. Ever since the second industrial revolution's labor-saving devices caused a drop in our level of general physical activity, the desire to be fit, or at least look that way, has grown. Jack LaLanne opened his first gym in 1936 and later took his act to TV. The '80s made heroes of bodybuilder-turned-actor Arnold Schwarzenegger and actress-turned-aerobics-instructor Jane Fonda. The 1990s saw a return to old regimens like yoga and Pilates and the emergence of newer ones like Tae-Bo and mountain biking. There are no longer any excuses for ignoring those dollar-driven philosophers of sports marketing who urge us to "just do it."

Why buy a home gym when train wheels (above) and mountains (left) can be fitness equipment?

For many people, their first home computers were little more than typewriters with screens. By the 1990s, with the wide use of the Internet, we used them to do banking without leaving the house, to do research without going to the library, and to revive the art of letter writing with E-mail. :)

PERCENTAGE OF AMERICAN HOUSEHOLDS WITH COMPUTER GAMES
1998: 26

PERCENTAGE OF AMERICAN HOUSEHOLDS WITH COMPUTERS
1998: 51

PERCENTAGE OF AMERICAN HOUSEHOLDS THAT ARE ONLINE
1998: 37.3

COPIES OF MICROSOFT WINDOWS 98 IN USE
1998: 22,332,700

COPIES OF MYST SOLD IN U.S. AS OF JUNE 1999
4,950,000

The eighty members of the department received a base salary, a safety net, of $120,000 a year each. This was regarded as a laughably small sum. The rest of their income came from commissions and profit-sharing. Sixty-five percent of the department's profits went to Pierce & Pierce. But 35 percent was split among the eighty bond salesmen and traders themselves. All for one and one for all, and lots for oneself! And therefore . . . no slackers allowed! no deadwood! no lightweights! no loafers!—Tom Wolfe [3], *The Bonfire of the Vanities*, 1987

THERE WAS NOWHERE TO HIDE. Everyone's oxygen had long since run out, making the group more vulnerable to the wind-chill, which exceeded a hundred below zero. In the lee of a boulder no larger than a dishwasher, the climbers hunkered in a pathetic row on a patch of gale-scoured ice. "By then the cold had about finished me off," says Charlotte Fox. "My eyes were frozen. I didn't see how we were going to get out of it alive."
Jon Krakauer [6]
Into Thin Air, 1997

MEN ARE FROM MARS, Women Are from Venus.
John Gray
Title of his best-selling book
MEN ARE FROM EARTH, women are from Earth. Deal with it.
Internet joke list

WE WILL REBUILD, and we will be stronger, and we will be in it together.
Pat Owens
Mayor of Grand Forks, N.Dak., after his city was ravaged by flood and fire, 1997

THE RHYMES WE say / they set a trend because a devastating rap / is what we send Every jam we play / we break two needles There's three of us / but we're not the Beatles
Run-D.M.C.
"King of Rock," 1985

WHEN [TIGER WOODS] NEEDS a 120-yard shot to go under an oak branch and over a pond, he doesn't visualize the shot, as most golfers would. He looks at the flag and pulls everything from the hole back, back, back . . . not back into his mind's eye, but into his hands and forearms and hips, so they'll do it by feel. Explain how he made the preposterous shot? He can't. Better you should interview his knuckles and metacarpals.
Gary Smith
"The Chosen One," *Sports Illustrated*, 1996

SARAJEVO, THE CAPITAL of neighboring Bosnia, is where World War I began. World War II and the Holocaust engulfed this region. In both wars, Europe was slow to recognize the dangers, and the United States waited even longer to enter the conflicts. Just imagine if leaders back then had acted wisely and early enough. How many lives could have been saved? How many Americans would not have had to die?
Bill Clinton [1]
On Kosovo, 1999

ROSE: TEACH ME to ride like a man.
Jack: And chew tobacco like a man.
Rose: And spit like a man!
Jack: What? They didn't teach you that in finishing school?
Leonardo DiCaprio and Kate Winslet [4]
As Jack and Rose, in *Titanic*, 1997

FIVE YEARS FROM NOW, people won't need to be computer-literate. Computers will be people-literate.
Esther Dyson [5]
1984

WHAT MOSES BROUGHT down from Mount Sinai were not the ten suggestions; they are commandments. Are, not were. The sheer brilliance of the Ten Commandments is that they codify in a handful of words, acceptable human behavior. Not just for then, or now, but for all time. Language evolves; power shifts from nation to nation; messages are transmitted with the speed of light. Man erases one frontier after another, and yet we and our behavior, and the commandments which govern that behavior, remain the same.
Ted Koppel [2]
1987

Index

Picture Sources